The
EVERYTHING®
Dog Health Book

Dear Reader:

With our canine companions becoming beloved family members, we obviously want to provide the best possible care for them. We want them to share our lives for as long as possible. We would like our puppies to have the right start in life and our senior dogs to finish out their lives in dignity and comfort. As a veterinarian and an experienced dog lover, we will guide you through the planning of your dog's health care.

Our job is to provide you with key information to make you the best possible health-care advocate for your dog. Knowing what care is important, how to provide the best care, and what questions to ask your veterinarian are all important tools for you. You know your dog better than anyone else, so you are her first line of defense against health problems. Anything you notice that is a change from her normal routine or is unusual may need to be brought to your veterinarian's attention. Then, as a team, you can customize a treatment plan to give your dog the best possible care!

Kim Campbell Thornton

Debra Eldredge, D.V.M.

The EVERYTHING® Series

Editorial

Publishing Director	Gary M. Krebs
Managing Editor	Kate McBride
Copy Chief	Laura M. Daly
Acquisitions Editor	Kate Burgo
Development Editors	Christina MacDonald
	Michelle Chard Rizzo
Production Editor	Jamie Wielgus

Production

Production Director	Susan Beale
Production Manager	Michelle Roy Kelly
Series Designers	Daria Perreault
	Colleen Cunningham
	John Paulhus
Cover Design	Paul Beatrice
	Matt LeBlanc
Layout and Graphics	Colleen Cunningham
	Daria Perreault
	Monica Rhines
	Erin Ring
Series Cover Artist	Barry Littmann
Interior Illustrator	Mark Divico

Visit the entire Everything® Series at *www.everything.com*

THE
EVERYTHING®
DOG HEALTH BOOK

A complete guide to keeping your
best friend healthy from head to tail

Kim Campbell Thornton and
Debra Eldredge, D.V.M.

Adams Media
Avon, Massachusetts

An Everything® Series Book.
Everything® and everything.com® are registered trademarks of F+W Publications, Inc.

Published by Adams Media, an F+W Publications Company
57 Littlefield Street, Avon, MA 02322 U.S.A.
www.adamsmedia.com

ISBN: 1-59337-320-1
Printed in the United States of America.

J I H G F E D C B A

Library of Congress Cataloging-in-Publication Data
Thornton, Kim Campbell.
The everything dog health book / Kim Campbell Thornton and Debra Eldredge.
p.   cm.
(An Everything series book)
ISBN 1-59337-320-1
1. Dogs. 2. Dogs—Health. 3. Dogs—Diseases. I. Eldredge,
Debra. II. Title. III. Series: Everything series.

SF427.T49 2005
636.7'0893—dc22
2004026900

This publication is designed to provide accurate and authoritative information with regard to the subject matter covered. It is sold with the understanding that the publisher is not engaged in rendering legal, accounting, or other professional advice. If legal advice or other expert assistance is required, the services of a competent professional person should be sought.

—From a *Declaration of Principles* jointly adopted by a Committee of the American Bar Association and a Committee of Publishers and Associations

Many of the designations used by manufacturers and sellers to distinguish their products are claimed as trademarks. Where those designations appear in this book and Adams Media was aware of a trademark claim, the designations have been printed with initial capital letters.

This book is available at quantity discounts for bulk purchases.
For information, please call 1-800-872-5627.

Contents

Dedication

I would like to dedicate my part of this book to the two wonderful dogs I lost this year—my incredible Kuvasz Bubba and my dearest soul mate, my Belgian Tervuren Beep. The world is a darker place without you! And to the two Belgian Tervurens and the elderly Corgi who helped me through my loss—my wonderful Dani; Beep's son, Hokey Wolf; and my devoted Susan. May you live long and full lives!

This book is dedicated to all the wonderful dogs who have shared my life and especially to my dearest Bella, Darcy, and Twyla, who make every day special. May we have many happy, healthy years to come.

Acknowledgments

With thanks to the many dogs who have shared our lives—
both as part of our families and as friends and patients.
We have learned from each one of you!

Top Ten Ways
to Keep Your Dog Healthy

1. Invest in preventive health care, such as regular veterinary exams, and consider purchasing veterinary health insurance to help cover your dog's veterinary expenses.

2. Feed your dog a high-quality diet appropriate for his life stage.

3. Exercise your dog daily, and measure his food so he doesn't become overweight.

4. Protect your growing dog's bone and joint development by restricting high-impact exercise until he's fully mature.

5. Spay or neuter your dog to prevent unwanted puppies and to reduce the incidence of certain hormone-related diseases.

6. Keep your dog's immune system strong with appropriate vaccinations.

7. Learn about dog anatomy to better understand how to care for your dog.

8. Protect your dog from parasites.

9. Ask your veterinarian about the latest methods of pain relief when your dog has surgery or is in pain from an injury or illness.

10. Recognize signs of illness so you can catch and treat problems early.

Introduction

▶ Twenty years ago, an evolution and a revolution began in what was known about dog care and health. People were taking more interest in their own health and nutrition, and they had the same interest in seeing their dogs live longer, healthier lives. After all, dogs are our best friends. Advances in veterinary medicine and canine nutrition helped move this trend along. Today, our dogs live longer than ever, and we know much more about taking good care of them than we ever have.

In fact, veterinary medicine has been transformed. Pet medicine is at a level undreamed of just twenty years ago, thanks to advances and changes in anesthesia, pain management, surgical techniques and tools, dental care, nutrition, parasite control, cancer treatment, diagnostic techniques and equipment, vaccination protocols, and the advent of specialist care. Our dogs today have access to magnetic resonance imaging (MRI) technology, computed tomography (CT, or cat) scans, orthodontics such as braces to correct malformed bites, and cryotherapy, chemotherapy, and radiation to treat cancer.

One of your most important tasks as a dog owner is to keep your pet healthy. Working with your veterinarian you can help to ensure your dog lives a long, happy life, and you can work toward preventing health problems before they begin.

Knowing your dog's habits is a good place to start. When you know his normal eating, play, and exercise routines, recognizing a problem is easier. Any change in your dog's normal routine may indicate a problem and should sound an alarm for you to keep a close eye on him.

A healthy diet, a solid exercise routine, and lots of love and play will help your dog grow happy and healthy. On top of that, regular trips to your veterinarian for preventive and maintenance health care will help keep him in top shape.

Besides introducing you to what's new in veterinary medicine, *The Everything® Dog Health Book* will help you understand your dog's anatomy, health needs, nutritional requirements, and more. You can refer to it throughout his life, from puppyhood through old age. In it, you'll find answers to your questions about illnesses and injuries that can affect your dog, what to do for them, and ways to keep him safe and sound. Our goal in writing this book is to help you take the best possible care of your dog so that the two of you will share a long, lasting, and loving relationship.

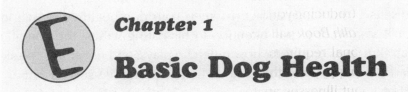

Chapter 1

Basic Dog Health

Keeping your dog healthy is one of your most important tasks as a dog owner. In partnership with your veterinarian, you can take steps to prevent health problems altogether or to recognize them before they become serious. The best way to do this is to watch for signs of good health as well as signs of illness, to know your dog's normal appetite and habits, and to schedule regular veterinary exams. Preventive health care also includes regular vaccinations and spay/neuter surgery for dogs that aren't used for breeding.

Preventive Care

An ounce of prevention is worth a pound of cure. It may be a cliché, but it's true nonetheless. Use a high-quality dog food with meat protein as the first ingredient, brush your dog's teeth frequently, make sure he gets plenty of exercise, dog-proof your home so he doesn't hurt himself, and protect him from disease with vaccinations. To keep your dog healthy throughout his life, you'll also want to pay attention to his eating habits; the condition of his coat, skin, eyes, and ears; how much he plays; and how much he sleeps. Familiarity with all your dog's habits helps you notice sooner rather than later when something's not right.

Here's more good news—preventive medicine keeps your wallet healthy, too. When you catch problems early, they're usually easier and less expensive to treat.

Monitor Your Dog's Appetite

In most cases, your dog's appetite is one of the most obvious signs of good health. The average dog is, well, a chowhound. Each dog is an individual, of course, and some dogs—and even some breeds—have a reputation for being picky. In general, however, you can expect your dog to eat heartily twice a day (more often if he's a young puppy). Perhaps Miguel Cervantes' character Sancho Panza in the novel *Don Quixote* said it best: ". . . she never seems to chew, but bolts and swallows all that is put before her, for she has a canine appetite that is never satisfied."

Signs of Good Appetite

A dog with a good appetite reminds you when it's mealtime. She dances excitedly around your feet as you prepare her food. If you've taught her good dinner manners, she sits impatiently, tail thumping, until you set her dish down and give the okay for her to dig in. She eats avidly, and when she's done she licks her chops and does the "happy dance," rolling ecstatically on the floor and then thoroughly wiping her mouth on your favorite carpet or upholstered furniture.

Signs of Poor Appetite

There's a difference between picky eaters and dogs that have lost their appetite. Picky eaters might "pick" at their food, only eating a little at a time, but they eventually finish it. Sometimes they eat well one day and refuse the same meal the next, having learned that they often get something different or special when they act this way. Other dogs are picky eaters until competition in the form of another dog is introduced; then they eat voraciously to protect their food from the newcomer.

Whether your dog is a chowhound or a picky eater, be concerned if you notice lack of appetite accompanied by depressed or lethargic behavior, especially if it seems to come out of nowhere. It's not unheard of for dogs with healthy appetites to skip a meal occasionally—usually when the weather is hot—but if your dog turns up his nose at food more than once in twenty-four hours and just doesn't seem himself, it's time to take him to the veterinarian. Loss of appetite is often a sign of disease or dental problems.

Increased Appetite

Sometimes dogs eat more simply because they have increased nutritional requirements. Show dogs, pregnant dogs, dogs that participate regularly in canine sports, and dogs that hike, jog, or hunt frequently with their people need more food than the average canine couch-potato. They may also eat more in response to cold weather, especially if they spend a lot of time playing outdoors. These are all normal instances of increased appetite.

Diabetes is among the diseases that can cause increased appetite. Others include diseases of the intestinal wall that interfere with food absorption and diseases that affect the hunger centers of the brain or that cause increases in hormones secreted by the adrenal glands.

On the other hand, some diseases can cause a dog to eat more than usual. That's because the disease process interferes with the way the body digests, absorbs, or converts food to usable energy. In other instances, it increases the rate at which the body uses energy. If your dog becomes ravenous, and the change can't be traced to a factor such as increased activity, see your veterinarian. This is especially important if your dog is eating a lot but still losing weight.

Know Your Dog's Habits

Other clues to your dog's good health can be found in her everyday actions. Paying attention to how she spends her days, her level of play and exercise, how she greets and interacts with family members, and even when and how often she potties can all help you keep a finger on the pulse of your dog's health. Consider keeping a diary of your dog's days. You'll find it's easier to spot changes in behavior or to see patterns if you can refer to a written record.

Play and Exercise

The amount of exercise dogs need and desire varies by breed and individual. Sporting dogs (the group that comprises retrievers, setters, spaniels, and pointers) tend to enjoy high levels of exercise every day. The same is true of terriers, most herding breeds, and some of the hound breeds. Most other dogs, including some of the toy breeds, usually have a moderate energy level. They enjoy daily walks and playtime, but to use an automotive metaphor, they run on gasoline, not rocket fuel.

ALERT!

Any unusual change in your dog's behavior is something to be aware of and to mention to your veterinarian, especially if it occurs in conjunction with lethargy or a change in appetite.

Lethargy is defined as an unusual lack of energy or vitality. You'll know it when your high-energy dog is feeling lethargic. He won't want to play his favorite games or go for a walk or run, and his eyes may seem dull. Lethargy may be a little less obvious in a dog whose energy levels are moderate or low to begin with. You might attribute his behavior to the heat or just to an off day. Even dogs have off days, after all. Whatever your dog's energy level, don't ignore lethargic behavior for too long. If he's uninterested in his usual favorite activities for more than a day, it's a good idea to take him in for a veterinary exam. Lethargy is a common sign of many different diseases.

Actions and Interactions

Changes in behavior and personality can also signal health problems. If your dog normally greets you happily at the front door when you come home from work, take note if he stops doing this. If your dog normally loves meeting people, be concerned if he suddenly shows no interest in them or even seems aggressive. Pay attention if your Labrador retriever turns away from tennis balls, your beagle stops sniffing anything and everything, your pug's tail loses its curl, or your Cavalier King Charles spaniel stops seeking out a lap.

Potty Behavior

It may not be what you thought you signed up for when you acquired a dog, but paying attention to a dog's urinary output and fecal composition is a big part of dog ownership, especially when it comes to keeping a dog healthy. Knowing your dog's normal patterns of urination and defecation allows you to notice quickly when they change. That's one of the many reasons it's a good idea to take your dog out to potty on leash instead of just sending him out into the back yard by himself to do his business.

What's normal? The average dog will welcome the opportunity to urinate every four to six hours. That's first thing in the morning, around noon, again later in the afternoon, and in the evening before bedtime. If need be, however, most healthy adult dogs can go eight hours between potty trips. Male dogs tend to urinate small amounts in different areas, marking their territory. Females usually empty their bladders all in one go, although it's not unheard of for them to scent mark as well. Dogs normally defecate once or twice a day. Stools should be small and firm.

Signs of possible problems include changes in the frequency of urination, the amount urinated, whether the dog seems to strain to urinate, and whether there appears to be blood in the urine. (Bloody urine is something you might miss unless your dog has an accident in the house and you see a pink tinge on the carpet.)

A constant need to go out, accompanied by straining during urination, could indicate a bladder infection. A big increase in the frequency and amount urinated, accompanied by an increase in water consumption, could indicate diabetes or kidney disease. Loose or liquid stools (diarrhea) can occur after a sudden change in diet or after eating garbage, as a result of certain internal parasites, or as a symptom of a serious infection, such as parvovirus. If he's straining to defecate and producing hard, dry stools, he may be constipated. All of these conditions require veterinary care, so you can see why it's a good idea to keep tabs on your dog's potty habits.

If your perfectly house-trained dog suddenly starts having accidents in the house, don't scold him for breaking training. He may be trying to tell you he doesn't feel well. Take him to the veterinarian to rule out any health problems, such as a urinary tract infection.

Regular Veterinary Checkups

Your veterinarian is your number-one partner in caring for your dog. If you're looking for one, get recommendations from shelter staff, breeders, and friends with dogs. If possible, go and check out the clinic and staff yourself. You want a clean facility that provides emergency coverage, with friendly staff who welcome your questions, and a reputation for good medical care.

An annual veterinary exam (plus visits as needed for illness or injury) is the best way to keep your dog healthy from nose to tail. Although you know your dog best, your veterinarian will often see or feel things that you might miss. Your veterinarian also has specialized instruments to fully examine your dog.

During the annual exam, you and your veterinarian should discuss the following aspects of your dog's health:

- Physical condition
- Vaccination status
- Parasite control
- Dental health
- Nutrition
- Behavior

If you've been keeping a diary of your dog's health and behavior, bring it with you. If your dog has been showing any signs of problems, such as discharge, redness or itching affecting the eyes and ears, skin problems, or changes in exercise tolerance, the dates and specifics can help the veterinarian figure out what's going on. She may ask what you feed your dog, how often he eats, whether you give any supplements, and how much and what kind of exercise he receives. Be prepared to answer any and all questions about your dog's habits. The better your veterinarian knows you and your dog, the better she can take care of him.

FACT

Behavior problems, especially housetraining issues or unusual aggression, sometimes indicate that something is physically wrong with your dog. Always be sure to mention them to your veterinarian, just in case.

During the exam, the veterinarian will listen to your dog's heart and respiration rate; examine the eyes and ears; palpate (examine by touch) the body to check the condition of the internal organs and make sure there are no unusual lumps or bumps; and test your dog's joint and muscle condition by moving his legs to check his range of motion. You will also want to bring in a stool sample so the veterinarian can examine it for the presence of parasites. (See more about parasites and their prevention in Chapter 12.)

Once the physical exam is complete, you and the veterinarian can discuss how your dog is doing and whether any changes should be made in his care. This is also a good time to mention any behavioral problems you might be having with your dog. If your veterinarian doesn't find an underlying medical cause for the behavior, she should be able to refer you to a veterinary behaviorist or experienced trainer who can help.

Vaccinations

There are several different ways a dog's body protects itself from disease. When puppies are born, they become temporarily protected from disease by nursing from their mother. The first milk she produces, called colostrum, contains maternal antibodies that protect the pup during the first weeks of life. Dogs can also acquire what is called natural, or active, immunity if they become ill with—and survive—a particular infectious disease. The antibodies formed from natural exposure usually last for life.

QUESTION?

Are vaccines 100 percent effective?
Not always. Vaccines can fail if they are handled or stored improperly, if the dog's immune system isn't functioning well because of malnutrition or immunosuppressive drugs, or if maternal antibodies neutralize the effect of the vaccine. Nor will vaccines protect a dog that is already infected with a disease.

Vaccination provides what is known as acquired immunity. A vaccine is a substance that, when injected, provides immunity against infectious diseases caused by bacteria, viruses, and other organisms. It does this by challenging the body with modified disease organisms, provoking the immune system to form antibodies against those particular organisms. Vaccinations don't necessarily provide lifelong immunity and must be repeated at certain intervals.

Necessary or Optional?

The decision to vaccinate a dog against a particular disease depends partly on the dog's age, breed, and potential exposure to the disease. It also has a lot to do with the distribution and virulence of the particular disease. Certain canine diseases are widely distributed, highly contagious among dogs, and serious or sometimes even fatal. Once a dog has acquired them, no treatment other than supportive therapy can help. These diseases are canine parvovirus, canine distemper virus, canine adenovirus, and rabies (which besides being fatal is also transmissible to humans, making it a public health threat). The vaccines against these diseases are referred to as core vaccines, meaning that they are recommended for all puppies and dogs.

Other vaccines are considered optional. When deciding whether to give them, you and your veterinarian should take into account the geographic distribution of the disease and your dog's risk of exposure. For instance, if your beagle is a show dog that never sets foot in field or forest, she's not at very high risk for Lyme disease. The non-core vaccines are those against canine parainfluenza virus, Bordetella bronchiseptica (for canine cough, also known as kennel cough), leptospirosis, giardiasis, and Lyme disease. The distemper-measles combination is also considered a non-core vaccine.

According to the vaccination guidelines of the Veterinary Medical Teaching Hospital at the University of California at Davis, vaccination with these non-core vaccines is generally less effective in protecting against disease than vaccination with the core vaccines. Some of these diseases are not common in many areas of the country, so there's no reason to give them unless your dog is at risk. Your veterinarian can tell you which are necessary in your area.

When to Vaccinate

Puppies receive vaccinations against parvovirus, distemper, and adenovirus-2 (canine hepatitis) at six to eight weeks of age, again at nine to eleven weeks, and at twelve to sixteen weeks, for the final series. A dog older than four months of age with an unknown vaccination history needs one dose of vaccine against these diseases. After a booster shot at one year, most authorities recommend revaccination every three years.

The first rabies vaccination is generally given at sixteen weeks (four months) of age. Boosters are usually given at three-year intervals, although a few states require annual rabies vaccination. Adult dogs with an unknown vaccination history need a rabies vaccination as well.

How Often to Vaccinate

Most vaccine labels recommend that the vaccine be administered annually. No scientific studies support this frequency of vaccination, however, and there's good evidence that the effects of vaccination last for much longer. While your dog still needs an annual exam, there's usually no reason for her to receive annual vaccinations. Frequent vaccinations may be advisable under some circumstances, so be sure to speak to your vet. For example, the Bordetella vaccine (which is given nasally) does not appear to last very long. If you kennel your dog frequently, or she often comes in contact with strange dogs at shows or dog parks, she may need this vaccine up to twice a year.

Reactions to vaccines are rare, but they can occur. Keep a close eye on your dog for the first few hours after she receives vaccinations to make sure she doesn't develop any serious allergic reactions. Keep Benadryl (diphenhydramine) on hand, and ask your veterinarian how much to give in case your dog develops hives, swelling, redness, or itchiness. The vaccines that are most commonly linked to reactions are those for leptospirosis, rabies, and parvovirus.

Why wouldn't you want to vaccinate every year? Better safe than sorry, right? Actually, that's not always the case. Too-frequent vaccination has been associated with autoimmune diseases such as autoimmune hemolytic anemia, and many veterinarians and dog owners are concerned that overvaccination can have other ill effects that are not yet known or understood. Before you schedule your dog for revaccination against distemper, parvovirus, or adenovirus-2, you may want to have her titer levels tested. A titer is the concentration of an antibody in blood serum. If these levels are still high, she probably doesn't need to be revaccinated.

New Developments in Vaccines

A new type of immunization, called a recombinant vaccine, is created by splicing gene-size fragments of DNA from a virus or bacterium. The recombinant vaccines that have been developed so far—for distemper, rabies, and Lyme disease—are safe and effective. They work by delivering specific antigen material to the dog on a cellular level, reducing the risk of vaccine reactions, which sometimes occur with vaccines that contain the entire disease-causing organism. When recombinant vaccines become more widespread, it may be necessary to reconsider the age at which vaccines are first given, as well as the interval between vaccines.

Spay/Neuter Surgery

If you don't plan to breed your dog—and you shouldn't, unless you have a superb example of the breed whose characteristics would improve the gene pool—you have two options for preventing puppies. The first is abstinence. This requires a high level of responsibility and maturity on your part, because it's a sure thing that your dog isn't going to show any restraint when it comes to satisfying those reproductive urges. You'll need to make sure your female is securely confined during estrus (heat). This is trickier than it sounds, because she will make every effort to escape in search of male companionship—and every male for miles around will be trying to get to her as well. And, of course, you'll need to make sure your male doesn't have any opportunity to impregnate the local females.

FACT

Spay/neuter surgery can be safely performed as early as six weeks of age. It is often done this early on puppies adopted from animal shelters. Animals this young don't require as much anesthesia as older puppies or adult dogs, and they recover rapidly from surgery.

The second option is spay or neuter surgery. Spay surgery, or ovariohysterectomy, is the removal of the female's uterus and ovaries. Neutering is the removal of the male's testicles, to prevent the production of sperm. Traditionally, spay/neuter surgery is performed just at or before the onset of puberty. Many veterinarians like to schedule spay/neuter surgery at four or five months of age, when puppy vaccinations have been completed.

Benefits of Spay/Neuter Surgery

Besides its main purpose of birth control, spay/neuter surgery has health benefits. Females that are spayed before their first estrus cycle are much less likely to develop breast cancer later in life than females spayed after one or more cycles. They are also spared the risk of developing ovarian cysts or uterine infections. Neutered males have no risk of testicular cancer and are at reduced risk for prostate enlargement and perianal adenomas, which are tumors of glands found around the anus. Dogs that are spayed or neutered are also more likely to get along better with other dogs and less likely to roam (unless they are scent hounds, in which case they are genetically programmed to follow tantalizing scents).

What You Need to Know

Before surgery, the veterinarian may recommend running a blood panel to make sure your dog is in good health. If your dog is young and has no known health problems, the only blood work will mostly likely be a simple test for blood urea nitrogen (BUN) levels, total blood protein, and a hematocrit, which is the ratio of packed red blood cells to whole blood. An aging dog or one that's not in tip-top health may need more extensive blood work.

Emergencies such as a reaction to anesthesia or a change in heart rate are rare. Thanks to improvements in anesthesia and monitoring equipment, veterinary surgery is very safe.

During surgery, the veterinarian or a staff member should monitor your dog's breathing and heart rate. Ask if they take the precaution of placing an IV catheter in a vein. This safety measure allows drugs to be injected quickly in the event of an emergency.

You'll also want to make sure the veterinarian provides your dog with pain-relief drugs before, during, and after surgery. The use of these drugs ensures that your dog suffers as little pain as possible and recovers more quickly. Some veterinarians don't believe pain relief is necessary for routine surgeries such as a spay or neuter procedure, but more progressive veterinarians know that a dog who's given pain relief will rest better and be at less risk of tearing an incision. (See Chapter 10 for more on medicating for pain.)

Recovery

During the first few days after surgery, your dog may be tired and a little sore, even with pain medication. Other dogs are as frisky as ever, running around and bouncing off the walls. Whether your dog feels well or not, it's important to keep him as still as possible. Rest will help the incision heal more quickly. You can limit activity by keeping your dog on leash or confining him to a crate.

ALERT!

To keep your dog from licking or biting at her stitches, you may need to use what's known as an Elizabethan collar. This plastic, cone-shaped collar (which resembles a lampshade) fits around your dog's neck, preventing her from reaching the sutured area. The drawback is that dogs hate wearing these collars and will shake their heads frequently in vain attempts to remove them. They may also be more likely to run into furniture while wearing the collar.

Some swelling at the incision site is normal, especially if the veterinarian uses absorbable sutures. Depending on the type of suture, swelling may last for six to eight weeks. This swelling may be more noticeable on a dog with thin, delicate skin. Redness, obvious inflammation, or any discharge (other than a little pinkish stuff the first day or so) are signs of possible infection, and your veterinarian should take a look.

Medications

No matter how hard you work to keep your dog healthy, she's sure to need medication at some time in her life. To make sure medication is effective, you'll need to know how to give it, how much to give, and how long to continue giving it. Each is essential in ensuring your dog's return to good health.

Your dog's medication may come in the form of a pill, liquid, or drops for the eyes or ears. Before you leave the veterinarian's office, make sure you understand when to start giving the medication, whether it should be given with food or on an empty stomach, and how often you should give it each day. You should also inform the veterinarian of any herbal or holistic remedies or other medications your dog is taking. They might interfere with the effectiveness of the prescribed medication.

FACT

The safety margin of a medication depends on such factors as the dog's age and whether her liver and kidneys are functioning well. Young puppies have immature organs, so they don't process medications as effectively as adult dogs. Senior dogs may have decreased liver or kidney function, which impairs the movement of drugs through the system.

Whatever form the medication takes, it is important to give your dog the full course of it, even if she seems to be better after the first few days. Her body needs to build up a certain amount of the drug in the bloodstream for it to be fully effective. That's also why drugs need to be given at specific intervals, such as every eight hours. So don't assume that your dog is well and decide to save the medication for "next time."

How to Give Pills

The easiest way to give pills is to hide them inside something tasty. Peanut butter, cream cheese, and canned dog food are all excellent "carriers" for pills. Before you follow this plan, ask your veterinarian if it's okay to do this. Some medications shouldn't be mixed with certain foods; for instance, tetracycline shouldn't be given with dairy products like cream cheese.

If you have a dog that eats the yummy coating and spits out the pill, or if the pill should be given on an empty stomach, you'll need to move to Plan B and give it by hand. Holding the pill in your dominant hand, use the other hand to hold the dog's mouth open. Place the pill toward the back of the tongue, close the mouth, and stroke the dog's throat to encourage swallowing. When you think she has swallowed, do a finger sweep inside her mouth to make sure she hasn't tucked the pill in her cheek to spit out later. Then give her a small treat or a few minutes of play with a favorite toy. The reward will encourage her to look forward to pill time.

ALERT!

Don't crush pills and sprinkle them on the dog's food. Crushed pills can have a bitter flavor that might make her reluctant to eat, and you won't have any way of knowing if she gets all the medication.

How to Give Liquids

Most liquid medications come with a dropper for dispensing them. If they don't, you can use a plastic syringe (the kind without a needle), as long as it has the proper measurement markings. Fill the dropper or syringe with the appropriate amount of medication, and hold it in your dominant hand, using your other hand to open the dog's mouth. Place the dropper in the mouth, aiming it at the cheek pouch, and pinch the lips closed. Slowly release the plunger and continue holding the lips closed until the dog swallows. Follow with a reward.

Eye Drops or Ointment

Administer eye drops straight from the bottle. Tilting the dog's head upward, hold the bottle in your dominant hand and squeeze the prescribed number of drops into the eye. Try not to touch the eye with the applicator tip. To apply an ointment to the eye, hold the head still with one hand, and pull the lower eyelid downward. Using your dominant hand, squeeze a small amount of ointment onto the eyelid, then release the eyelid and gently rub the surface of the closed eye to distribute the ointment over the eyeball. Again, be careful not to poke the dog in the eye with the applicator. It may help to have someone else hold her head for you.

Ear Drops or Ointment

Ear medications often need to go deep into the ear, so they usually come in a tube or bottle with a long, narrow applicator. Place the applicator inside the ear and dispense the appropriate amount. Be sure you have a firm grasp on your dog's head while you do this. Before he can shake his head and send the medication flying, fold the ear over and gently massage it to make sure the medication is thoroughly distributed.

Chapter 2

Breeding, Pregnancy, and Birth

Breeding your bitch or using your male dog at stud is a major decision on your part. All dog breeders need to be very responsible about breeding only dogs of top quality structure, temperament, and health. You must also be prepared to put extensive time and effort into giving the puppies the best possible start in life. Responsible breeders carefully screen prospective homes and are always prepared to take a puppy of their breeding back, even at ten years of age or more. Breeding a litter can be fulfilling, but it requires lots of work and dedication!

Is Your Bitch Top Notch?

Most breeders start off by owning a bitch they plan to breed. Before you even head out to check out the stud dogs available, you need to very objectively evaluate your bitch. She should be purebred and pedigreed through a reputable registry. The pedigree information helps you to avoid close breedings and any known health problems in the breed.

At a minimum, you need a three-generation pedigree on your bitch and the stud dog to plan a breeding. A three-generation pedigree will show your dog's parents, grandparents, and great-grandparents. Think of these as architectural plans!

Health Considerations

A bitch used for breeding should be at least two years old so that permanent health screenings can be done. Virtually every dog used for breeding needs to have orthopedic clearances, up-to-date eye checks, and a current thyroid level evaluation. Different breed clubs stress different clearances, so be sure you are familiar with the genetic problems in your breed. For example, responsible Dalmatian breeders evaluate their breeding dogs and any puppies they produce for deafness, a genetic defect in this breed. Basic responsible breeding means trying to minimize the chances that you might produce an unhealthy pup.

Before your bitch goes into heat, you should double-check to be sure her vaccinations are up to date. A fecal check and preventive wormings should be done now as well. You want her pups to start life with good maternal immunity and to be as free from parasites as possible.

Vaccinating a pregnant bitch, especially with a modified live vaccine, could lead to birth defects in the puppies. Always vaccinate your bitch well ahead of time, after discussing all options with your veterinarian.

Structure and Temperament

As well as being healthy, you want your bitch to be a good representative of the breed both in structure and in temperament. If possible, have a respected mentor in your chosen breed objectively evaluate her—this is often the person who bred her in the first place. Dog shows are another way to get an evaluation of your dog. Has she earned a conformation championship? In many breeds, it is also expected that your bitch has shown she is a competent example of her breed. For herding dogs, that means competing in herding trials, while sporting dogs are expected to compete in field trials or hunt tests, sight hounds are expected to do lure coursing, and terriers should have been in earthdog trials. All breeds should be capable of earning obedience titles and possibly doing some agility. There are plenty of homeless dogs out there, so if you are going to breed a litter, you want to produce only the best!

Selecting the Right Stud Dog

When looking for your bitch's Mr. Right, you need to make many of the same judgments you did when you evaluated your female. Any male dog used at stud should be at least two years of age and have the expected health clearances that are standard for your breed. Virtually all breeds should have basic orthopedic clearances, up-to-date eye checks, and current thyroid level testing. Any dog with a serious genetic defect, including ones that aren't easily noted (such as epilepsy) should not be bred! You should ask to see the clearance certificates and the stud dog's pedigree. A responsible stud dog owner will want to see all of those things from your bitch as well.

You should meet and evaluate the stud dog in person ahead of time. This lets you evaluate his temperament and look at his structure. Ideally he will have been shown successfully and done some performance work, earning titles for his expertise.

Again, if you are a novice, ask for the opinion of a respected mentor, especially if that person knows your bitch as well. You want to be sure you don't double up on any undesirable traits or health problems. This is where studying pedigrees and following dog family lines is invaluable.

FACT

If possible, try to meet some progeny already produced by the stud dog. Evaluating them will give you an idea of what traits he may pass on. Always factor in the bitch's contribution, too—so try to look at puppies or dogs produced from breedings done with bitches similar to yours.

The Mating Cycle

Now that your homework is done, you need to wait until your bitch is ready to breed, or until she is "in heat" or "in season." The first heat usually occurs when she is between six and fourteen months of age. Most bitches cycle roughly two times a year, but each is an individual. Some only cycle once yearly or even every eighteen months. A few bitches cycle every four months. Once again, the breeder of your bitch is an invaluable source of information. Most bitches will follow the cycle of their dam.

Stage One

There are four stages in a bitch's reproductive cycle. The first stage is proestrus. This stage, which lasts about nine days, is when the pituitary starts producing hormones that influence reproduction, such as follicle stimulating hormone (FSH) and luteinizing hormone (LH). The FSH causes the follicles (capsules around the ovum or egg) to increase in size so the ovum can develop, and the LH helps the ovum to mature. The vulva will start to swell, and your bitch may have a bloody discharge. Be aware that some bitches are so fastidious they clean all the blood up right away, so you may not notice drops on the floor. If you think your bitch may be coming into heat, you might want to do the "white Kleenex test" every morning. Take a clean white tissue and gently touch the vulva to see if you find any blood droplets.

Stage Two

The second stage, also usually about nine days in length, is estrus. This is the time of peak conception rates and when your bitch is most likely to accept the male. The cells in her vagina will change, and her progesterone levels will rise. Once progesterone levels peak, your bitch will ovulate two days later. Now is the time to breed!

Knowledgeable breeders and veterinarians work together, checking progesterone levels and looking at vaginal cells under the microscope to determine the best dates to breed. Ideally your bitch will be bred at least twice during this time of maximum fertility.

Estrus is also the time to be careful to keep your bitch sequestered away from unwanted male suitors! During this time, she should only be walked on leash and never left alone with a male that you don't wish to breed to.

Stage Three

Unless she has become pregnant, your bitch's reproductive system will switch over to diestrus about six days after ovulating. The progesterone level will drop again. Due to the hormone fluctuations, this is the time she is most prone to develop uterine infections (known as pyometras) if she isn't bred. This stage lasts about two months, the time it takes for your bitch to whelp her litter (give birth) or for her hormone level to fade.

Stage Four

After diestrus, the bitch's reproductive tract goes into a resting stage called anestrus. During this time, the body replenishes itself and prepares for another round of possible reproductive activity. This stage is the most variable of the reproductive stages and can last four months or more.

If your bitch stops eating, starts to vomit, has a greenish vulvar discharge, and acts lethargic, she may have a uterine infection called a pyometra. Call your veterinarian right away! Pyometras can require surgery and can be fatal if left untreated.

Care During Pregnancy

Now that your bitch is pregnant, it is important that you give her the best possible prenatal care. This is very important both for the health of your bitch and her future puppies. Routine care such as grooming and exercise must be continued, and special attention should be paid to nutrition and preventive health care.

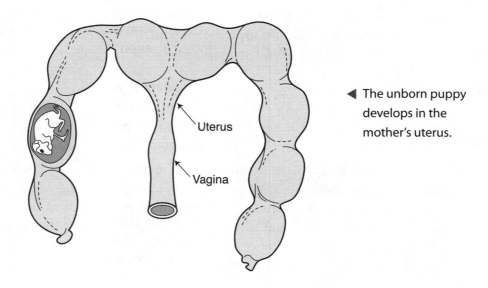

Uterus

Vagina

◀ The unborn puppy develops in the mother's uterus.

Prenatal Health Care

You certainly want your bitch free of any parasites. If you live in an area known for fleas and ticks, you need to continue preventives for these pests. The same is true for heartworm preventives. These are all important medications for the health of your bitch, and if she isn't healthy, her pups won't be. Check with your veterinarian for products that are safe to use.

Your veterinarian may also recommend a preventive deworming, even if your bitch has a negative fecal check. Parasites such as roundworms can encyst in your bitch's tissues, becoming active during her pregnancy and infecting the puppies in utero.

Prenatal Nutrition

What should you feed a pregnant dog? For the first six weeks of pregnancy, most bitches do just fine on their regular high-quality food. A bitch should have a hearty appetite, but don't let her get too heavy. Pregnancy is not a time to try new or exotic diets or additional supplements. Always check with your veterinarian before adding anything extra. Your veterinarian may approve some extra calories, but the diet must be carefully balanced.

Some bitches will experience morning sickness around two to three weeks into their pregnancy. They may act nauseous and refuse a few meals or only eat a small amount of their normal ration. For most bitches, this stage lasts only a couple of days.

For the last three weeks or so of pregnancy, you will need to gradually increase food. If your bitch has a large litter, she may need multiple small meals instead of two larger meals. Again, this should be a top-quality balanced diet. Talk to your veterinarian about any supplements you want to add.

Do not go overboard supplementing calcium! This can cause the bitch to develop eclampsia and other problems after whelping. Ideally a bitch should mobilize some of her internal calcium to meet the needs of the growing pups in utero.

Pregnancy Workout

Exercise is important for a pregnant bitch. She should be in good shape, fit, and able to handle the stress of whelping. Long walks are excellent exercise. Once the pregnancy is more than a couple of weeks along it would be best to avoid stressful running, jumping, and twisting. Agility and lure-coursing plans should be put on hold!

Preparing for Whelping

Preparations for the big day include getting the bitch used to her whelping box or area. This box should be easy to clean and should have side rails to protect pups from a rolling mother. The side rails come out from the whelping box about four inches up so that if the mother rolls over, the pup will be pushed under the rail to safety. The box should also have an area for early housetraining of the pups. Its sides should keep the pups in, out of drafts, and safe, but the dam should be able to step over them. The bitch should start sleeping or resting in this box ahead of time so she is comfortable there. It is worth taking the time to do this so to avoid her whelping on the new living room sofa!

You need to watch your bitch closely for any unusual vulvar discharge that could indicate infection (greenish) or premature labor (reddish). Another important step is knowing how many pups to expect. Ultrasound examinations are routinely done at around twenty-eight days. This is an excellent way to confirm pregnancy, but the actual puppy count isn't always accurate this early on. Most breeders will have an X ray (radiograph) done about a week before the due date to count skeletons and get an accurate count of how many pups to expect. Knowing the exact number of pups can give you some relief, since you'll know when the last pup is out safely!

FACT

In some breeds, you will need to arrange for a C-section as the pups may not be able to be delivered naturally. This includes breeds such as bulldogs, where the puppies' heads are so large that many bulldog bitches can't whelp them on their own.

Getting Through Labor and Whelping

About a week ahead of your bitch's due date (about sixty-four days after breeding), you should start checking her temperature twice daily with a rectal thermometer. A dog's normal temperature is 101 to 102 degrees. Within twenty-four hours of whelping, a bitch's temperature will drop to about 98 degrees. When this happens, call work and tell them you won't be in! If you have never whelped a litter before, ask an experienced breeder to be available to assist you, and be sure to stay in touch with your veterinarian.

First-Stage Labor

During the first stage of labor, the levels of progesterone (which have kept the uterus from contracting) drop. The cervix starts to dilate, and the uterine muscles gear up. This stage could take two to twelve hours. While some bitches simply lie quietly through it, others will pant and pace.

Birth

The second stage of labor is when the puppies will actually be born. The uterus contracts and your bitch will lie down, panting and visibly straining. The pressure of the first pup in the pelvis stimulates the release of oxytocin (a pituitary hormone also called pitocin). The oxytocin makes the uterus contract faster and harder. Puppies will be born in a thin amniotic sac that the bitch should tear open, and if she doesn't, you must! She will also chew the umbilical cord in two. A good bitch will then lick her pup to stimulate breathing and dry it off. As the pups dry off, they will move over to nurse. The nursing stimulates the release of more oxytocin and keeps the uterine assembly line moving. Some bitches need injections of oxytocin or calcium to help with delivery, which will require the involvement of your veterinarian.

A bitch may need veterinary assistance if she has had hard contractions for an hour or more with no pup being born, or if she has rested for three or four hours and appears to have stopped contractions even though you know at least one more pup is expected. This is why it is so important to know how many pups are expected.

Generally puppies are born at thirty- to sixty-minute intervals. Some bitches deliver quickly, while others take long rests in between pups. A bitch that has whelped before is usually faster.

Along with puppies, your bitch may pass some dark green fluid, which is from old blood in the placentas. Any thick, dark discharge could indicate a stillborn puppy. Call your veterinarian if you see any unusual discharges!

It's better to call about a minor thing than to wait too long and need a C-section to remove a stillborn pup.

Stage-Three Labor

By the third stage of labor, all the pups should be born. The bitch now has to pass any placentas left inside. Some bitches want to eat the placentas, and experts go back and forth as to whether allowing her to do this is really a good idea. It undoubtedly comes from the days back in dogs' evolutionary development when a whelping bitch would be stuck in her den with her litter and might not get any additional nutrition for a few days. Letting her eat a placenta or two should be fine, but most veterinarians and breeders do not recommend letting the bitch clean up more than that.

Pups Are Now Here!

Once the pups have all made an appearance, you still have work to do. First, identify all the pups so you can keep track of weights and growth. Some breeders use nail polish, either using different colors or marking different toes. Others give each puppy a tiny rickrack collar in a different color. Newborn pups should be checked for serious genetic defects such as cleft palates (a hole in the roof of the mouth that leads to aspiration pneumonia and usually death without extensive surgery). These pups and any with other serious deformities may need to be euthanized, one of the difficult decisions breeders must make.

Judging Progress

For the first week or two, pups should be weighed daily on a scale with gram measurements. You should see some increase in their weight every day. If pups aren't growing well, the dam may not be producing enough milk. She could have mastitis (inflammation or infection of the mammary glands), or the pups may have problems.

You need to keep a close eye on your bitch to be sure she is eating well and that her mammary glands stay a healthy pink and not too firm. If the litter is large, pups may have to eat in shifts. Again, it is important to identify all the pups so you can be sure everyone gets a fair share!

Puppies may need paper or bedding changes multiple times per day. They will eliminate upon waking up, whether it is from a nap or a longer overnight sleep, after activity, and after eating. They must be kept warm but not overheated. Puppies also should have gentle handling daily to accustom them to people and to being handled.

It is important to check each individual pup at least twice daily to be sure they are all nursing well. Gently tent up the puppy's skin with your fingers to check for dehydration; well-hydrated skin will snap right back into place. You should also feel for a nicely rounded little belly. If pups aren't getting enough milk, you may need to tube feed or supplement with a bottle.

Tails and Toenails

If it is customary with dogs of your chosen breed to dock tails or remove dewclaws, you need to arrange with your veterinarian for this to be done. These procedures are often carried out on three- to five-day-old pups. They are not mandatory, however. Many breeds are now changing their standards to allow dogs with undocked tails and uncropped ears to be shown.

Puppies Are Growing Up!

By three weeks of age, your puppies will have their ears and eyes open. They will be starting to toddle around and may be quite noisy! Your cleanup chores will increase dramatically, and the pups may need to start with some food supplements. Discuss what to feed with your veterinarian or an experienced breeder. Many breeders move pups of this age to a whelping box that provides for a separate area where pups can go to eliminate, possibly with wood chips or shredded paper. The bitch will often help guide her pups to use that area.

Singletons, or puppies that are the only ones in their litter, need extra attention and socialization. They miss out on the important littermate interactions that help dogs fit in with other dogs. The dam is important, but other mature dogs that are gentle with puppies can be valuable "nannies."

Learning about the World

At this time, the pups start to become little sponges of information. They need to be exposed to a number of people and experiences—always keeping their safety and health in mind! Friends of a variety of ages should come over and gently handle the pups after first washing their hands and removing their shoes to prevent tracking in any disease agents. Pups should be exposed to various surfaces to walk on, such as carpet, linoleum, and outside in a clean area.

Many breeders play music or tape recordings of city sounds, sirens, and storms so that these sounds are not frightening to the pups when they go out into the world. Puppies should have little playground areas with things to climb over, crawl through and under, and play hide-and-seek around.

This is an ideal time for pups to start learning about crates, taking short car rides, and being taken out separately for play and attention. Exposure to dog-savvy cats can occur now, but only under supervision. Remember, your job as the breeder is to produce the best possible puppies and then prepare them as best you can for their future lives with their new families!

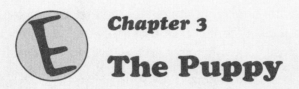

Chapter 3
The Puppy

Adding a new puppy to your family is a very exciting event! Dogs are social animals, just like people, and are happiest when they are included in as many family activities as possible. They can provide companionship for a lonely senior citizen, a wonderful sounding board for an upset teenager, company for the empty nester, and a buddy for everyone!

Is a Puppy Right for You?

Just like young children, puppies thrive on love and attention. They need frequent bathroom breaks, lots of play time, training time to get the basics learned while they are so open to new things, socialization outings, and exercise—both for your sake and theirs. You should only get a pup if you are willing to put in a major time commitment for the first six months and a fair amount of time for the six months after that. After all, you're interested in getting a puppy because you want to spend time together and develop a wonderful bond, right?

Unless your heart is set on a puppy and you are sure you have the time, energy, and proper situation to deal with raising a baby dog, consider bringing home an adult dog. Breeders sometimes have young adults that need new homes if they aren't working out as show dogs. Rescue groups foster and screen dogs carefully, and nice dogs are turned in to shelters for reasons such as divorce. These dogs are often already housetrained. They know how to walk on a leash, may be past the chewing stage, and don't hold as many surprises. You will know their full-grown size, temperament, and activity level for sure, so what you see is what you get.

However, if you still think a puppy is what you want, and as long as you have the time and energy to devote to training a young dog and provide a safe, healthy, loving environment for her to grow up in, all you need to know is how to choose the right puppy.

Selecting Your Puppy

An important part of having a canine family member is choosing the right puppy for your family to begin with. Do your research ahead of time! There are excellent books and Web sites that can help you choose the right puppy for your lifestyle. Talk to your veterinarian, animal shelter staff, and try to attend a dog show locally. Meet as many dogs as you can of a variety of breeds. And don't forget to meet adult dogs of the breeds you like as well as just puppies! While an Old English sheepdog puppy is a cute teddy bear, an adult may be a bit overwhelming for the average family. When you think you know what breed or type of dog would be perfect for your family, make sure you also find a healthy puppy of that breed! Look for a bright-eyed, active pup with no signs of diarrhea or parasites—don't fall for the sickly pup hanging back in a corner even if you feel sorry for her.

Things to Consider

Make a list of priorities for your family and lifestyle. Do you enjoy grooming? Or are you an immaculate housekeeper who would prefer not to deal with dog hair? Can you afford the regular grooming appointments needed to keep some breeds comfortable and looking their best? How about exercise requirements? Is yours an outdoorsy family that likes to hike and camp, or do you prefer to spend your weekends curled up with a good book? It is important to consider these and many other factors to help you choose a dog you will enjoy and who will be happy living with you!

If you're acquiring a dog for your kids' sake, be sure you will enjoy having one too. Dogs are fun, but they're also a lot of work and responsibility. Your children will love the dog, but she'll rely on you for most of her care.

When you begin to consider a certain type of dog, learn all you can. Weigh all factors of the given breed carefully, including the following:

- Size
- Grooming requirements
- Exercise needs
- Special equipment needs (such as a very large crate for a giant-breed dog)
- Ease of training
- Behavior around children
- Type of temperament (friend to all or a bit of a guard dog?)
- Activities you may want to share with your dog, such as agility or obedience

Luckily, dogs have an incredibly wide range of variation. There are pure-bred dogs of virtually every possible size, coat, color, and temperament combination. When you add in the amazing mixed breeds, there is sure to be a puppy somewhere that is just right for you!

Choosing a Healthy Puppy

There are some basic things to look for when adding a dog to your family. The puppy should be clean and in good condition. Some breeds tend to be roly-poly as pups, but being too fat is not good, and a very distended belly could be a sign of roundworm infestation. Beware of pups with diarrhea, goopy eyes, lackluster coats, and sneezing or coughing. Avoid puppies with reddened skin and those that are itching more than an occasional scratch. Any open sores should be a warning to you that the pup may have skin or immunity problems. The pup's skin should be elastic and snap back into place after you tent it up gently; this shows that the puppy is not dehydrated. Look for hernias—out-of-place bulges—usually near the umbilicus (generally a minor problem) or in the groin (a more difficult problem that needs to be fixed surgically).

You can't always judge the adult size of a pup by its feet. Some medium-sized dogs like English springer spaniels have large paws, while a Siberian husky has tight, smaller feet.

The pups should be active and energetic. Look for a puppy with a middle-of-the-road attitude—one that comes up to greet you but isn't frantic—and avoid the pup hanging back in the corner alone.

Follow the Breeder's Advice

Many breeders will do a puppy temperament test to see which pups may be easier or harder to train, as well as which would do best in a family, fit into a working home, and so on. While these tests are not infallible, when you combine them with the breeder's own impressions of the litter, they can help you get a true feel for the personalities of the puppies. Unless you are very experienced at evaluating puppies, expect the breeder to guide you in your choice or even pick out a pup for you.

A good breeder is an invaluable resource for health-related information as well. While all dogs have many of the same care requirements, certain breeds have unique needs. Large-breed puppies need careful diet plans to help their bones develop properly. Toy-breed puppies may need extra nutritional snacks to keep their blood sugar up. Dalmatians need to avoid foods that could cause bladder-stone formation. Your breeder can tell you these sorts of things and also give you guidelines to see if your pup is growing normally. Each breed is unique in many of its characteristics, and a reputable breeder knows her breed inside and out.

Do Your Homework

Once you've narrowed the field to a breed or even a particular pup, try to meet both parents of the litter if you can. The father may not be local, but you should at least get to meet the dam. (Don't be surprised if the mother dog looks a bit worn in coat and thin—raising puppies is hard work!) The mother may be cautious, but she should be basically friendly.

From doing your homework, you should know what genetic problems can occur in the breed you're interested in. Ask to see certifications that the parents are free of hip dysplasia, elbow problems, and eye problems if those are common in that breed. Ask about other problems that have been seen in that breed. If the breeder assures you their breed or their dogs never have problems so they don't need to do any screenings, beware! As your mother always said, if it sounds too good to be true, it probably is.

Try not to fall in love with and purchase the first puppy you see. The more litters you look at, the better idea you'll have of which puppy will fit best in your family. Of course, with some rare breeds, this isn't possible, but you should still interview several breeders—even if they don't have puppies available—to get a good feel for the breed.

Reputable breeders will ask you as many questions as you ask them. Don't be put off by this. It is a sign that they put a great deal of thought and love into breeding their dogs and they only want the best possible homes for their pups. Good breeders will also have you sign a contract so that if anything goes wrong, the puppy will come back to them. They feel responsible for creating this new life. That even applies many years later, when your "puppy" is ten years old!

Nutritional Needs

A puppy has different nutritional needs than an adult dog. Growing requires extra amounts of certain vitamins and minerals, and these must be present in the correct ratios. Growing pups need different amounts of protein and energy sources as well. Too much can be as bad as too little! Your pup's food should say "Balanced and complete for all life stages" or be specifically labeled as a "puppy food." The best foods will not only have a complete nutritional analysis on the label but will state somewhere that they were tested with feeding trials. A laboratory analysis is not a substitute for actually testing a diet by feeding it to dogs.

FACT

Don't assume that a special diet for large-breed puppies is simply a marketing gimmick. A regular puppy food provides complete and balanced nutrition for any size dog, but a food formulated for large-breed puppies is fine-tuned to meet the precise growth needs of those puppies.

Dogs that will weigh 50 pounds or more at maturity need a special diet that will help them grow slowly and not put weight on too quickly, which can cause skeletal problems in a still-maturing dog. Large- and giant-breed dogs need a carefully balanced calcium diet with fewer calories and lower levels of protein to help them mature at a controlled rate.

Before you bring your new puppy home, ask your breeder what food he has been using. You should try to use that food at least for the first week or so to make the new home transition easy for your pup. If you intend to switch foods, do so gradually over a week or so. Resist the temptation to ply your new family member with exotic and wonderful goodies.

Puppy Growth

Puppies grow very rapidly. Small breeds may attain their adult size by six to eight months, while giant breeds may continue to grow for eighteen to twenty-four months. They all need adequate nutrition in terms of calories, vitamins, and minerals. Premium dog foods have been thoroughly tested and will fit the bill. Puppies need more calories per pound than an adult dog. It is important not to let your pup get overweight, though. Extra weight adds stress to those growing bones and can lead to arthritis problems later in life.

How Much to Feed and When

Your veterinarian and your breeder can help you work out the best diet for your pup. Discuss what amount to feed and how often, as well as what foods are best. Remember that the amounts written on dog food bags or cans are simply guidelines. You need to feed your pup as an individual. Most pups do best with three meals a day until four months or so, and then stay on two meals daily for the rest of their lives. Very small toy-breed puppies may need extra snacks to keep them growing well.

Make sure your puppy isn't getting too fat. When you look down at him, you should see a clearly defined waistline. If he looks more like a plump little sausage, you might be feeding too much.

Specific meal times are preferred to feeding free choice (leaving a bowl of food out for your dog to graze on). With set meals, you know right away if your pup isn't feeling well. You can easily keep track of just how much your pup is eating, and it helps with housetraining on a schedule. Puppies should have access to fresh water almost all the time. You may want to limit water shortly before bedtime or an hour or two before heading out on a long car trip.

Puppy Treats

Let's face it—as well as his regular food, your puppy will be getting treats and chew items. Treats can help train your pup and help develop your close bond. Remember that if you use a lot of treats in training, you may need to cut back on your pup's mealtime amounts. Most puppies are happy to use their regular food as training treats, but if you want special treats, talk to your veterinarian. Don't forget that pieces of chopped apples or carrots are good and healthy treats for your dog. They're low-calorie and good for his teeth!

Your Puppy's Basic Supplies

Your new pup will need a set of basic supplies to help him settle in to your home. A crate is very important. This is a metal or plastic cage that serves as your pup's bedroom. He will sleep in this at first, take naps here, and rest safely while you are busy or away from home. A crate can double as a safe carrier on car trips or airline flights. It will also help with housetraining—puppies don't like to mess in *their* room, even if they don't mind going on your best rug! A crate can be moved around your house so your pup can still be involved with the family, even at night or during mealtimes.

FACT

A plastic crate gives your dog some privacy and is necessary if your pup will be traveling by air at some point. A wire crate provides good ventilation and can be folded up for storage, but it's not suited for air travel. Wire crates can be covered for privacy.

A crate also serves to keep your pup safe. If you are busy and can't be watching him closely, your pup could be chewing on poisonous plants, biting into electrical cords, or chewing on dangerous household items. Tucked into his crate with a blanket and a chew toy, he is safe and so is your house! It is very sad to learn of puppies left tied out behind the house alone because they did damage in the house. That is a much crueler fate than resting in a crate for a few hours. Many dogs will go into their crates for a rest even as adults with the run of the house. For them it is a safe den—a quiet retreat from guests, too much activity, and other pets.

Collars and Leads

The collar should be one with a buckle, plastic snap, or safety release—not a chain or prong collar. The collar should have identification tags to help your pup return home if she gets lost, and a rabies tag, once she is vaccinated. When it comes to a leash, a leather or canvas lead is easier on your hands than a chain or nylon one. Also, for now at least, stay away from flexible or retractable leads. These are not good for puppies. You don't want your pup to learn to pull on the leash, and retractable leads always have some tension. It is also easy for people and dogs to get tangled up and hurt by the thin line.

Microchips are an additional form of identification that are inserted under the skin with a needle. Each tiny chip has a unique number that can be read with a scanner. This number is linked to the information necessary to return your dog home. With a collar and tags and a microchip, your dog is doubly protected if she gets lost. Tags are visible, but they can fall off or be removed. A microchip provides backup identification if this happens.

Grooming Tools

Grooming equipment varies among different breeds, but every dog needs to have her nails trimmed, ears cleaned, teeth brushed, and coat brushed. A thin hound cloth works for dogs with short, tight coats, such as greyhounds, while a long-coated dog like a collie may need a slicker brush and a pin brush. Talk to your breeder or the shelter staff about the right brushes for your pup. Soft cotton balls, a child's soft toothbrush, and some dog toothpaste (not the people kind—that is designed to be spit out, plus it doesn't come in great flavors like poultry) are important. It is also nice to have some "dog towels" for quick drying after a walk in the rain.

Toys

Favorite toys will vary from dog to dog. A tiny Chihuahua pup may not be interested in a tennis ball, while a Labrador retriever will be thrilled. Make sure the toys are "puppy safe," that is, filled with nontoxic stuffing. Plastic that will break is not safe. Make sure your pup doesn't swallow any squeakers if she is tearing up a toy. With the exception of toys like Kongs and Gumabones or Nylabones, which are exceptionally tough, very few toys should be left with an unsupervised pup.

Other Supplies

Your pup will also need a comfortable bed and bowls for food and water. Her bed can be an elaborate cedar-filled pillow or a comforter purchased at a garage sale. Above all, it should be soft, fluffy, and easy to wash. When it comes to bowls, stainless steel is nonallergenic (unlike some plastics) and easy to clean. Beautiful pottery bowls should wait until your pup is a bit older. You don't want her chewing on and breaking her bowls.

Puppy-Proofing Your Home

Keeping your puppy and your home safe from each other can be a challenge. Your goal is to keep your pup with you as much as possible. Supervision is key to prevention, as is keeping your pup out of places where he can cause trouble. Baby gates work wonders. These are adjustable gates that can block off doorways. These gates can be used to separate pets, so your cat doesn't feel threatened by this unmannerly newcomer, and to keep the pup off your heirloom Oriental rug.

ALERT!

If your puppy thinks furniture legs taste good, there are a couple of things you can try to protect them. Wrap them in aluminum foil; it's not pleasant to bite down on that. If that doesn't suit your décor, coat the furniture legs with Bitter Apple to repel your dog. The paste form often works better than the spray.

Dangerous household items such as bleach and cleaners should be in locked cupboards. Electrical cords need to be moved out of reach or covered with plastic hosing for extra protection. Anything the pup shouldn't have must be put out of his reach. (Your children will learn to pick up and put their toys away after he makes one or two attempts to chew their things.) Shoes need to be in closets, and even books should be put where the pup can't easily reach. A large-breed pup will quickly grow big enough to reach the kitchen counters, so check there, too.

Don't forget to protect your doorways. You need to make sure right from the start that your pup can't barrel past you out into an unfenced yard or the street. It is helpful to use gates and start training the "Wait" command very early on.

Set Rules and Routines

Just like human babies, puppies do best on a routine. This keeps the fussing to a minimum and really helps with housetraining. Keep in mind that your pup has no sense of the days of the week. If you get up at 6 A.M. on Monday through Friday to give him a short walk and breakfast, don't expect him to sleep in until 8 A.M. on Saturday. Think of it this way—you have even more hours to enjoy your new companion!

To keep your pup from wandering and getting into trouble, without crating him, keep him on leash inside the house so he stays at your side. This is a good way for him to learn to look to you for guidance.

Along with a feeding and walking routine, you need to establish family limits for your pup. Everyone must agree on these things so the pup doesn't get confused. These rules include whether or not the pup is allowed on furniture and if so, which furniture. Is the pup allowed to sleep on a bed if he behaves properly, or is it best for all if he sleeps on his own soft bed next to yours?

Do remember that it might seem cute now for your little Saint Bernard pup to curl up on your lap to watch television, but that might not be so much fun when your pup is a 150-pound adult. Decide on house rules now, and make sure the whole family sticks to them!

Grooming

Grooming can be a wonderful time for you to bond with your new pup. Start by just gently using a soft brush or cloth to rub over your pup's back. If she resists, feed her a treat while you do this. It also helps to talk to your pup in a positive voice—telling her how beautiful she is and how she will look even more beautiful when you are done. That sounds silly, but dogs truly respond to your voice and the emotions it conveys even if they don't understand every word.

If you have a longhaired pup, try to do just a little grooming every day. That way the pup isn't bored, and you stay on top of any tangles or mats. If you are not willing to take care of a long coat such as that on a Shih Tzu, you should make the commitment for regular grooming or clipping appointments with a professional groomer. Mats can be quite painful for your dog, and they can cover up skin problems that need attention.

Some puppies, such as cavalier King Charles spaniels, don't acquire their full coat length until they're eighteen months to two years old. That means you have more than a year to help them learn to enjoy grooming time—before it gets to be more involved than just a simple brushing.

How to Brush

Make sure when you brush that you are not just brushing the hair on the dog's back. You need to hold the hair up, brush underneath down to the belly, and even brush out any feathering on the legs. Many pups enjoy a good belly rub, and that can be a good time to do a little grooming there too. The tail needs to be gently brushed as well as the area around the face and ears. Even short-coated dogs need a wipe with a damp cloth to pick up loose hair and any dirt buildup.

Trimming the Nails

If you've gotten your pup used to having his feet handled, nail trimming should not be traumatic. Carefully removing the tips of the nails will not hurt. Some people use grinders to trim nails instead of clippers. Be sure to have your veterinarian or breeder demonstrate how to do nails correctly and safely. This is another time when generous treats are important to make your pup comfortable with you handling his feet and doing his nails.

Dogs with long, hanging ears, such as spaniels or retrievers, often develop ear infections. The inside of the ears is warm and moist, an ideal home for bacteria to flourish. To prevent problems, keep the ears clean and dry, especially if your dog loves to go swimming.

Cleaning Eyes and Ears

Pups should also be comfortable with you carefully wiping any discharge from their eyes with a damp cloth and checking their ears. This daily routine, followed with a small treat, will make it much easier for you and your veterinarian if your dog ever has a problem. When you clean the eyes, check for any redness or squinting that could indicate irritation or injury. Sniff the ears to make sure they don't smell bad. If they do, your puppy might have an ear infection that needs veterinary attention.

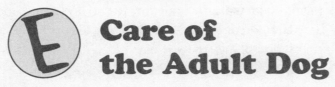

Chapter 4

Care of
the Adult Dog

Dogs reach physical and emotional maturity at eighteen to twenty-four months of age. They may look fully grown long before then, but they're still developing, so be patient with their puppy-like enthusiasm and adolescent testing of your authority. As dogs reach maturity, their nutritional and exercise needs change. If they're longhaired, their coat comes into its full glory. Appropriate diet, grooming, dental care, and exercise are all essential to keep your adult dog in peak condition throughout his life.

Nutritional Needs

Your dog's nutritional needs depend in large part on his breed and size. Some dogs reach physical maturity much more rapidly than others, with large-breed puppies taking the longest to mature. Although the growth of any dog starts to slow at about six months of age, large and giant-breed dogs don't reach full physical maturity until they're two and sometimes even three years old. They should eat a large-breed puppy diet or a diet customized by your veterinarian until they're two years old.

Typical dog foods come in canned or dry forms. Most people feed dry food because it's convenient, but it's okay to mix in a little canned food for flavor. Your pup will lick his chops!

Small and medium-size dogs have special needs as well. Small dogs of any age, especially those that weigh less than 20 pounds, have a higher metabolic rate than large-breed dogs, so they burn energy more quickly. They need a nutrient-dense diet that gives them a lot of nutrition in a small amount of food. That's because their stomachs just aren't that big relative to their needs. Most small and medium-size dogs can start eating a food formulated for adult dogs at nine months to one year of age. At this age, their skeleton will be full size, or almost there. The exceptions to this rule are the small but stocky breeds, such as pugs, that are also prone to skeletal problems if they grow too quickly. They can start eating an adult food as early as five months of age.

Determining Mature Weight

What if you don't know how big your puppy is going to be? Mixed-breed puppies adopted from animal shelters don't come with papers detailing their parents' breed or size. But there's a rule of thumb that will get you in the ballpark. Take the puppy's weight at eight weeks. Multiply by four or five, and the result is an estimate of his adult size. For example, an eight-week-old pup that weighs 15 pounds is likely to weigh 60 to 75 pounds as an adult. This estimate is probably a little on the low side, but it can help you figure out whether you need to feed a food geared for a large or small breed.

Switching Foods

When it's time to switch your dog from puppy food to adult food, or if you simply want to change brands, always do so gradually. Dogs have sensitive stomachs, and a rapid dietary change can bring on vomiting or diarrhea. Begin by adding small amounts of the new food to your dog's regular food over a period of five to ten days. The more different the foods are from one another, the more gradual the change should be.

For instance, if you're switching from Brand A puppy food to Brand B adult food, the change should go more slowly than if you're changing within the same line of food; say, from Brand X puppy food to Brand X adult food. Also change gradually if you're switching from dry food to canned food or vice versa. Allow plenty of time for the dog's gastrointestinal system to fully adapt to the new diet. Whatever you choose to feed your dog, be sure that it offers complete and balanced nutrition for his life stage.

FACT

Some manufacturers add ingredients such as glucosamine and chondroitin to diets for large-breed puppies and adult dogs. These nutrients are believed to help improve joint cartilage, and they remain stable in foods for long periods.

Nutrition for Older Dogs

A healthy older dog can continue to eat the same diet as long as he maintains a good weight and his coat and skin remain in good condition. One of the signs that your dog might need a change in diet is weight gain. Like people, dogs tend to become less active with age, so they need fewer calories to maintain an appropriate weight. Because their aging body is less able to metabolize protein efficiently, they need a food with reduced levels of fat and calories, but high levels of protein. Added fiber can also help reduce the calorie count, while still giving your dog the feeling of a full belly.

Older dogs can also develop a thinner coat or dry, itchy skin. Certain nutritional supplements may help, such as essential fatty acids, vitamin E, and zinc. Ask your veterinarian for a recommendation. Checking thyroid levels is important on older dogs with weight gain or coat changes as well.

Grooming and Skin Care

If you introduced your puppy at an early age to being groomed, your adult dog will be well-behaved during grooming sessions. He will probably even look forward to them. After all, what's nicer than having someone else brush *your* hair, getting deep down and giving you a scalp massage? It feels just as good to your dog, as long as you're careful not to yank on tangles or scratch delicate skin. Brushing is also great for keeping your dog's skin in good condition. It promotes blood circulation and new hair growth.

A complete canine grooming session involves brushing and combing the coat; checking the skin for signs of itchiness, parasites, or injuries; cleaning the eyes and ears; and taking care of the nails. Depending on your dog's coat type, size, and lifestyle, grooming can take as little as five minutes to as much as twenty or more minutes each day.

You may want to consider investing in a grooming table. This is a good way to keep your dog at eye level, so you don't strain your back when you're working on him. Choose one with a grooming arm and noose to hold him in place. If a grooming table isn't an option, try placing your dog on a picnic table or on top of your washer or dryer.

Simply to keep the level of shedding hair at a manageable level, most dogs should be brushed daily. Among the breeds that shed heavily are German shepherds, Dalmatians, Labrador retrievers, and pugs. They have coarse hairs that weave themselves into fabrics and are difficult to remove.

By brushing daily, more hair goes onto the brush and into the trash instead of floating off onto furniture and clothing. If your shorthaired dog doesn't shed heavily, a weekly brushing is sufficient.

Brushing Shorthaired Dogs

A good brush for most shorthaired dogs is a rubber curry brush that fits over the hand. Known as a hound mitt or glove, this brush is covered with nubby bristles. A curry brush should fit comfortably in your hand and may have a strap to help you keep a firm grip when brushing. You can find a good selection of curry brushes and hound mitts at well-stocked pet-supply stores. Also get a steel comb with wide and narrow teeth to help remove tangles.

If your dog is shedding heavily, brush him thoroughly, give him a warm bath, then blow dry him, brushing as you go, until he's completely dry. This will help loosen and remove excess hair.

Hold the brush firmly, or put on the hound mitt, and rub it over the coat in the direction the fur lies. Don't just run it over the top of the coat. Brush all the way down to the skin to remove dirt, skin-cell debris, and loose hairs. You may be amazed at the amount of hair you remove. This is a good grooming task for outdoors or in the garage. If that's not possible, brush the dog while he's standing on a sheet so you can simply gather it up and throw it in the washing machine when you're through.

Breeds that shed heavily may also benefit from the use of a shedding blade, shedding comb, or wire slicker brush. These tools have sharp edges or teeth that remove excess coat. Use them once or twice a week, after first brushing with the curry. Move it over the body in the direction the hair lies. Don't bear down too hard, or the sharp edges may injure your dog, and don't use it on the legs or areas where the hair is thin and fine, such as the belly. Avoid using shedding tools too often or you'll remove too much coat, leaving your dog with a flaky or scaly appearance.

Brushing Longhaired Dogs

Longhaired dogs are prone to mats and tangles. Daily brushing helps keep these problems under control. Tools you'll need for a longhaired dog include a pin brush, a shedding comb, a wire slicker brush or shedding blade, and a bristle brush. A pin brush, which has long metal "pins" coming out of the pad, helps lift out loose hair and skin debris without removing a lot of undercoat. When you're finished grooming, you can use the pin brush to fluff the coat by brushing against the direction the hair lies. A shedding or dematting comb helps break a mat into manageable sections so they can be combed through. You can also use the slicker brush to gently remove knots and tangles. The bristle brush brings out shine once the other tools have done their work. When your dog is "blowing," or shedding coat, a shedding blade comes in handy to remove all that excess hair.

If you purchased your dog from a breeder, ask what grooming tools she recommends and how to use them. As your puppy matures and his coat grows out, the breeder may be willing to give you some grooming lessons so you can keep the coat looking beautiful.

Run the pin brush through the coat in the direction the hair lies. Check for mats behind the ears, on the backs of the legs, in the groin area, and on the tail. If necessary, use the shedding comb to remove any mats. Work at it slowly, starting at the bottom of the mat and working toward the skin, being careful not to pull your dog's hair. Try to avoid cutting the mat, because that will simply make the area more prone to matting. Spending just a few minutes each day to remove tangles before they get bad will save you time in the long run, and it will also save your dog pain. As a bonus, grooming is a great way to bond with your dog, and he'll look fantastic.

Grooming Wirehaired Dogs

Besides the usual brushes and combs, among the tools you'll need to groom a wirehaired dog are trimming and thinning scissors, a stripping knife or two, and a set of clippers. You can keep a wire coat in good condition with weekly brushing. Use a pin brush or a natural bristle brush. First brush in the opposite direction the hair lies, then brush with the direction. Care for leg and facial hair with a wire slicker brush. The slicker brush is also useful for removing undercoat.

QUESTION?

If I have a hairless dog, I don't need to worry about grooming at all, right?
You wouldn't think a hairless dog would need any grooming, but these breeds have special needs. Their skin is prone to acne and sunburn. Different hairless breeds have different skin types, so your dog's breeder is the best person to advise you about appropriate skin care.

To maintain its correct hard texture, a wire coat must also be stripped twice a year. No, that doesn't mean taking your dog in for a wax job. Stripping is a technique done to remove dead hair and shape the coat. You can strip the coat by hand or with a special tool called a stripping knife. Your breeder or a dog groomer can show you how to strip the coat and advise you on the types of stripping knives and scissors to purchase. If stripping seems like too much work, you can simply have the coat clipped, but be aware that this will soften the texture and color of the hair. Wirecoated show dogs are never clipped, and if you want your dog to maintain the proper wire look, stripping is the way to go.

Wirehaired breeds also have facial hair—eyebrows and a beard—that must be trimmed and shaped. Before you start, wash the furnishings (as facial hair is known) and work in some cornstarch or grooming chalk. Comb the hair forward and use scissors to trim as desired. For a pet, you'll just want your dog to have a neat appearance, but if you plan to show your dog, you'll need to get detailed advice from your breeder or another person experienced in the breed to achieve the correct look.

Skin Care for Hairless Dogs

Hairless dogs with good skin—smooth and clear with tiny pores—rarely need baths. Hairless dogs with larger pores or oily skin that's prone to acne may need baths with a mild shampoo every one or two weeks to keep their skin in good condition and oil production at a minimum. (By the way, contrary to what you may have heard, hairless breeds perspire only through their paw pads, just like other dogs.) If your dog is prone to acne, use a medicated shampoo or acne medication recommended by your veterinarian or breeder. Often, acne clears up after adolescence, just as it does in humans.

After a bath, you may need to moisturize the skin to keep it soft and supple. This is especially important if you live in a dry climate. You can use gentle products made for human use. Coat oil made for dogs can also help keep a hairless dog's furnishings—the hair on the head, feet, and tail—in good condition. Carefully brush the hair with a pin brush.

Hairless breeds also sunburn easily. Keep them indoors during the heat of the day, and make sure they're protected with sunscreen if they do go outside. Choose a sunscreen that's safe if your dog licks it off, or purchase one that's specially made for dogs—yes, there is such a thing! Look for it at pet-supply stores, your veterinarian's clinic, or at online pet-supply sites. Just go to your favorite search engine and type in the words "canine sunscreen."

FACT

Any dog can get sunburned, not just hairless breeds. If your dog will be spending lots of time in the sun, protect his skin with sunscreen. Apply it to nose, ears, belly, and any other areas that aren't well protected by hair.

The Bath

There are two truths about giving a dog a bath: One, it's easier if you're organized; and two, even if you're organized, you will still get wet. When getting organized, be sure to gather everything you'll need before you even think about running water and calling your dog. That means two to three towels; a washcloth for cleaning the face; cotton balls to place inside the ears; mineral oil to put around the eyes to protect them from soapy water; dog shampoo (and conditioner if you use it); a rubber mat to place on the floor of the tub or shower to provide sure footing; and a blow dryer that's plugged in and ready to go wherever you plan to dry the dog.

Now brush your dog thoroughly. Work out any mats or tangles you find. If they get wet, they'll tighten up and become even more difficult to remove. Then take your dog to the bath area. A large walk-in shower with a seat and a handheld nozzle is ideal for your small or medium-size dog. Small dogs (up to about 20 pounds) can also be bathed in the kitchen sink, which is easier on your back than bending over a tub. To repel water, dab mineral oil around the eyes, and place cotton balls inside the ears.

Never call your dog to come for a bath (or anything else unpleasant, such as getting medication). He'll quickly get the idea that coming when you call is a bad idea. Instead, go and get him. That way, he won't associate the "Come" command with doing something he doesn't like. Of course, if your dog loves getting baths, this advice doesn't apply.

In the Suds

Using warm water, wet your dog down to the skin, starting at the head and working your way back. Apply shampoo, again starting at the head and working back. Massage it in thoroughly. Rinse with warm water until no more suds are running out of the coat. Shampoo that remains in the coat can make it look dull and flaky, so rinse thoroughly. Apply conditioner if you use it, and rinse again.

Grab a towel and start drying your dog. Stop for a minute, and more than likely he'll shake, removing even more water. If you have a longhaired dog, squeeze the water out of the hair on the ears, legs, and tail. By now your first towel is probably pretty wet, so grab another one and dry your dog some more before you let him out of the shower or tub.

Drying Time

Blow-drying your dog is best done with him on a grooming table, picnic table, or other surface that puts him at eye level. It's easier on your back and allows you to dry him more thoroughly. If you have a small dog, an option is to sit on the floor of the bathroom with the dog in your lap and blow-dry him from that position. Whichever spot you choose, be sure your dog can't get away. This means using the noose on the grooming table, closing the door of the bathroom, or having a helper hold the dog while you dry him.

Never trust your dog to stay in place when you're grooming him, especially if you have him up on a high surface. If you must leave to go get something, take him down first.

Set the dryer on warm, not hot. Hold it several inches away from your dog's body, and keep it moving so you don't accidentally burn the skin. Brush through the coat as you dry to remove more loose hair, using a curry for shorthaired dogs and a pin brush for longhaired dogs. You can dry him completely, or you can get him mostly dry and let him finish drying in his crate. Be sure it's not in the path of any drafts.

When you finally turn him loose, he'll probably go running through the house, rolling on the carpet in an attempt to rid himself of the funny shampoo/conditioner smell. And be warned, if you let him outdoors right after a bath, he'll probably go roll in the first dirty thing he can find.

Dental Care

One of the biggest complaints people have about their dogs is bad doggie breath. Not surprisingly, periodontal disease is one of the most common problems veterinarians see in dogs. To paraphrase Shakespeare, the answer, dear owner, lies not in our dogs but in ourselves. Your dog can't brush his teeth himself, so it's up to you to do it for him. Brushing your dog's teeth daily—or at least several times a week—will help prevent the build-up of bacteria-trapping plaque, which hardens into ugly brown tartar and eventually causes gum disease. Your dog's breath will smell much better, and he'll keep more of his teeth as he ages. He'll have fewer bacteria circulating in his system. Also, he'll need fewer expensive veterinary cleanings. It's a win-win situation.

Brushing the Teeth

Use a toothbrush and toothpaste made especially for dogs. Look for a toothbrush with a long handle, soft bristles, and an angled head for ease of brushing. Some dog toothbrushes have two ends, one large for cleaning the front teeth and one small for cleaning the teeth way in the back of the mouth. You can also use a small, nubby rubber brush that fits over your finger like a thimble. This may be the best choice for puppies or small dogs. Doggie toothpaste should contain enzymes to fight plaque. Some varieties have fluoride to help control bacteria. Avoid using toothpaste made for people, which can contain baking soda, detergents, or salts that can upset your dog's stomach. Many dog toothpastes are flavored like beef or chicken to add to their appeal.

FACT

If your puppy enjoys chewing, encourage the habit throughout his life. Chewing helps keep the teeth clean. Provide your dog with chew toys that assist in dental care, such as enzymatic chew sticks and ridged Kong chews.

If your dog wasn't introduced to tooth-brushing as a puppy, work up to it by wiping out his mouth daily with a damp washcloth or piece of gauze. After a couple of weeks, he'll be used to having you touch his mouth and teeth, and you can introduce the brush and toothpaste. Starting where the teeth and gums meet, hold the brush at a 45-degree angle and gently move it in an oval pattern. Be sure to get the bristles between the teeth as well as at the base of the tooth. It's not necessary to brush the inside of the teeth, just the outside. The upper teeth in the back are most important, but try to get all teeth if possible.

Veterinary Cleanings

When yellow or brown plaque has built up on your dog's teeth, he needs more help than home tooth brushing can provide. Schedule an appointment with your veterinarian for a professional cleaning. Groomers may offer to remove plaque or tartar with a dental scaler, but they can't get to the diseased area below the gum line. A veterinary cleaning, done under anesthesia, has three purposes: to immobilize your dog for a more thorough cleaning; to prevent him from feeling any pain during the cleaning; and to allow the veterinarian to place a tube into the windpipe, which prevents bacteria from entering the respiratory system.

QUESTION?

Should I be concerned about anesthetizing my dog?
Remember that today's veterinary anesthetic agents are very safe. Preanesthetic blood work can help to plan the safest anesthetic procedures for dogs with health risks. A good veterinarian will also have equipment to monitor your dog during the cleaning to provide even greater safety.

Before a professional cleaning, the veterinarian will give your dog a physical exam. He may order preanesthetic blood work, depending on your dog's age and condition. Once your dog is anesthetized, the veterinarian will thoroughly examine his mouth, remove tartar, scale the area below the gum line, polish the teeth, rinse the mouth, and apply fluoride. Afterward, he may prescribe antibiotics to ward off potential bacterial infections. The cost for a professional cleaning varies, depending on the condition of your dog's teeth and whether he needs lab work before the cleaning and antibiotics afterward.

Exercise and Play

From the tiniest toy breeds all the way up to the giants of the canine world, all dogs need exercise and play to keep them healthy and mentally sharp.

A dog that simply lies around all the time becomes dull and depressed. Dogs are active animals that need and enjoy interaction with people and other dogs. Daily walks, indoor and outdoor play, and training sessions all contribute to your dog's physical health and mental well-being.

The amount of exercise your dog needs depends on her age, breed, and individual activity level. In any case, your goal is to keep your dog from becoming soft and flabby. Every dog should have firm muscles and a nice waist that you can see when you look down at her.

Puppies of all breeds need lots of free play—running loose in an enclosed yard or chasing balls, for instance. This helps build strong muscles and bones. Puppies also need to practice walking nicely on leash. Protect puppies from jumping on and off furniture and running on hard surfaces, both of which can injure their growing bones and joints.

The most active adult dogs tend to be members of the sporting, working, terrier, and herding breeds. Expect to give them at least thirty minutes to an hour of good, hard exercise every day. Jogging and dog sports such as agility and flyball are great ways to give these dogs the action they need.

As your dog enters his golden years, exercise continues to be important. He doesn't need the high levels he enjoyed in his prime, but walks and play help him to remain alert and mobile. With dogs as with humans, the phrase "Use it or lose it" says it all.

Geriatric Dogs

As you've learned, dogs age at different rates, depending on factors such as their breed, the care they receive, and their environmental surroundings. In general, canine old age is considered to begin at seven years, although some dogs still seem young for several years beyond that age. The same factors that affect aging also affect a dog's life span. A small or medium-size dog that receives excellent veterinary care, exercise, and nutrition is likely to live twelve to sixteen or more years, while a large or giant breed that receives the same good care will probably live only ten to thirteen years.

Whatever the case, you can take steps to enhance and extend your geriatric dog's life.

Keep Your Dog Comfortable

Dogs tend to get a little slower and a little creakier the older they become. Their joints don't work so well anymore, and they have a little more trouble jumping up on the bed or sofa to be with you. Consider getting a ramp for the furniture so they can walk up or down instead of stressing painful joints by jumping. If your dog doesn't already have a nice soft bed, provide one to cushion aging bones. Some dog beds come with heating elements that provide soothing warmth to ease aches and pains. Take your older dog out to potty more often, too. His bladder and sphincter muscles aren't as strong as they once were. Adjust the length and pace of your walks, if necessary. They're still important, but your dog might not be able to go as far or as fast as he once could. If your small or medium-size dog isn't able to walk very far but still enjoys getting out and seeing things, consider pulling him in a child's wagon. It's good exercise for you and good stimulation for him.

Old-Age Health Problems

Arthritis, cancer, heart disease, hypothyroidism, organ failure, and even senility are all problems of older dogs. These aren't really new problems; we just see them more often these days because dogs are living longer, thanks to the great care they receive. To make sure you catch health problems before they become serious, plan with your veterinarian to start screening for them when your dog turns seven years old. A physical exam, annual blood work, and other diagnostic tests can help keep your dog in peak health as he grows older.

Chapter 5
Dog Anatomy

Anatomy is the structural makeup of the body, including the skin, muscles, bones, joints, and individual body systems such as the respiratory or digestive tract. A basic knowledge of anatomy is essential to understanding how your dog's body works, which will help you take better care of her. What follows is a guide to your dog's skin, fur, bones, joints, musculature, oral cavity, eyes, and ears.

Appearance and Stature

Dogs may well be the most genetically diverse species on earth. How many other species can claim such a range in size, appearance, and coat type? No matter what the breed or mix, though, every dog has certain external features.

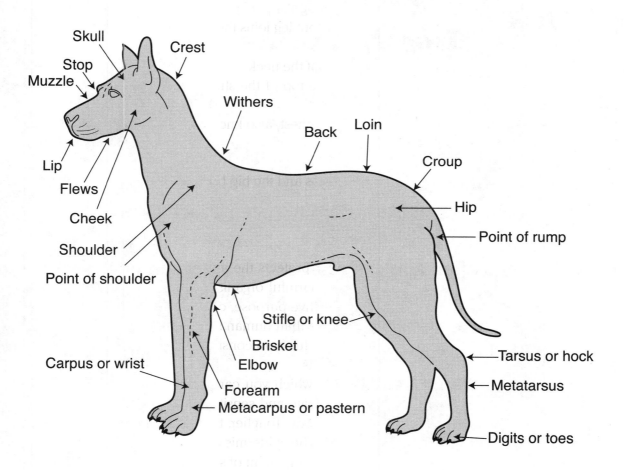

Skull

Crest

Stop

Muzzle

Lip

Flews

Cheek

Shoulder

Point of shoulder

Withers

Back

Loin

Croup

Hip

Point of rump

Stifle or knee

Brisket

Elbow

Carpus or wrist

Forearm

Metacarpus or pastern

Tarsus or hock

Metatarsus

Digits or toes

▲ Become familiar with the terminology used to refer to the different parts of a dog's anatomy.

Here are a few important anatomical terms:

- **Stop:** The indentation between the eyes where the nasal bones and skull meet (where the muzzle rises up to become the skull)
- **Muzzle:** The area in front of the eyes, consisting of the nasal bones, nostrils, and jaws
- **Ear leather:** The flap of the ear
- **Flews:** The hanging part of a dog's upper lip
- **Carpus:** The area where the front leg joins the paw (corresponds to the human wrist)
- **Crest:** The upper arched part of the neck
- **Withers:** The high point at the top of the shoulders from which a dog's height is measured
- **Brisket:** The lower part of the chest; also known as the breastbone or the sternum
- **Stifle:** The knee
- **Loin:** The area between the ribs and the hip bone

Your Dog's Skin

The skin contains your dog's body. It protects the internal organs, bones, and joints from injury and prevents harmful organisms from entering the body. Although it does serve a protective purpose, canine skin is thin and sensitive, more susceptible to damage than human skin. That's one of the reasons it has a protective covering of fur. Skin consists of three layers: the epidermis, the dermis, and the subcutis.

The epidermis is the outer layer, which you can see beneath the fur. Some parts of the epidermis are delicate and sensitive, such as the groin or the area where the legs meet the body. Tougher, thicker sections of epidermis cover the nose and paw pads. The epidermis contains cells that produce keratin, a protein that's a major component of skin, hair, and toenails; melanin, which gives skin its color; and cells that help the skin generate immune responses.

The middle and thickest layer of the skin is called the dermis. It consists mainly of collagen fibers, with some elastic fibers to keep the skin supple. Among the cell types found in the dermis are mast cells, which help control inflammation. Also part of the dermis are the epidermal appendages: hair follicles, which produce hair; sebaceous glands, which secrete sebum, an oily substance that helps lubricate the skin and coat; and sweat glands. Dogs have two types of sweat glands. The apocrine sweat glands, found throughout the body, produce a scented fluid that may play a role in sexual attraction. The eccrine sweat glands, located in the paw pads and the nasal pad, help dogs regulate their body temperature.

Supporting the dermis and the epidermis is the subcutis, which is also known as the hypodermis. It's made up of fat cells and connective tissue, through which nerves and blood vessels supply the skin.

Your Dog's Fur

Skin is protected by a layer of hair, or fur, referred to as the coat. Dogs come in a variety of coat types. There's the long, silky coat of the Afghan hound or papillon; the short, thick coat of the pointer or Great Dane; the hard, dense, wiry coat of the giant schnauzer; the curly or wavy coat of the Portuguese water dog or American water spaniel; the straight, coarse, medium-length coat of the rottweiler; the profuse double coat of the Samoyed or chow chow; the woolly corded coat of the puli; the distinctive lamblike coat of the Bedlington terrier, with its crisp mixture of hard and soft hair; the smooth, flat, hard coat of the smooth fox terrier; the short, smooth, fine coat of the Boston terrier; and the suede-like smooth body of the Chinese crested, adorned with a plumy tail, furry feet, and the crest on the head. The reason there are so many coat types is because different breeds produce different sizes and numbers of primary and secondary hairs.

Hair Production

No matter how different the various types may appear, all hair is produced by hair follicles, living cells that lie beneath the skin. Formed by proteins, hair originates in a part of the follicle called the hair bulb and passes through the follicular sheath to emerge at the surface of the skin. Each individual hair is called a hair shaft. Although follicles are living cells, hair itself is a dead structure.

FACT

Every hair shaft has three layers. The outside of the hair is called the cuticle. Inside the cuticle is the cortex. The inner layer is called the medulla. A structure known as the hair root anchors the shaft to the skin.

Each follicle produces bundles of seven to fifteen hairs. These bundles usually consist of one long, stiff primary, or guard, hair and a number of finer secondary hairs, which are also called underhairs.

Different breeds of dogs have different numbers of hairs. The density of hairs per square inch varies from breed to breed. The dogs that we tend to think of as heavy shedders have either long hair or a dense undercoat. Don't be fooled if your dog doesn't seem to shed. All dogs shed hair; it's just more apparent with longhaired dogs or dogs with thick undercoats. Paradoxically, dogs with short hair shed the most.

The Importance of Hair

For a dog, hair isn't just decoration. Hair has a protective function, keeping the skin safe from physical traumas such as cuts and scrapes, sun damage—yes, dogs can get sunburned!—and chemical irritants with which the dog might come in contact. It also helps insulate the dog from temperature extremes. All in all, the coat has a tough job. Dogs spend a lot of time scratching at and lying on their coats. In addition, all that abuse from sun, air pollutants, and scratching takes a toll on fur, so periodically the body sheds the old and damaged hairs and replaces them with new hairs.

Ever wonder why poodles and bichon frises don't seem to shed?
The secret to their nonshedding reputation is that their hair has a longer growth cycle than that of other breeds, so hair isn't replenished as often. If you're a lousy housekeeper, you can go about a month without vacuuming before you start to see poodle dust bunnies.

Hair Growth Cycle

The life cycle of hair is one of growth, rest, loss, and replacement—a process that's called shedding, or blowing coat. Hairs in different parts of the body grow to genetically determined lengths. This growth period is known as the anagen phase of hair growth. Once hair reaches its predetermined length, it rests, a period known as the telogen phase. After this rest period, new hair begins forming. As these new hairs rise through the follicular sheath, they push out the old hair, which is when it lands on your clothes, floor, and furniture.

You may notice that hair seems to grow and shed at certain times of the year. That's because hair growth and loss is affected by the number of hours of daylight to which it's exposed. Hair grows thick in the fall, in preparation for cold winter months. As the days grow warmer and longer, all that excess hair falls out, to be replaced with a cooler summer coat. If your dog spends most of his time indoors, his coat is less subject to these seasonal cycles, and he will probably shed small amounts year-round.

Hormones also affect shedding. Females that aren't spayed usually shed twice a year, at the same time they're in heat. Spayed females, on the other hand, usually develop a very full coat because they don't have that periodic surge of hormones. They're more likely to shed year-round than seasonally.

What's Normal?

The first time you see the shed of an Alaskan malamute, chow chow, or other breed with a heavy double coat, you may think the dog has an awful skin disease. The fur comes out in big clumps, and the coat can look pretty patchy and ratty. Don't worry! Unless the dog has actual bald spots, this is normal.

On the other hand, hormonal diseases such as hypothyroidism, certain hereditary abnormalities, and even stress can cause dogs to shed abnormally. Dogs with hypothyroidism often develop symmetrical hair loss on the body. For instance, the dog might lose hair on both of its rear legs. The coat doesn't look healthy, either. It becomes thin or sparse and falls out easily. Dogs whose bodies produce too much cortisone (Cushing's disease) also tend to have this symmetrical hair loss. When stress is a factor, hair loss often occurs in specific areas, such as the rear end, where hair typically grows quickly.

Muscles, Tendons, and Ligaments

Rippling beneath the skin are the muscles. Muscles are body tissues made up of long fibers that contract when they're stimulated, producing motion. The muscles are connected to the underlying bones with fibrous tissues called tendons. Ligaments are dense, stiff, stable bands of fibrous tissues that support and stabilize the joints—the places where two bones meet. In other words, they attach one bone to another. Ligaments limit range of motion, which is why your dog's front leg, for instance, bends backward but not upward.

Your dog's body has three types of muscles. Skeletal muscle plays a role in movement; smooth muscle enables the contractions of hollow organs such as blood vessels, the gastrointestinal tract, the bladder, and the uterus; and cardiac muscle ensures that the heart keeps beating. Skeletal muscles are the only ones that your dog can actually control. Smooth and cardiac muscles operate under the direction of the nervous system.

What the Muscles Do

Dogs have five muscle groups: the head and neck muscles; the dorsal (back) muscles; the thoracic, abdominal, and tail muscles; the forelimb muscles; and the hind-limb muscles. The muscles of the head and neck enable your dog to move his ears forward, up, or back. One muscle depresses the eyelid, while another raises the upper lip and dilates the nostrils. Muscles are also involved in chewing, moving the head and lower jaw, and flexing the neck and extending the shoulder. The dorsal muscles—the trapezius, the latissimus dorsi, and the lumbodorsal fascia—work to raise the head and shoulder, flex the shoulder, and anchor other muscles. The thoracic, or intercostal, muscles connect the ribs. The pectoral muscle helps to flex the shoulder, while abdominal muscles are important for a strong back and to stabilize the entire body. Your dog is able to wag his tail with the help of the caudalis and sacrococcygeus muscles. The various forelimb muscles are involved in flexing and extending the shoulders, supporting the shoulder joints, flexing and extending the elbows, and moving the front paws and toes. Your dog's rear end is controlled by the hind-limb muscles, which flex and extend the hip and knee joints and extend the foot.

Musculature Injuries

Dogs can suffer muscle sprains and strains and tendon injuries. If your dog is limping, he may well have one of these injuries. These are common in canine "weekend warriors"—dogs that aren't well conditioned and then get taken out for strenuous exercise, such as a long walk, a trip to the park to chase flying discs, or a hike that involves jumping over obstacles such as fallen trees.

Sprains are partial or complete tearing of a muscle or ligament. Torn knee ligaments are especially common. Sprains often occur when a dog slips or slides on a hard, slick surface or falls off a piece of furniture. Once a dog has suffered a sprain, it's likely to recur, so keeping your dog in good condition is important.

Recurring sprains can cause joints to become unstable and may lead to arthritis. Never take the blasé attitude that "It's just a sprain." Sprains can be difficult to heal, often more so than a fracture. Signs of a sprain include tenderness in the area of the injury, swelling, bruising, and lameness. X rays can rule out a fracture and help evaluate the injury to the soft tissue.

Sprains are treated with rest. The easiest way to do that is to confine your dog to his crate or to a small room such as a bathroom or laundry room. Cold packs applied to the injured area for the first twenty-four hours can help bring down swelling. Use a gauze wrap to attach a chemical cold pack or a bag of frozen peas to the affected area, leaving it for fifteen to thirty minutes. Do this three or four times during the day. On the second and third days, apply warm—not hot—compresses to the area on a similar schedule. Your veterinarian may prescribe pain relievers (nonsteroidal anti-inflammatory drugs), but these can have the negative effect of causing your dog to use the limb before the injury has healed. Continue to rest him, and take him out to potty on leash to prevent him from running or jumping. Sprains can take as little as three weeks to heal or as long as several months. Healing occurs when the body replaces the torn portion of the ligament with new fibrous connective tissue.

Tendon injuries usually occur when the dog suddenly wrenches or twists a limb. The most common injury of this type in dogs is a ruptured Achilles tendon and is often seen in canine athletes such as racing greyhounds, hunting dogs, or agility competitors. Tendons can also become inflamed (tendonitis) after extensive running or other overuse of the leg. Tendon injuries have much the same signs and treatment as sprains. The exception is the ruptured Achilles tendon, which must be repaired surgically.

Bones and Joints

The skeleton is the frame that supports and protects the muscles and other soft tissues. It also stores minerals the body needs, such as calcium. The leg and pelvis bones contain bone marrow, which produces the red and white blood cells the body needs to function. Bone is a living, renewable component of the body that contains blood vessels and nerves. It's covered with a thin sheath of sensitive tissue, the periosteum, which plays a role in bone growth, repair, and protection.

The joints are the areas where two bones meet. Your dog's major joints are the knees, hips, and elbows. The joints are cushioned by cartilage, a specialized type of connective tissue.

The skeletal system has two major parts. The appendicular skeleton is made up of the leg and pelvis bones (known as the long bones), and the axial skeleton consists of the skull, vertebrae, ribs, and sternum. The long bones have growth plates that produce cartilage, which is converted to bone as the dog grows. At puberty, this bone growth slows, and the growth plates close when the dog reaches physical maturity, allowing no further growth.

FACT

A dog's body has 319 bones. That's about 100 more bones than humans have. Whether they're big or small, all dogs have about the same number of bones, although the size and shape of the bones do vary.

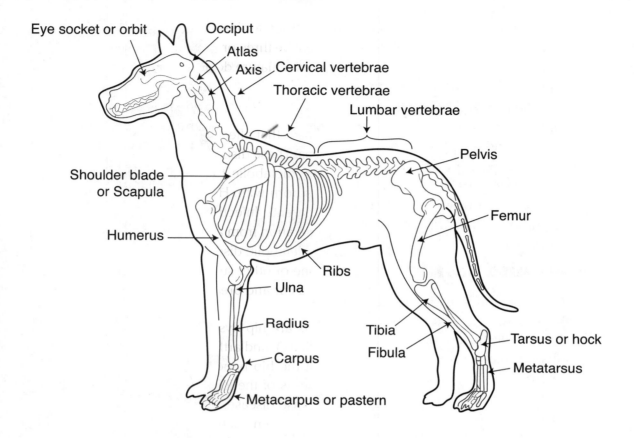

Eye socket or orbit
Occiput
Atlas
Axis
Cervical vertebrae
Thoracic vertebrae
Lumbar vertebrae
Pelvis
Shoulder blade or Scapula
Femur
Humerus
Ribs
Ulna
Radius
Tibia
Fibula
Tarsus or hock
Carpus
Metatarsus
Metacarpus or pastern

▲ The skeleton is the framework that supports the body.
More than 300 bones make up the canine skeleton.

Puppy Skeletal Development

Depending on the breed, a puppy's bones continue to grow and develop until he's anywhere from a year to two years old. He'll grow rapidly until he's about six months old and then more slowly, with occasional growth spurts, until he reaches physical maturity. Small and medium-size dogs mature at about seven months to one year of age, while large and giant-breed dogs might not be fully grown until they're eighteen months to two years old. You'll notice that your dog goes through a gangly stage—often referred to as the ugly period—usually between six months and two years of age. He might look higher in the rear than in the front, for instance, but eventually everything will all come together. He might be three or four years old before he has the complete body and muscling of a mature dog.

Skeletal Disorders

Dogs are prone to a number of diseases that affect the skeletal system, resulting in lameness or bone deformities. These diseases can be congenital, hereditary, infectious, or inflammatory, metabolic, traumatic, or neoplastic. A congenital disease is one a dog is born with. Hereditary conditions are passed on from one or both of the parents. Infectious or inflammatory diseases can be caused by injury, degeneration from age, or bacterial contamination of a joint through a wound. Metabolic diseases result from too much or too little of a particular hormone or other substance in the body. Traumatic injuries include getting hit by a car and breaking a leg. Neoplastic diseases are caused by cancer.

The most common skeletal disorders are hip dysplasia, intervertebral disc disease, patellar luxation (all hereditary), and arthritis (inflammatory). Hip dysplasia occurs when the head of the hip bone doesn't fit properly into the hip socket. The resulting looseness of the joint causes inflammation, pain, and lameness. Intervertebral disc disease, known as IVDD, is a ruptured disc (the cushion of cartilage between each vertebrae) that puts pressure on the spinal cord or a nerve root. Some skeletal disorders, such as patellar luxation (dislocation of the knee), are easily diagnosed simply by observation of the dog's hoppity gait and range of motion. Others require X rays or other diagnostic tests. Sometimes they can be corrected surgically, but often rest and pain relief are the only treatments available, especially for such conditions as arthritis.

You can help reduce the risk of your dog developing a skeletal disorder by purchasing your puppy from a reputable breeder who makes sure all breeding stock tests clear of skeletal problems. Also, not overfeeding your puppy or adult dog, and preventing your puppy from doing a lot of jumping or running on hard surfaces before his growth plates close help reduce the risk of developing a skeletal disorder.

Your Dog's Mouth and Teeth

A dog's mouth is much like your own. Dogs have lips and cheeks, a slurpy tongue, four pairs of salivary glands, a larynx and pharynx, and an epiglottis. The lips, of course, are where food enters the mouth. The tongue is a multipurpose organ that responds to taste and sensation and plays a role in cooling the dog's body (panting). The salivary glands produce saliva, which is transported to the mouth by means of tiny drainage tubes. Saliva starts the digestive process by moistening food so the body can break it down, and it produces enzymes that help rid the mouth of harmful bacteria. When dogs pant, the saliva on the surface of the tongue evaporates, providing a cooling effect.

The larynx gives voice to your dog's barks and howls and is the entrance to the respiratory system. Both air and food pass through the muscular tube that is the pharynx. It helps propel food into the esophagus and ensures that food doesn't go down the wrong way. The epiglottis is a thin flap of flexible cartilage that prevents food from entering the respiratory tract.

Let's not forget the teeth. Besides the lolling tongue, the teeth are probably the first thing you notice about a dog's mouth. Puppies are born toothless. The twenty-eight baby (deciduous) teeth start erupting when they're two or three weeks old. Puppies start losing their baby teeth at about three months old and usually have all their adult teeth by four to seven months of age.

FACT

Eight pairs of muscles and five pairs of nerves control the tongue's movements. The canine tongue responds to three flavors—salty, sweet, and sour. The bumpy projections on the surface of the tongue are called papillae. Black spots on the tongue are common and don't have any medical or other significance.

Adult dogs have forty-two teeth: twelve incisors, four canines, sixteen premolars, and ten molars. That's twenty-two in the lower jaw and twenty in the upper jaw. These teeth fit pretty well into the mouth of a medium-size or larger dog, but small dogs often have dental problems because all forty-two teeth are crammed into such a tiny mouth. And some short-faced breeds, such as pugs or bulldogs, may have fewer teeth because there's no room in their mouth for the last molars. Some breeds, such as Doberman pinschers, carry a mutation for missing teeth, and some spaniels and hounds may develop extra teeth. These extra teeth should be pulled so they don't crowd, twist, or overlap the normal teeth.

Mouth Problems

The most common mouth problems in dogs are gum inflammation (gingivitis) and periodontal disease, an inflammation of the deeper tooth structures. Other mouth problems include incorrect bites (malocclusions), a hereditary swollen jaw (craniomandibular osteopathy), and inflamed or infected lip folds (lip-fold pyodermas). Mouth injuries range from foreign bodies lodged in the mouth or throat to infections from quills or splinters stuck in the mouth to electrical or chemical burns. Abscessed or broken teeth are also common.

Gingivitis and periodontal disease are preventable with regular tooth brushing and veterinary cleanings as needed. Dogs that have an overshot jaw (one in which the upper jaw protrudes beyond the lower jaw) or an undershot jaw (in which the lower jaw protrudes beyond the upper jaw) may need orthodontic treatment if the problem is causing the teeth to become crowded or displaced. Dogs whose bites must be corrected orthodontically should not be bred, to keep them from passing on the deformity. In most cases, however, an incorrect bite doesn't cause serious problems, and no treatment is necessary. In fact, for some breeds, such as the Shih Tzu, an undershot bite is desirable.

Craniomandibular osteopathy, or CMO, is a painful inherited condition that's seen in certain terriers, as well as some other breeds. It usually develops in puppies at four to ten months of age and results from excess bone deposits along the underside of the jaw and on other parts of the jaw and skull. Puppies with CMO usually run a fever, drool, and have little appetite. Aspirin in amounts prescribed by your veterinarian can help control the pain, and the condition sometimes improves with maturity, although complete recovery is rare.

ALERT!

Cancers of the mouth are rare in dogs, but they can occur. Types of cancer that can affect the mouth are melanomas, squamous cell carcinomas, granular cell tumors, and mast cell tumors. They are treatable if caught in time, but may require surgery and radiation therapy.

Care of the Mouth

To keep your dog's mouth healthy, examine it weekly for signs of injury or illness. Things to look for include raised or bumpy tissue, sores, broken teeth, and bruises or bleeding from the tongue, gums, or roof of the mouth. Look under the tongue to make sure nothing is wedged beneath it. And, of course, check your dog's mouth any time he's drooling or pawing at his mouth or throat. That's dogspeak for "Help! I'm choking!" Your dog probably loves chewing on sticks, but they're not good for him. Splinters can get stuck in the mouth or tongue, causing an infection. Buy him regular chew toys instead.

The Eyes

The business of seeing is a complicated process made possible by the eye. Housed in a socket called the bony orbit, and protected by the upper and lower eyelids as well as the third eyelid (called the haw or sometimes the nictitating membrane), the eyeball is a delicate yet powerful organ of sense. Your dog needs his eyes to chase after and fetch balls or birds, find his way in darkness, and look lovingly at you.

The eye is made up of three layers. The fibrous outer layer of connective tissue contains the cornea (which bends incoming light rays and focuses them onto the retina) and the white of the eye, called the sclera. A middle layer called the uvea contains blood vessels and nerves as well as the light-regulating iris and a muscle called the ciliary body located behind the iris. The job of the iris is to control the amount of light that enters the eye. It does this by adjusting the size of the opening in its center, the little black dot known as the pupil. And it's the iris that gives your dog's eyes their color. The inner layer of the eye contains the light-sensitive layer of cells known as the retina, which contains specialized light receptors known as rods and cones. Their job is to convert incoming light into nerve impulses, which are then relayed via the optic nerve to the brain to be processed into an image. Amazingly, all of this occurs in a split second.

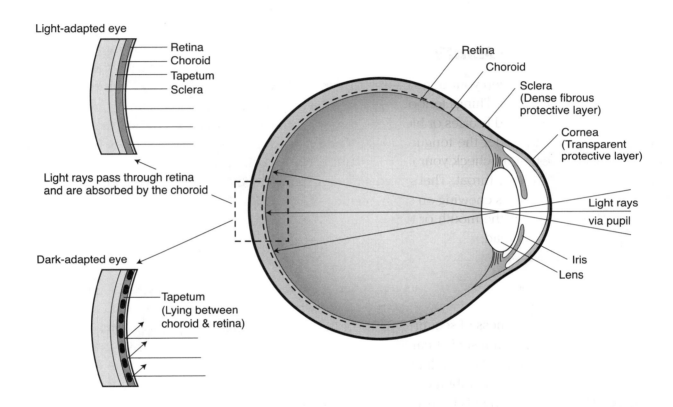

Light-adapted eye

Retina
Choroid
Tapetum
Sclera

Light rays pass through retina and are absorbed by the choroid

Dark-adapted eye

Tapetum
(Lying between
choroid & retina)

Retina

Choroid

Sclera
(Dense fibrous
protective layer)

Cornea
(Transparent
protective layer)

Light rays
via pupil

Iris
Lens

▲ Knowing the anatomy of the eye will help you understand
diseases of the eye that may affect your dog.

FACT

Lubricating the eyes are the lacrimal glands, which produce tears. Besides keeping the eyes from drying out, tears contain immune substances to help fight infections. Each eye has two lacrimal glands.

The Sense of Sight

Vision involves the perception of light as well as the intensity of that light. Different wavelengths of light appear as different colors. Vision also requires perception of forms, or images. All of these perceptions are integrated by the brain's visual center, connected to the eyes via the optic nerves, to produce sight.

Although a dog's senses tend to be more sensitive than those of a human, they have relatively poor eyesight. Because dogs evolved as hunters, their eyes are located in the front of their head, which allows them to focus on their prey. This eye placement is good for coordination and accuracy, but it's not so good for peripheral vision. Dogs can focus well on what's in front of them, but they have to look around more than a person would to see the rest of the picture. A dog's eye anatomy makes him good at detecting and following movement, as well as seeing in poor light, but he's not so good at recognizing details or differentiating colors. Dogs can see color, but not to the same extent as humans.

Eye Diseases

Dogs can suffer from a number of eye diseases. Eye problems can result from anatomical anomalies—such as too many eyelashes—irritation or injury, infections, or congenital or hereditary conditions. Common signs of eye problems are pain, discharge, redness, and filminess or cloudiness of the eye.

There are ways to tell if your dog's eyes are hurting him. Dogs indicate eye pain in many ways. You may notice that the eye is tearing more than usual or that your dog is squinting or seems sensitive to light. He may paw at his eye or whine. The eye may also look red or irritated. Take your dog to the veterinarian if his eye appears to be painful.

Common eye problems include extra eyelashes, which irritate the eye; eyelid defects such as entropion or ectropion; cherry eye, a congenital defect in which a tear gland bulges out from beneath the eyelid; conjunctivitis, or pink eye; dry eye; corneal injuries; cataracts; glaucoma; and retinal diseases. Depending on the condition, your veterinarian can address the problem with surgery or medication. Unfortunately, some eye diseases, such as progressive retinal atrophy, have no treatment and lead to eventual blindness. On the up side, dogs can get around very well without sight by making more use of their senses of smell and hearing.

The Ears

One of the reasons dogs are such great companions to humans is because they alert us to so many things that we would otherwise overlook. This includes sounds that our own hearing isn't sensitive enough to catch. A dog, on the other hand, has an acute sense of hearing, thanks to the structure of his ears. Simply looking at the variety of dog ears is a reminder of the range of canine anatomy. A dog's ears can be pricked in the air or folded over like the dog-eared page of a book. They might be large or small, long or short. But on the inside, every dog's ear is a masterpiece of acoustics.

Ear Anatomy

Sound is energy, or vibrations, that is transmitted by waves through the air. You may have noticed that your dog can wiggle his ears much more than you can yours. He can rotate his ear flap (known as the pinna) to capture sounds, which then travel into the ear canal. From there the sound flows through the ear canal downward and inward until it arrives at the eardrum, or tympanic membrane. A chain of small bones called the auditory ossicles then transmits the sound to the inner ear, which has been described as resembling a series of bony canals. The inner ear is the essential organ of hearing and contains the cochlea. Coiled like a snail shell, the cochlea is filled with fluid that converts the vibrations making up sound into waves that in turn become nerve impulses transported to the auditory nerve where they are interpreted by the brain. As with the process of sight, all of this occurs instantaneously.

Ear Problems

As much as 20 percent of a veterinarian's practice consists of treating ear infections and other ear problems. Ears can become infected with bacteria, fungi, or yeast. They can sustain injuries in fights or play, and they can become infested with mites. Allergies can cause ear problems, and dogs can suffer congenital or acquired deafness.

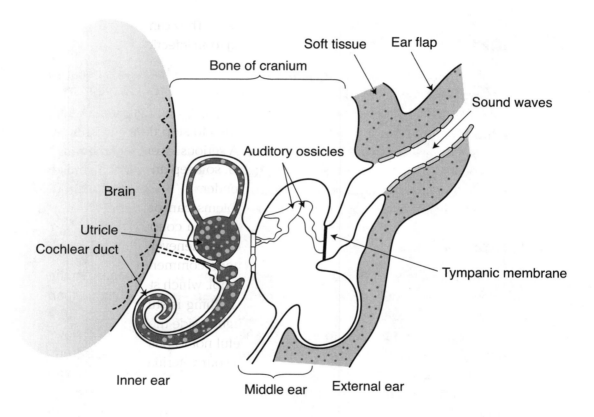

▲ Except for the external ear, dogs and humans have similar ear anatomy, but dogs can hear high-pitched sounds that are inaudible to humans and can hear sounds from a much greater distance than people.

If your dog frequently shakes his head and paws at his ears, he may have an infection. Ear infections are treated with antibiotics. Your veterinarian will need to culture the buildup in the ear to determine what's causing the infection. This allows her to prescribe the best antibiotic for the job. Itching and inflammation caused by allergies calls for use of the big guns: antihistamines and corticosteroids.

Don't use cotton swabs to clean your dog's ears. They can push debris deeper into the ear and block air flow, leading to an infection. Use them only to clean the folds of the outer ear.

If your dog's ear flap is wounded, you'll need to stop the bleeding and apply antibiotic ointment to the injured area. A serious laceration may need stitches. Bite wounds often become abscessed, so keep an eye on the area to make sure it doesn't become swollen and tender.

With good care, however, many ear problems can be avoided. Keep your dog's ears clean and dry. Wipe them out with a cotton ball after your dog has a bath or goes swimming. Clean the ears whenever you see a build-up of wax or dirt in the ears. Use an ear cleaner recommended by your veterinarian and avoid products that contain alcohol, which stings.

Check the ears frequently to make sure nothing is stuck inside them. Dogs can get grass seeds or other objects caught inside their ears. If they're not removed, an infection can begin. Be careful not to push the object further into the ear. If necessary, take the dog to your veterinarian to have the object removed.

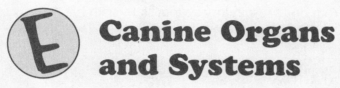

Chapter 6

Canine Organs and Systems

Our canine companions are composed of a number of organs and systems. This is another way of saying that a lot of parts go into making the whole that is your dog! Ideally, these parts all function together as a well-oiled machine. To understand your dog's health, it helps to know about the different systems and the main organs that make up each one, as well as some of the more common problems that occur with each. These organs and systems must all work properly on their own and also interact in order to keep your dog in top condition.

Respiratory System

The respiratory system is an incredible series of passageways that works to take oxygen out of the air and deliver it to the bloodstream, where red blood cells then carry it to individual cells throughout the body. The respiratory system works with the cardiovascular system to remove carbon dioxide waste as well. Your dog's respiratory system starts with her nose as fresh air goes in, and it ends with her nose as carbon dioxide is breathed out.

Airways

What better place to start a trip around your dog's body than with the nose? Your dog's nose is an unparalleled scenting machine, capable of detecting much more than a human nose can. Even more importantly for your dog, it is the starting point of the respiratory system. While dogs can breathe through their mouths if necessary, such as when they are hot or tired, they generally breathe through their noses.

FACT

Dogs with short muzzles, such as pugs and bulldogs, are referred to as brachycephalic, meaning short-headed or broad-headed. Dogs with long muzzles, such as greyhounds, are called dolichocephalic. The word comes from *dolichos*, the Greek word for long.

As air comes into her nose, your dog separates out all the fascinating smells (and perhaps even runs off to go follow one!). At the same time, her many nasal sinuses help to moisturize and warm the air to body temperature so her lungs won't get a shock from too-cold air. Dust, viruses, and bacteria can all enter the nose too, but the nasal passages are lined with fine hairs to catch debris and infection-fighting cells to trap any troublemakers.

From the nose, air travels into the larynx, the pharynx, and on to the trachea, or windpipe. The trachea is a tunnel of cartilage that leads from the upper airways into the lungs. The trachea should be composed of about three-quarters firm cartilage, with the remainder being soft tissue that stays taut but gives the trachea some flexibility. However, some breeds of dogs have tracheal collapse. In these cases, the cartilage is defective, or the soft tissue area too large or too loose. When the dog breathes in deeply, the soft area pulls down into the trachea or the tracheal rings themselves flatten. This reduces the area available for air to move through—picture squeezing a cardboard tube partially closed—and therefore the body receives less oxygen. This condition can be helped medically or surgically, depending on the exact problem.

Lungs

From the trachea, air moves into progressively smaller airways, called bronchi and bronchioli. These airways end in tiny areas called alveoli. Here, oxygen is added to the blood when your dog breathes in and carbon dioxide removed when your dog breathes out. Lungs contain miles of these passageways along with many blood vessels, all to make sure your dog's cells get the oxygen they need. Your dog's lungs have two main lobes on the left side and four lobes on the right side. To breathe, your dog needs the assistance of a specialized muscle called the diaphragm, which separates the chest from the abdomen. This muscle helps to pull air into the lungs and expel carbon dioxide.

Like most of your dog's respiratory system, the lungs have cells to fight infection as well as fine hairs called cilia that separate out debris and try to push it up and out. Your dog can only get the most benefit from breathing if the air she breathes is clean. Smog and secondhand cigarette smoke can all lead to respiratory problems in dogs.

Digestive System

Your dog's digestive system starts right off at the mouth and ends at his end—the anus. This system of your dog's body is designed to take in nutrients, utilize those nutrients in the best and most efficient way, and then get rid of waste products. Dogs are extremely good at surviving on even poor-quality food (though you will eventually pay the price with health problems such as skin allergies and bone development abnormalities). Dogs are also very clever at locating food sources, so remember to keep enticing treats off the counter. Close your cupboards, and keep garbage out of reach.

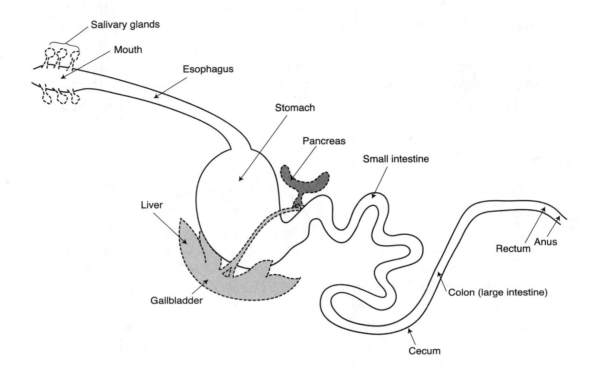

Salivary glands

Mouth

Esophagus

Stomach

Pancreas

Small intestine

Liver

Gallbladder

Rectum

Anus

Colon (large intestine)

Cecum

▲ The digestive tract goes through the entire body, starting at the mouth and ending at the rear. Dogs tend to bolt their food and have an expanding esophagus to accommodate the sometimes big chunks of food that come down it.

Teeth

The normal adult dog has forty-two teeth (twenty-eight for puppies). This holds true for all dogs, from the huge Irish wolfhound to the tiniest Chihuahua. Toy breeds may lose teeth easily due to crowding, and some dogs may be born missing teeth or even with extra teeth, but ideally there should be forty-two. This includes twelve incisors (the small teeth in the very front) that are used for delicately grasping things. The large canine teeth come next— two on the bottom and two on top. The canines are used for biting (both for protection and to catch food), to help keep the tongue in the mouth so it doesn't dry out, and to carry things. Following the canines come the premolars. These teeth get progressively bigger as you go back in your dog's mouth and are used for shearing and chewing. There should be sixteen pre-molars total, but these are the teeth that seem to be missing most often. The last teeth are the molars—four on the top and six on the bottom.

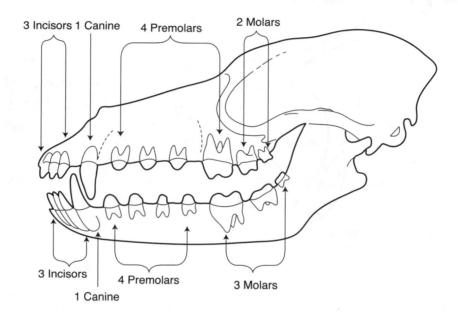

3 Incisors   1 Canine   4 Premolars   2 Molars

3 Incisors   4 Premolars   3 Molars

1 Canine

▲ A dog's teeth are designed to bite, tear, cut, and grind. The incisors (the front teeth) are the biting teeth, while the canines (the fangs) are used to grasp and hold food and tear off muscles and skin. The side and back teeth (premolars and molars) cut and crush food.

Tongue and Salivary Glands

The tongue is one of the strongest muscles in the body. While dogs don't use their tongues to make the wide variety of sounds that people make, their tongues help them to lap up liquids, aid in temperature control when they pant on hot days, and help them express how they feel, such as when they lick you with delight when you walk in the front door.

The salivary glands produce the drool that your dog leaves when trying to convince you to share your hamburger. Saliva also starts the process of digestion and helps food move easily down through the esophagus. It may help to heal wounds in the mouth, and a dog with sores or injuries to the mouth will drool more than usual.

Esophagus and Pharynx

The pharynx is part of the pathway from the mouth to the esophagus. The esophagus is a tube of muscle running from the mouth down to the stomach. It runs through the chest but does not help in breathing at all; it is solely a food tube. Sometimes the muscles or nerves in the esophagus can have problems, and food does not move steadily along but gets trapped. In these situations, the esophagus may stretch into a megaesophagus (think of baggy pantyhose). With a megaesophagus, your dog can't get nutrients into the stomach efficiently and may vomit and aspirate some of the food, leading to pneumonia. This problem can develop as the result of disease later in life or show up as a congenital defect in puppies.

Stomach

The stomach is a massive muscular food grinder that contains digestive enzymes to help break food down into molecules that your dog's body can use. Food enters the stomach via the esophagus and leaves through the pylorus (a muscular ring) to enter the first part of the small intestine, an area called the duodenum. Just like people, dogs can develop ulcers or get gastritis. Also, due to the way the dog's stomach is attached to the body wall, the stomach may twist. This shuts off the blood flow to the area, causing tissue death and possibly even the death of your dog! This condition, known as bloat or gastrointestinal volvulus, is an emergency situation and usually requires surgery.

ALERT!

If your dog appears bloated, tries unsuccessfully to vomit, and paces uncomfortably, assume she may be bloating. Call your veterinarian immediately! This problem is more common in deep-chested breeds such as Great Danes, Irish setters, and dachshunds.

Small Intestines

The small intestines have three parts—the duodenum, the jejunum, and the ileum. These long tubes are the workhorses of digestion. Using their own enzymes, plus enzymes from the pancreas, the small intestines digest food and absorb the nutrients. There is a population of "good bacteria" that work and help in digestion as well. If things are not right, poor digestion or poor absorption (malabsorption) can lead to diarrhea, vomiting, and weight loss.

The small intestines have many projections, or villi, into the open tube that increase the surface area of working cells. The villi secrete enzymes and other substances, absorb nutrients, and help guard against harmful substances and infectious bacteria and viruses.

Pancreas

The pancreas is a small organ that lies next to the stomach and small intestines. It produces the serious enzymes for digesting food, plus some important hormones such as insulin that help the body make use of nutrients. The pancreas is sensitive to stress, such as that caused by feeding a lot of fatty foods, and the resulting inflammation of the pancreas, known as pancreatitis, can be fatal. If the pancreas does not make its usual digestive enzymes, your dog will have diarrhea and have trouble maintaining weight, as he can't utilize the food he is eating very well. Dogs with subnormal amounts of insulin are diabetic and will typically need insulin injections and special feeding regimens.

Liver and Gallbladder

Your dog's liver works to process nutrients and filter out toxins. Together with the gallbladder, which produces bile to help digest fats, the liver is an essential part of your dog's energy production system. Liver problems can show up as malnutrition, life-threatening infections, and even neurologic signs if toxins build up in the blood. Dogs with liver problems may appear jaundiced, with yellow coloring in their skin, eyes, and gums, or they may vomit.

Large Intestines

The large intestines are divided into parts known as the ascending colon, transverse colon, descending colon, and the cecum. The large intestines help to retain water and any nutrients missed by the small intestines. They concentrate waste and produce stool. Problems with the large intestine primarily show up as diarrhea or constipation.

Cardiovascular System

The cardiovascular system includes your dog's heart (the "cardio" part) and the blood vessels (the "vascular" part). There are two types of blood vessels—the arteries, which move blood away from the heart, and the veins, which move blood back to the heart. The cardiovascular system works with the lungs to bring oxygen to cells and take away carbon dioxide, as well as to carry nutrients to the cells and remove wastes.

Heart

A dog's heart is very similar to a human heart. The heart has four chambers—a right and left atrium and a right and left ventricle. The chambers on the right side receive blood from the body and send it out to the lungs, to be enriched with oxygen. Blood returns to the heart from the lungs on the left side, and the strong left ventricle then pumps the oxygen-rich blood out to the body.

A puppy may be born with a defective heart. The chambers may be malformed or missing, the blood vessels in and out of the heart too small or in the wrong place, or the heart valves between the chambers may not be right. Older dogs can develop heart failure due to infections, stress, dietary problems, or genetic predispositions. There are now many medications to help dogs with heart problems, and even pacemakers, but canine heart transplants are not an option yet.

Blood Vessels

Dogs have literally miles of blood vessels. These include the large arteries that travel to the abdomen, head, and heart, along with the tiny capillaries that join the arteries and veins. Arteries are the muscular blood vessels that move oxygen and nutrients from the heart to the rest of the body. When you feel a pulse, you are feeling that action along an artery. The veins bring blood that has been depleted of oxygen back to the heart and lungs.

FACT

If your dog cuts an artery, the blood will spurt due to the muscle action passed along from the heart. The blood will be bright red from the fresh load of oxygen it carries. The blood from a cut into a vein runs rather than spurts and is darker in color as it carries carbon dioxide, not oxygen.

Blood

Blood itself is made up of various components. Red blood cells carry oxygen; white blood cells fight infection; and platelets help with blood clotting, along with the fluid called plasma. Many substances are transported through the bloodstream. Hormones, nutrients, waste products, and even medications are delivered to cells via the blood. Disorders with the different blood components can cause several different kinds of problems. Too few red blood cells can result in anemia, while too few white blood cells may lead to infections. Dogs that don't have enough platelets or clotting factors can have bleeding disorders, such as von Willebrand's disease. These problems can be side effects of other diseases, or they may occur as congenital defects.

Nervous System

Think of your dog's nervous system as the control center for his body. The brain, spinal cord, and roadmap of nerves that travel to every inch of your dog's body tell him what his senses detect and which muscles to move. They also help him learn. The nervous system also includes the intangibles that make each dog's personality unique. So along with relatively understandable disorders, such as movement problems, behavior disorders also start here.

Brain

The brain has three main areas—the cerebrum, the cerebellum, and the brain stem. The delicate tissue of the brain is protected with a sturdy covering of tissue called the meninges as well as the bones of the skull. While those coverings form important shields, they can cause problems with brain trauma as they don't allow room for swelling. Secondary pressure is often more damaging to brain tissue than the original injury. If your dog has serious brain trauma, he may need holes drilled into the skull so these shields can be opened to allow for expansion.

ALERT!

Do *not* put your hand into the mouth of a dog having seizures! Dogs don't have the risk of swallowing their tongues like people do. If you get bitten, you'll need to take yourself to the emergency room as well as get your dog to the veterinary hospital.

The cerebrum is the part of the brain where learning takes place. It collects input from your dog's senses (such as vision and smell) and controls emotions. Epileptic seizures originate in the cerebrum; these seizures are basically a short circuit of the neurons there.

The cerebellum is the part of the brain that helps your dog with balance and movement. A problem in the cerebellum might show up as a wobbly gait or clumsiness. The brain stem controls many of the body's most basic functions. For example, directions for breathing originate here.

Spinal Cord

The spinal cord runs through the bony vertebral column down your dog's back. This is a very important pathway for nerves that travel from the brain, carrying information for individual muscles and cells. Information is also carried as feedback from muscles and cells back to the brain. For example, say your dog is running, and the footing suddenly changes from grass to rocks. The brain has been directing long, hard landing strides. Now, the feet pass back the information that the surface has changed. The brain quickly changes its message to accommodate the poor footing, and the dog shortens and lightens his stride.

An injury to the spinal cord may lead to paralysis or death. Ruptured spinal column discs that put pressure on the spinal cord often have permanent effects on the nerves involved. Discs can rupture from severe trauma, such as being hit by a car, or from repeated low-level damage due to wear and tear. Some breeds (such as the long, low-backed breeds like dachshunds and basset hounds) are predisposed to disc problems from the way their bodies are formed.

Nerve Cells

Your dog has great numbers of nerves throughout her body. These nerves continually send messages back and forth from the brain and body. Many of these functions are subconscious. Your dog doesn't have to think carefully to breathe. When nerve cells are damaged, pain reports go back to the brain. If conditions change, the news is passed on to the brain so adjustments can be made.

Excretory System

You've already learned that solid food wastes pass out of your dog via the large intestines. Wastes from water and many metabolic processes leave via the excretory system. This system is led by the kidneys, which work with the ureters, bladder, and urethra.

Kidneys and Ureters

The kidneys are the prime organs of the excretory system. Your dog has two, one on each side, tucked up in front of the hind legs near the spinal column. They are bean-shaped (as in kidney beans!) and are real workhorses. The kidneys remove metabolic wastes and toxins from the blood while taking up some of the fluid and any nutrients that pass through them. Kidneys can concentrate urine or dilute it, depending on how much your dog is drinking and if there are any health problems. Urine made by the kidneys is then passed down tubes, the ureters, to the bladder.

Dogs may be born with congenital kidney defects, or the kidneys may be damaged by toxins or infection. Dogs with kidney problems may vomit as a result of toxin buildup, or they may drink a lot with excessive urination or no urine production at all. About two-thirds of the kidneys must be damaged before your dog shows signs of illness. Dogs can survive very well with just one healthy kidney at work.

Bladder and Urethra

The bladder is a pouch that receives the urine flowing from the kidneys via the ureters. The bladder collects and holds urine until the amount is big enough to stimulate your dog to urinate. Obviously, in a puppy, that's not very much! Older dogs can often hold their urine much longer, but as they lose muscle tone with age they need to relieve themselves more often.

Dalmatians have a unique uric acid metabolism that predisposes them to developing urinary tract stones in the kidney or bladder. These stones can cause urinary blockages, especially in males. Miniature schnauzers are susceptible to a different type of bladder stone. Special diets may help to prevent stones in these breeds.

Bladder problems that dogs can have include loss of muscle tone, hormonal influences, infections, cancer, and even developing bladder stones. Stones are often diet related and may require surgery or a special diet.

The urethra is the membranous passageway for urine from the bladder out via the vagina or penis. This is usually a trouble-free area of the excretory system, though stones can block the urine flow.

Endocrine System

The endocrine system consists of the organs that produce hormones. Hormones help to regulate body functions, from hair growth to reproduction and everything in between! Most of these endocrine organs are regulated themselves by an internal feedback system. When enough of a hormone is produced, the organ receives a signal and production stops for a while. When the level drops, the organ gets the signal to produce again. The endocrine system includes some organs that also belong in other systems, such as the pancreas and the reproductive organs, as their main functions are not just hormone production. Other glands, such as the thyroid, parathyroid, adrenal, and pituitary, are mainly hormone producers.

Thyroid Gland

The thyroid is a two-lobed gland lying by the trachea in the neck. This gland is responsible for making the thyroid hormones that can be so important to a dog's health. Thyroid hormones help regulate a dog's metabolic rate (how fast calories are burned), influence coat growth, and are important for fertility and physical activity levels.

Dogs often have too little thyroid hormone. Dogs with low thyroid levels may be inactive and overweight, with poor coats. Males may be sterile, and females may have trouble conceiving and carrying a litter to term.

Parathyroid Glands

The two small parathyroid glands lie next to the thyroid. While small in size, these glands produce important hormones, such as parathormone, which regulates the metabolism of calcium. Calcium is important for bone growth, nerve function, and muscle function. Too much or too little can have disastrous consequences!

If your dog has surgery on the thyroid or in this area of the neck, your veterinarian will closely monitor your dog for a few days to be sure the parathyroid was not damaged. Calcium metabolism must be carefully regulated for good health.

Adrenal Glands

The adrenal glands are another pair of small but mighty endocrine glands. These glands are located next to the kidneys. They produce three classes of hormones. The glucocorticoids, such as cortisol, act on carbohydrates and help with stress and inflammation. The catecholamines, such as epinephrine (adrenaline), prepare dogs for fight or flight by dilating arteries, increasing heart rate, and opening airways. Finally, the mineralocorticoids, such as aldosterone, regulate sodium and potassium levels in the body. Various other hormones, including some of the reproductive hormones, are also manufactured here as well as in the reproductive organs.

Pituitary Gland

The pituitary is a two-part gland located at the base of the brain. The adrenal glands and thyroid all get their working orders from the front part of the gland, the anterior pituitary. In addition, the anterior pituitary produces growth hormone, which acts directly on cells.

The posterior pituitary isn't nearly so busy. Its primary productions are oxytocin, which stimulates uterine contractions at labor and milk letdown for nursing, along with antidiuretic hormone, which acts via the kidneys to regulate how much water is resorbed.

Reproductive System

The reproductive system is important for preserving the species, but it is not vitally important for the health of an individual animal. Unlike the organs of most other systems, a dog can survive quite well without testicles or a uterus. Along with the obvious purpose of producing puppies, the reproductive system also produces hormones that influence a dog's secondary sex characteristics. For instance, in many breeds the males are larger and have more coat.

Male Reproductive System

The male reproductive system starts internally with the prostate gland, which is located next to the bladder. This gland adds secretions to any ejaculate of semen that help to keep sperm alive. The urethra (part of the excretory system) then carries secretions out to the penis. In dogs, the penis has a bony section as well as vascular areas that swell with erection. The penis lies in a skin sheath called the prepuce.

Dogs normally have two testicles enclosed in a skin pouch outside the body called the scrotum. This is located under the tail. Each testicle stores the sperm it produces. The testicles also produce testosterone, which gives intact male dogs their fuller coats, interest in female dogs, and other characteristic behaviors.

Dogs with a retained testicle (one left inside the body—not dropped out into the scrotum) should be neutered, as the internal testicle may become cancerous. These dogs are called cryptorchids.

Just as in people, the prostate gland can get become enlarged (known as benign hypertrophy) and cause problems by putting pressure on the bladder. It can even develop cancer in rare cases.

Female Reproductive System

Female dogs have two ovaries, which are small organs located internally near the kidneys. This is where eggs are produced, as well as the hormones estrogen and progesterone. The activity of the ovary is controlled by hormones from the pituitary gland. When the ovary has mature eggs, they travel via the fallopian tubes to the uterus. The uterus is where the eggs are fertilized and puppy embryos develop.

The uterus has two long horns to accommodate multiple growing puppies. When puppies are being whelped, they pass along the uterus, through the cervix into the vagina, and out the vulva under your dog's tail.

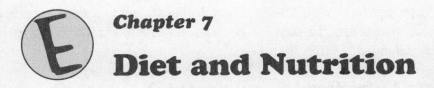

Chapter 7

Diet and Nutrition

Dogs have a long history of scavenging their meals. In fact, some experts theorize that the canine propensity for raiding human garbage sites may have played a role in the domestication of the dog. As dogs learned that humans were the source of easy meals, and humans learned that dogs could ward off other predators or sound the alarm, the two became partners in survival and food gathering. Now, of course, our dogs depend on us entirely for their meals, and we know a lot more about the best ways to feed them.

Nutritional Requirements

Dogs are omnivores. That means they can survive by eating a variety of foods. (Cats, on the other hand, are obligate carnivores, which means they must have meat in their diet.) A balanced diet for dogs contains all the essential nutrients their bodies need to function, in the correct quantities and proportions. With all the research that's gone into canine nutritional requirements over the past few decades, it's safe to say that our dogs probably eat more healthily than we do.

Who Sets Nutritional Requirements?

The nutritional requirements for dogs are set by two organizations: the National Research Council (NRC), and the Association of American Feed Control Officials (AAFCO). NRC recommendations are made by an international committee of animal nutrition experts and are updated as needed. The committee's report includes such information as how a dog's body metabolizes nutrients, the diseases related to poor nutrition, signs that a dog is suffering a nutrient deficiency, and the minimum daily nutrient requirements for dogs. The nutrient requirement recommendations are based on a dog's activity level and life stage (such as puppy, adult, or senior). Both of these factors have a large influence on a dog's nutrient needs.

FACT

The nutritional adequacy statement on a dog food label must say which life stage the product is made for: growth/lactation (puppies or pregnant/lactating females), maintenance (adults), or all life stages (any dog). AAFCO recognizes only two life-stage profiles, growth/lactation and maintenance. Therefore, a food labeled for "seniors" or "large breeds" simply meets their requirements for adult dogs.

When they're formulating foods, however, dog-food manufacturers rely on nutrient profiles from AAFCO, which are based on commonly used ingredients. These provide recommendations for practical minimum and maximum levels of nutrients in dog foods. The NRC recommendations come from studies in which higher-quality nutrients are used. Without input from the AAFCO, pet foods might be nutritionally deficient.

When you look on a bag or can of dog food, somewhere on the label should be a statement that the food is formulated to meet the nutritional levels established by AAFCO, or that feeding tests using AAFCO procedures substantiate that the food provides complete and balanced nutrition. Ideally, the manufacturer uses feeding trials to prove that a food is complete and balanced rather than simply mixing together a recipe without actually feeding it to dogs. The 2003 NRC recommendations contain new information about canine nutritional needs, so it's possible that AAFCO nutrient profiles will change in the near future.

Dog-Food Ingredients

The manufacture of pet foods is governed by the federal Food, Drug, and Cosmetic Act, which mandates that pet foods, like human foods, be pure and wholesome, contain no harmful or deleterious substances, and be truthfully labeled. Dog-food ingredients must be "generally recognized as safe" (GRAS for short), and dog foods must have labels listing all the ingredients. An ingredient list is useful for telling you what's in a food, but it can't tell you the quality of the ingredients. However, there are some tricks to reading a label that will help you be a more informed dog-food shopper.

Dietary protein contains ten essential amino acids that dogs cannot make on their own. The best dog foods have meat protein as the first ingredient. Protein from meat is higher in quality than protein from grains. Forms of meat protein include meat by-products and meat meals, which is meat that's been heat-processed to remove fat and water.

Ingredients are listed by weight, in descending order. That means the food should have more of the first ingredient than anything else. While some dog foods may list meat as the first ingredient, if you look farther down the label you may notice that it also lists a particular grain in several different forms, such as wheat flour, flakes, middlings, or bran. Individually, each form of wheat might make up only a small part of the food, but together they may outweigh the meat it contains. Look for a food that contains a balance of meat and grain proteins.

The Feeding Schedule

Dogs do best when they eat regular meals at specific times every day because they're less likely to eat too much. Consistent meal times also help with potty training. Physiologically, dogs have the urge to go after they eat, so by scheduling meals and taking your dog out immediately afterward, you can accustom him to eliminating at certain times. Finally, dogs are creatures of habit. They like knowing that meals will appear at certain times every day.

When to Feed

Adult dogs do well on two meals a day, morning and evening. Puppies typically eat three or four meals a day. That's because they're growing, so they need more nutrients than adult dogs. If you aren't able to provide mid-day meals, don't worry. Simply divide the amount of food the puppy needs for the day into two meals, and he'll do just fine. The exception might be a small toy-breed puppy. These little dogs sometimes need a snack between meals to keep their energy levels up. You can do this for any dog by filling a treat ball or cube with kibble. Your dog will occupy himself by trying to get the kibble out, and he'll get the snack he needs even if you're not home to feed him.

Proper Eating Habits

By helping your dog develop good eating habits, you can avoid problems with obesity and teach manners at the same time. The first good habit is one you need to learn: Measure your dog's food. Don't just fill his dish until it's full. Use a measuring cup or a kitchen scale so you feed an appropriate amount. If you're using a measuring cup, give a level cup instead of a heaping one.

FACT

If your dog "inhales" his food, spread it out on a flat surface such as a cookie sheet (use one with raised edges to keep the food inside it). This forces him to slow down and eat at a more moderate pace.

Unless your dog is really low to the ground, it's a good idea to use raised feeding dishes. They have all kinds of benefits for you and your dog. For one thing, your dog is less likely to slosh water or drop food on the floor. He's also less likely to develop intestinal gas. When dogs have to bend down to swallow their food, they swallow air with it, which later becomes stinky intestinal gas. Raised dishes are also recommended for deep-chested dogs that are prone to bloat, or gastric dilatation volvulus. Dogs that have a large, flaccid esophagus—a condition called megaesophagus—can benefit from raised feeding dishes, which make it easier for food to move from the esophagus to the stomach. Best of all, raised dishes are not only more comfortable for your dog to eat from—especially if he's old and creaky—they're also easier for you to put down and pick up because you don't have to bend over so far.

ESSENTIAL

Wash your dog's dishes regularly. Nobody likes eating off smelly, food-encrusted dishes. Choose metal or ceramic dishes that are dishwasher-safe, and keep extras on hand so you have one set to use while the other is in the dishwasher.

Next, teach your dog to wait politely while you prepare his food. Dogs love mealtime, and they'll whirl around in circles or jump up on you while you fix their food to show their appreciation. Channel this energy by asking your dog to sit while you prepare his food. Put the bowl down, tell him to stay, and then give him permission to eat by saying "Okay!" or "Chow!" This makes meal preparation more pleasant for you, and it's a good opportunity for Rex to practice his manners and get an immediate reward.

Commercial Foods

Dogs used to eat whatever scraps people gave them. The first commercial dog food was developed a little over 140 years ago by James Spratt, in the form of a biscuit. Spratt's dog biscuits were popular, and other companies also began to manufacture pet foods. At first, these foods were available only in feed stores, but by the 1930s they could be found in grocery stores as well. Canned foods were most popular, but the invention of the extrusion process to create dried food pellets propelled dry foods to the top spot in dog owners' hearts. Dry food was less expensive and easier to feed. Today, dog owners can choose from a wide variety of commercial canned, dry, frozen, and dehydrated dog foods.

What Type of Food Is Best?

Dogs are individuals, and different dogs do better on different types of foods. Whether you choose a canned, dry, or other type of dog food depends not only on your dog's needs, but also on your budget, what's most convenient for you, and how you feel about certain types of ingredients. Consider all these factors when you're choosing a food. Each type has advantages and disadvantages.

FACT

If you have leftover canned food, don't leave it in the can. Place it in a plastic storage container or in a plastic storage bag with all the air squeezed out. Refrigerate it until the next use.

Dogs like the taste of canned food, and it may make you feel as if you're offering a substantial meal. It has a long shelf life until it's opened. On the down side, canned food is expensive, and it must be refrigerated after it's opened. Dry food is easy to scoop out, measure, and serve. It's less expensive than canned food and doesn't need to be refrigerated, even after it's opened. And dogs often like the crunchy texture. Dry food doesn't have much of a down side, although most dogs, if given a choice, will prefer canned food. There's nothing wrong with adding a little flavor to a dry meal by mixing it with some canned food. That can help you stretch your dog-food budget and satisfy your dog's taste buds.

More recently, manufacturers have begun preparing frozen and dehydrated foods for dogs. Frozen diets are prepared fresh, made into rolls, cubes, or loaves, and flash frozen so they don't need artificial preservatives. The lack of heat processing preserves heat-sensitive vitamins and amino acids that would otherwise be damaged. The disadvantage is that you have to remember to thaw it before use (although many dogs are satisfied to just gulp it down frozen).

ALERT!

Remember that too much of a good thing can be harmful. If your dog is eating a food that's complete and balanced, avoid giving him vitamin or mineral supplements without first checking with your veterinarian or a veterinary nutritionist.

Dehydrated foods (which have all the water removed from them) are prepared at a temperature low enough to preserve the value of the vitamins, minerals, and other nutrients yet high enough to kill any bacteria. Just mix them with warm water, and they're ready to feed. Dehydrated foods have the long shelf life and easy storage of canned and dry foods. Rehydrated food must be refrigerated if your dog doesn't eat all of it at one sitting, but it's easy to prepare only the amount you need so he doesn't have any leftovers.

Popular, Premium, Natural, and Organic Foods

What do these terms mean? That's a good question. Lots of labels are applied to dog foods, but they don't always have a clear-cut meaning or government-approved definition. Dog food is often categorized as popular, premium, or generic. Popular foods are the national or regional brands that you find in grocery stores. They're made by well-known manufacturers that spend a lot of money researching canine nutritional needs and testing their foods by feeding them to dogs. One potential disadvantage of these foods is that their formulas can vary from batch to batch, depending on the cost and availability of their ingredients. Some dogs suffer tummy upset when their diets change, so this is a factor to consider in choosing a dog food. In general, popular foods aren't as digestible as premium foods, but they're of better quality than generic foods.

QUESTION?

What is digestibility?
Digestibility is the proportion of nutrients in a food available for the body to absorb and use. It's determined over a period of days by measuring the amount of food a dog takes in and the amount of fecal matter he produces, which is then analyzed in a laboratory to see how much is nutrient waste and how much is normal metabolic waste.

Premium foods are found primarily in pet supply stores. They contain high-quality ingredients that provide good to excellent digestibility and are prepared according to fixed formulas, meaning that the ingredients don't change. Some premium foods may contain organic or human-grade ingredients. Premium foods are expensive, but because of their higher digestibility you can feed less of a premium food than of a popular or generic food, which brings down the cost per serving.

Premium foods are often labeled as organic or natural. That definitely sounds good, but it doesn't have any real meaning. The term "natural" doesn't have an official definition. Instead, it is usually used to mean that a food doesn't have any artificial flavors, colors, or preservatives. The term "organic" simply refers to the way plants were grown or animals were raised (usually without the use of pesticides or fertilizers or only certain types of pesticides or fertilizers).

Currently, the United States Department of Agriculture (USDA) does not have any rules governing the labeling of organic foods for people or pets, although this will probably change in the future. Just because a dog food is labeled premium, superpremium, natural, organic, or gourmet does not mean that it actually has to meet any higher or different standards than other foods. Call the manufacturer—companies are required to provide contact information on their labels—and ask for specifics on what their claim actually means.

All dog food labels must contain five pieces of information: the guaranteed analysis, which tells you the minimum and maximum levels of protein and fat the food contains; the nutritional adequacy statement; the ingredients, the feeding guidelines; and the manufacturer's name and address.

Generic Foods

Low-cost generic foods are attractively priced, but that's because they use poor-quality ingredients to keep costs down. The nutritional quality of generic foods is rarely confirmed through AAFCO feeding tests, and some may not even carry a nutritional adequacy statement. This is one of those instances in which you get what you pay for. In fact, because of the low level of digestibility, it's necessary to feed a lot more of a generic food than a popular or premium food to ensure that a dog receives adequate nutrition, so the savings are illusory.

Canine Health Foods

Nutrition plays an important role in overall health, and diet can be effective in managing certain illnesses. Certain diets, known as veterinary medical foods, are formulated to meet these needs and are available only from your veterinarian. Because they have specialized nutrient content, they're not appropriate as regular diets. Because a veterinarian supervises the use of veterinary medical foods, these diets are exempt from the AAFCO requirement that food labels include feeding directions. If this type of diet is prescribed for your dog, he may need to eat it temporarily or, in some instances, for the rest of his life. Conditions that may be helped by diet include cancer, diabetes, food allergies, or kidney or liver disease.

Don't Believe Everything You Read

You will often see foods that claim to promote "healthy skin" or a "shiny coat." Be aware that this type of claim doesn't have any real meaning; any good-quality food will give your dog healthy skin and a shiny coat.

The Food and Drug Administration's (FDA's) Center for Veterinary Medicine (CVM) monitors the health claims made for foods. Manufacturers may not state on a pet food label that a particular food can treat, prevent, or reduce the risk of a certain disease. Health-related information on the label must be supported by research and approved by the CVM. That's why you're unlikely to see claims that a food will "improve" skin and coat or "prevent" dry, flaky, or itchy skin. Certain substances such as omega-3 fatty acids may indeed help control inflammatory skin disease, but they aren't currently recognized as essential nutrients for dogs, so dog food manufacturers that include these fatty acids in their foods can't make unqualified claims on the label regarding the benefits of supplementation.

Acceptable claims include those for dental diets, such as "helps control plaque" or "helps control tartar." On the other hand, the label on a dental food may not claim to prevent or treat periodontal disease. Diets prescribed by your veterinarian to help treat a particular disease may not be labeled with drug claims, but the CVM does permit manufacturers to provide literature to veterinarians that will help guide them in using the product.

Home-Prepared Meals

Over the past decade, many people have begun to prepare their dogs' food themselves rather than rely on commercial products. They may do this because the dog has a health problem that requires a special diet or because they believe that home-prepared meals contain higher-quality ingredients. Homemade food can be raw or cooked. Raw diets are popular because they're thought to be more natural, thus better at meeting a dog's nutritional needs.

Table scraps are not appropriate as a complete diet for dogs. Your meals are not formulated to meet a dog's nutritional needs. It's okay to let him lick the egg yolk or a little gravy off your plate, but stick to commercial foods or an appropriate homemade food for his regular meals.

The down side to preparing a dog's food at home is that it's difficult to produce a meal that's nutritionally complete, and it's time-intensive. Many people don't have time to prepare healthy meals for themselves, let alone their dogs. It's also important to handle raw meat carefully to prevent bacterial contamination. Wash your hands and mixing bowls and utensils thoroughly after handling raw meat.

Recipes for nutritionally complete dog foods are available in a number of dog nutrition guides. (See Appendix A for suggestions.) Choose a recipe from an expert source, such as a veterinary nutritionist or a layperson with training in animal nutrition. You can also find commercially available raw foods (usually frozen) at pet-supply stores, including "base" mixes to which you can add your own meat and vegetables.

Obesity

The number-one health problem seen by most veterinarians is obesity. It's all too easy to overfeed your dog, especially when his big brown eyes are pleading for just a little more. But as in humans, canine obesity is linked to health problems such as diabetes, heart disease, and joint aches and pains. Keeping your dog at a healthy weight will help him live a longer life.

Recognizing Obesity

When you look down at your dog, you should see a defined waistline behind his ribs. If instead you see a solid chunk of flesh, your dog is probably overweight. Most breeds have an acceptable weight range for males and females. Check your breed's standard (at the American Kennel Club's Web site, *www.akc.org*) to see what's right for your dog. For instance, Labrador retrievers should weigh 55 to 80 pounds, with females on the smaller side. Cavalier King Charles spaniels should weigh 13 to 18 pounds. Bullmastiffs should weigh 100 to 130 pounds. Even if your dog is a mixed breed, you can compare his weight to that suggested for a similar size. Whatever his breed or mix, if your dog is over the suggested weight range, doesn't have a waist, and huffs and puffs at the slightest exertion, it's time for you to start him on a diet and exercise plan.

Canine Weight Loss

Before you do anything, talk to your veterinarian. He can help you devise a weight loss plan appropriate for your dog, taking into account his age, physical condition, and overall health. You can start by simply feeding your dog less. If you've been leaving out a bowl of food all day or giving heaping cupfuls of food, begin measuring portions and feeding meals at set times. Sometimes that's all you need to do. In other cases, you may need to switch your dog to a lower-calorie food.

FACT

According to the NRC, a growing puppy starts out needing about twice as many calories per kilogram of body weight as an adult dog of the same breed. A normal, active adult dog weighing 35 pounds should consume about 1,000 kilocalories a day.

A dry dog food labeled as "lite" may not contain more than 3,100 kilocalories per kilogram (kcal/kg), according to AAFCO regulations. Because canned foods are high in water, "lite" canned foods may contain no more than 900 kcal/kg. Manufacturers of reduced-calorie foods that don't meet the "lite" rules can make comparative statements, such as "25 percent fewer calories than our regular food." Similar rules govern foods labeled as "lean" or "low fat." These claims are based on maximum allowable fat percentages rather than number of calories.

Along with feeding less or providing a low-calorie diet, introduce more exercise into your dog's life. Start with short walks of five or ten minutes, depending on how out of shape he is. As his stamina improves, you can gradually increase the time and distance.

Treats and Snacks

It's pretty safe to say that dogs love treats. And what a dog considers a treat can range from pieces of his regular kibble to commercial treats to bits of hot dog, cheese, fruits or vegetables. Dogs are pretty much happy with anything you give them to eat, but not all treats are created equal. Here are some tips on treating your dog healthily:

- **Keep treats special.** Offer them only as a reward; don't just hand them out indiscriminately.
- **Limit treats.** They should make up no more than 10 percent of your dog's daily food intake.
- **Read treat labels.** Avoid those that are high in sugar and fat, or give them only in small amounts.
- **Vary treats.** Dogs like crunchy things, sweet things, and savory things. Offer bits of chopped apple, banana, or carrots, fresh or frozen berries, cubes of cheese or hot dogs, baked liver bits, and biscuits.
- **Tailor the treat to the occasion.** Use tiny bite-size treats for training, larger biscuits or long-lasting chews for going into the crate or doing something else that doesn't require instant follow-up.
- **Know what's not a treat.** Chocolate, grapes, alcohol, and onions are all toxic to dogs.

Dog treats are held to the same FDA and state labeling requirements as dog foods, but they're not required to be nutritionally complete. Biscuits are the exception to this rule, unless they're specifically labeled as a "snack" or "treat." Rawhide chews, pig ears, and similar items made from animal materials or parts are considered food by the FDA, but unless they claim some nutritional value, such as "high protein," their manufacturers aren't required to follow AAFCO pet food regulations. A treat product is required to list the manufacturer's address and to have an ingredient list if it contains more than one ingredient.

Among the great interactive toys for dogs are plastic balls or cubes that can be filled with kibble or other hard treats. When the dog pushes or rolls the toy, the food falls out through openings in the toy, which can be adjusted for difficulty. Hard rubber Kongs, which have an opening in the bottom, can also be used this way.

Signs of a Well-Fed Dog

Not sure if your dog's diet is the best it could be? There's an easy way to make sure. Examine your dog's overall condition. If you see the following things, your dog is eating well:

- Shiny coat with no hair loss or sores
- Healthy skin that's not itchy or inflamed
- Fresh breath, clean teeth, and pink gums
- Bright eyes with no discharge
- Clean ears with no redness or bad smell
- Small, firm stools
- Firm muscles and a visible waist behind the ribs

Don't be afraid to switch foods if your dog doesn't seem to be doing well on a particular diet. Remember that dogs are individuals, so a particular food, even if it has great ingredients, might not be the right choice for your dog. Try a different brand or protein source (chicken instead of lamb, for instance) to see if you get better results. Just remember to make the change gradually to give your dog's system time to adapt to the change.

Chapter 8

Exercise and Sports Medicine

Dogs that participate in agility competitions, earthdog events, field trials, herding tests, hunting, flyball, flying disc games, weight pulling, and other canine sports and activities deserve the title of athlete just as much as cyclist Lance Armstrong or soccer great Mia Hamm. They work hard, play hard, and are prone to injuries from their activities. Injuries may include broken bones, ligament tears, muscle sprains and strains, and more. You can't prevent every injury, but you can take steps to condition your dog so he's less likely to hurt himself.

Pre-Competition Screening

When people start a new sport or exercise program, they are usually advised to check with their doctor to make sure they're in good physical condition. You should do the same for your dog if you're planning to get her started in one of the many dog sports or even if you just want a canine jogging or bicycling companion. Your veterinarian can evaluate your dog's cardio-vascular fitness, make sure she doesn't have any vision problems, test her range of motion, and X-ray her hips and elbows to make sure they're not dysplastic. She can also advise you on whether the activity you've chosen is suited to your dog. Not all of us are cut out to be athletic superstars, and the same is true of our dogs. Your dog might be overweight or just not built right for a particular sport. It doesn't have to stop you from getting active together, though. Just because your pug isn't suited to jogging doesn't mean she won't excel in the more leisurely sport of tracking. Basset hounds, bull-mastiffs, and many other breeds aren't well suited to agility trials, but they can still compete as long as you take precautions and run them only on courses that don't have so many of the tight twists and turns beloved of some agility judges.

Conditioning Your Dog

All dogs need regular exercise to stay healthy, but canine athletes need conditioning to build up their stamina and improve their athletic performance. If you've ever gone out and done a strenuous hike or long bike ride after spending a sedentary week in your office, the soreness you experience the next day is a tipoff to the importance of conditioning. Top herding dogs can cover as much as 100 miles a day. Field trial and hunting dogs must run or walk for miles all day long, as well as retrieve from cold and sometimes rough water. Sled dogs may race 1,200 miles in less than ten days. All this should make you appreciate how much work goes into conditioning a dog. Help your dog avoid the weekend warrior syndrome by gradually increasing her level of activity and the length of time she spends doing that activity.

How to Start

A dog that's in condition has the appropriate level of physical fitness for the activity he does. Whatever sport you try, walking is the best and easiest way to start conditioning your dog. Depending on his age, size, and general level of health, begin with short walks on leash. Puppies or overweight dogs might start by walking a quarter mile, or whatever distance you can go in five minutes. (Most people can walk a mile in twenty minutes.) Gradually work up to a half mile and then a mile. Remember that high-impact exercise such as running or jumping on hard surfaces is detrimental to a young dog's musculoskeletal development. The growth plates of large-breed dogs don't close until they're fourteen to eighteen months old (small breeds at ten to twelve months of age), so avoid jogging, running, or taking your dog over high jumps until he reaches physical maturity.

Exercise Physiology

Once your dog is at a basic level of fitness, you can start conditioning him for a specific activity. Like any athlete, your dog needs strength, flexibility, and stamina. To help him achieve peak performance, it's important to understand your dog's musculoskeletal system and recognize signs of lameness. By monitoring your dog's response to workouts, you can help prevent the muscle aches and pains that come with too much exercise.

When he's competing, plan to exercise your dog half an hour every day (with one day off every week for rest). Dogs that compete only seasonally—in field trials, for instance—can stay in shape with a daily fifteen-minute workout, increasing to half an hour daily a couple of months before the season begins. Break up this chunk of time by focusing on different aspects of fitness.

Once your dog is at a basic level of fitness, you'll need to pick up the pace. Walk faster, break into a jog, and play games that involve running. Introduce sprinting by walking for a minute, then jogging for a minute, then dropping back to a walk. Gradually increase the distance you jog before returning to a walk.

Types of Exercise

To build up your dog's strength and stamina, take him jogging, run him alongside a bicycle, play fetch with a ball or dumbbell, take him swimming, or allow him to run off-leash in a safe, enclosed area. If you're highly motivated to condition your dog and you have money to burn, consider investing in a canine treadmill. Walking or running on a treadmill can improve your dog's strength, balance, and coordination, and it's convenient on rainy, snowy, or hot days.

ALERT!

Lots of dogs love to chase flying discs, but jumping and twisting to snatch them out of the air can cause injury. If you play this game with your dog, keep your throws low to the ground.

Working on flexibility can be flat-out fun. Teach your dog tricks, such as bows, spins, and waves. Walk him in circles and figure eights. All of these motions help keep your dog limber. Even if you don't compete in agility, consider setting up some weave poles in your back yard. Going through them increases flexibility, improves coordination, and helps strengthen your dog's back. If weave poles aren't an option, teach your dog to sit up for a treat. That's another good back-strengthener.

Other types of exercise can help your dog improve balance and develop specific skills. Have him practice stepping on and off objects and stepping over a bar (such as a broomstick) on the ground or a very low jump. Walk him on leash on both level and uneven surfaces so he's accustomed to both. Change pace frequently, moving from a slow walk to a fast walk and back again or from a walk to a trot and back to a walk. If you compete in obedience, make sure to teach your dog to heel on both sides so that he stays supple.

Mental Conditioning

With both human and canine athletes, stress is a given in competition. It comes not only from physical exertion but also from the psychological pressures of travel, noise, hot or cold temperatures, and the presence of spectators as well as other competitors. It's just as important to condition your dog mentally as it is physically.

The best canine athletes are confident and well socialized. They get lots of handling by people from the time they're born, and they're exposed to all kinds of different people, other animals, sights, and sounds. They become accustomed to riding in a car, going to the veterinarian, attending training class and play groups, and navigating crowded places such as outdoor shopping malls. All of these experiences help them become better able to deal with the stresses that accompany any performance sport. Other factors that affect your dog's ability to deal with stress include temperament, age, and overall health.

Mental conditioning also involves exposing dogs to the sights and sounds they'll experience in competition. Field trial and hunting dogs learn during puppyhood not to shy from the sound of a gun. Agility dogs become familiar with the feel and flapping sound of a closed tunnel and the thunk of a teeter-totter as it hits the ground. Young show dogs in training attend matches to get a feel for the ring.

Any athlete, canine or human, can experience burnout from working too hard or too long. If you notice that your dog is losing interest in his sport or seems less willing to work, back off your training schedule. He needs some time off just to relax and have fun.

Recognizing whether your dog has a desire to win is related to these efforts. It's a crucial aspect of being an athlete. A dog that doesn't have that drive can still have fun in agility, be a good hunting companion, or earn a championship, but even if physically he has everything going for him, it's unlikely he'll ever be one of the top competitors.

Most important, incorporate play into all of your dog's workouts. Make time for it in between practice sessions or make it part of his skills training. Play helps you build an unbreakable bond with your dog. Without it, he'll never reach his full potential.

Weight and Diet

Two factors that can affect performance are weight and nutrition. Every dog should be at a healthy weight, but the canine athlete should be lean and muscular. You can feel all his ribs, and he doesn't carry any extra fat. Gently pinch the skin on his back. You should be able to gather only a small amount with your fingers. A normal weight for the golden retriever that spends her days playing with the kids is probably way too heavy for the golden that competes in field trials. Additional weight, even if it doesn't seem like a lot, can contribute to injuries. Carrying too much weight causes or predisposes a dog to ruptured anterior cruciate ligaments, arthritis, and intervertebral disc disease, to name only a few.

Nutrition

Athletic dogs need special diets. With all the energy they expend, a nutrient-dense diet is a must. But beyond that, the type of food your athletic dog needs depends on his sport. Sprinters, such as agility or weight-pull dogs, need a diet high in carbohydrates. Nutritional needs vary for dogs involved in intermediate-level activities, which may last a few minutes to a few hours. A rule of paw is that the more work they do, the more dietary fat they need. And dogs that do endurance sports in extreme temperatures, such as sled dogs, need a diet very high in fat. It's also important to factor in whether your dog competes year-round or only seasonally. Off-season, a normal diet will serve him best to prevent weight gain.

Performance Diets

A number of diets are available to enhance a dog's athletic performance. Called performance diets, they usually contain about 20 percent fat, which provides more energy than carbohydrates and protein. At least one study has shown that athletic dogs fed a performance diet were better able to maintain their body weight and condition than dogs on a lower-fat maintenance diet, and they performed better. That said, high levels of protein are important, too. When athletic dogs get their energy from fat, their bodies can use protein for tissue repair and other functions, reducing the incidence of injuries. Remember that performance diets are suited only to dogs in competition. Your Labrador retriever may have a huge amount of energy, but if all he does is play fetch with your kids and go jogging with you occasionally, he doesn't need a performance diet.

Warm Up and Cool Down

Any time you exercise your dog, warm him up first and cool him down afterward. That's the best way to prevent injuries. To start, get the blood flowing with a short walk or jog. The warm-up stimulates the delivery of increased oxygen and nutrients to the muscles.

Don't forget stretches to limber up the tendons and ligaments. Encourage your dog to do some play bows—think downward-facing dog, if you're a yoga aficionado—and encourage some spins and waves. Teach your dog to do bends by having him face you and then reach to either side to get a treat. This is great for loosening the neck and body muscles. Give a quick all-over massage to loosen stiff muscles and joints.

If you are purchasing a puppy with the intent of competing in a particular dog sport, remember that genetics matters. Make sure the puppy's parents are sound and have tested clear of genetic disorders such as hip and elbow dysplasia, eye problems, and blood-clotting disorders.

After a workout or performance, your dog may want to guzzle some cold water and collapse in his crate. Don't let him! Cool him down first with a slow five-minute walk. This allows the muscles to release the waste products that can cause stiffness. Let him drink small amounts at a time as he cools down. Pay attention to your dog's gait as you walk to make sure he doesn't show any signs of stiffness or lameness. End the cool-down period by running your hands over his body to check for any sore areas that may need attention.

Common Sports Injuries

You've done everything right, but your dog has still suffered an injury. Unfortunately, that's pretty much a given in any activity. There's always the chance that something will go wrong. Dogs can suffer broken bones, tail injuries, anterior cruciate ligament (ACL) tears, and foot pad damage, to name only a few. The following sections describe some of the common problems that can affect different types of athletic dogs, how to recognize them, and what to do for them.

Musculoskeletal Injuries

Broken bones, knee injuries, and muscle sprains and strains are a fact of life for athletic dogs. A field dog can trip in a hole and break his leg, his back, or his neck. Knee injuries such as cruciate ligament tears can occur in any sport that involves jumping or twisting. Lots of dogs injure toes in any number of activities, particularly agility. Any dog that's not well conditioned or that doesn't get a good warm-up before activity is prone to muscle sprains and strains. An athletic dog's musculoskeletal system takes a beating, which is why it's so important to emphasize strength and flexibility.

ACL Tears

The anterior cruciate ligament (ACL), which runs from the thigh bone to the shin bone, is the knee's major stabilizing ligament. Canine athletes and working dogs such as sheepdogs are prone to ACL tears, rips in the tough, fibrous bands that hold the knee in place, and some dogs have a congenital or developmental predisposition to ACL tears. The wear and tear on limbs from participating in agility or advanced obedience puts dogs at risk for this type of injury, which occurs when the knee twists suddenly or hyperextends. The result is sudden rear leg lameness and a swollen, painful knee joint.

The latest surgical repair for this kind of injury is called a TPLO: tibial plateau leveling osteotomy. It involves new techniques and instrumentation that were developed relatively recently. Performing a TPLO allows veterinarians to provide a better, more dynamic repair, with much better results than were previously available.

FACT

It doesn't hurt to supplement your athletic dog with the nutraceuticals chondroitin and glucosamine as a preventive measure. They might not prevent injury, but they may help strengthen cartilage and ensure that injuries are less serious.

A TPLO involves breaking the shin bone, taking a wedge out, rotating the bone to level out the top part of the shin bone that interacts with the knee, putting a plate or two on, and then treating it as if it were a healing fracture. Now, if that sounds like an incredibly invasive and painful procedure, it is, but thanks to new pre- and post-surgical pain relief techniques (described in Chapter 10) it's much more bearable than it would have been in the past. For dogs with a blown ACL, this surgery allows them to regain full function of their knees and resume their careers as working or athletic dogs.

Hydrotherapy may be recommended for dogs recovering from ACL surgery. The main benefit of water workouts is that they reduce pressure on the joint. Working out in water, either by swimming or by walking on a hydrotreadmill, can help restore and maintain the joint's range of motion, relieve pain, and improve muscle and joint strength and function.

Bursitis or Tendonitis

As you can tell from the suffix "itis," these are inflammations of a bursa (a small sac between a tendon and a bone) or a tendon (a tough, fibrous band or cord of connective tissue). It's commonly seen in the biceps tendon, which in dogs translates to shoulder lameness, and is usually caused by chronic ongoing overactivity. Shoulder injuries are common in agility dogs, thanks to slamming their shoulders against rigid weave poles and lots of jumping. Any dog with a straight front (the forepart of the body, as it's viewed head-on) is more likely to be predisposed to shoulder injuries.

Bursitis and tendonitis are diagnosed by extending the shoulder and putting pressure on the biceps tendon or bursa. If it's painful, you'll hear about it from your dog. Therapies that can help include massage, stretching, hot and cold compresses, and therapeutic ultrasound.

Joint Sprains

Sprains occur when the ligaments surrounding a joint suddenly stretch or tear. Dogs with sprains have pain and swelling at the joint. They can usually put some weight on the leg but walk with a limp. If your dog can't put weight on the leg, he'll need X rays to rule out a fracture or dislocation.

QUESTION?

How do I keep the cold pack or warm compress on my dog?
Use some gauze wrap to loosely attach it to the affected area. Your other option is to spend some quality time with your dog by holding it in place for fifteen minutes, maybe while you're watching television.

Rest is the best treatment for a sprain. To help reduce swelling, apply cold packs (a chemical pack or bag of frozen peas wrapped in a towel) three or four times a day for the first twenty-four hours, leaving them on for fifteen to thirty minutes at a time. For the next two or three days, apply warm (not hot), moist compresses to the area, following the same schedule as for cold packs. Warmth increases circulation, which promotes healing. The following signs will help you recognize joint problems so you can seek veterinary advice:

- Lameness
- Swelling, tenderness, or heat at the joint
- Redness of the skin around a sore joint
- Favoring a particular leg or holding it up
- Reacting to touch of the painful area by holding the breath, turning the head rapidly, or even snapping

Muscle Tears, Strains, and Sprains

When a muscle is stretched beyond its normal length, the result can be a tear, sprain, or strain. This type of injury often occurs after strenuous field work or other activities that involve long periods of running. The injured area is often close to but doesn't involve a joint and is usually painful, hot, and swollen. Once your veterinarian rules out joint disease or a ligament tear as the source of the problem, she will probably recommend at least three weeks of rest, accompanied by cold and heat therapy. Massage or acupuncture may also help.

Broken Bones

A fracture can occur in any sport. All it takes is for a dog to fall off an agility A-frame, step in a hole, or otherwise suffer a bone-breaking trauma. Suspect a broken bone if your dog is unable to put weight on a limb. You'll know for sure she has a broken bone if it's a compound fracture, in which case the bone juts out from the skin.

ALERT!

In the event of a broken bone, splint it the way you found it. Don't try to straighten the limb out; you could make it worse. Keep the dog as still as possible, and get her to the veterinarian.

A dog with a fracture will need surgery to repair the broken bone. Until it heals, the bone will need to be held in position with pins and metal plates or with a splint and cast. It all depends on where the break occurs. Once the bone has healed, exercise, hydrotherapy, and other therapies can help rebuild muscle strength and flexibility.

Back and Neck Injuries

Tight, twisty agility courses and rigid weave poles are often the cause of back and neck injuries in dogs, as are the twists and turns of a lure course and the spinal compression that occurs every time an advanced obedience or flyball dog lands following a jump. Even if a dog isn't injured during a sport, the underlying arthritis caused by strain on the joints can precipitate problems later from a more trivial action, such as jumping off the sofa.

Intervertebral Disc Disease

Some dogs develop intervertebral disc disease (IVDD), which occurs with the degeneration of the gel-like cushions, called discs, that rest between the vertebrae. The discs serve as shock absorbers, but they can start to dry out and lose their elasticity. Trauma, even as mild as jumping off the sofa, can cause a degenerating disc to rupture. Two types of disc ruptures can affect dogs. The first type, seen most often in small dogs such as dachshunds, beagles, cocker spaniels, and Pekingese, occurs when the outside portion of the disc breaks open, allowing the cushy center to push out through the opening and put pressure on the spinal cord. The second type, which usually affects larger breeds such as German shepherd dogs or Labrador retrievers, occurs when the entire disc bulges outward, pressing on the spinal cord. In either case, the result is pain and sometimes partial or complete paralysis. Disc ruptures can come on gradually or suddenly.

Treating Back and Neck Pain

Rest and pain relief are often the best cures for IVDD. Rest doesn't just mean refraining from a sport; it means close confinement and only brief walks on leash so your dog can relieve himself. The typical rest period is two to four weeks. In addition to analgesics for pain relief, your veterinarian may also prescribe corticosteroids to help reduce swelling and inflammation. A dog with paralysis may need surgery to repair the damage. Stiffness and back pain from arthritis can be treated with rest and nonsteroidal anti-inflammatory pain relievers such as carprofen and etodolac.

Foot Injuries and Toe Trauma

From agility to field trials, herding to sled-dog racing, every canine athlete is prone to foot and toe injuries. Foot pads can become worn down (a common problem in herding dogs). Feet can get cut, and paw pads can become dry and cracked from overuse or exposure to cold. A toe injury might sound trivial, but it can be serious enough to lead to a dog's retirement from a sport. Retrievers and agility dogs are especially prone to toe injuries, which can range from a torn-off toenail to a sprained, dislocated, or broken toe. Dogs can get toe injuries from hitting the toe too hard against something, stepping in a hole, or landing wrong from a jump. Many agility dogs suffer toe injuries from A-frame slats.

To prevent broken toenails, keep your dog's nails trimmed short. If a toenail does tear off, all the bleeding may look scary, but it's not as serious as it seems. Just put pressure on the wound to stop the bleeding. If the nail doesn't break off on its own, your veterinarian may have to remove it. The toenail should eventually grow back.

To treat minor cuts, clean out the wound and bandage the foot. Give it time to heal before your dog returns to his activity. Keep dry, cracked paw pads well moisturized, and clean your dog's feet after he's been out in snowy or icy conditions. This helps remove harsh deicing chemicals that may be on sidewalks or roads. Toes may heal on their own but sometimes require surgery. An X ray may be necessary to spot hairline fractures.

Tail Trouble

A condition that commonly affects hunting dogs goes by a variety of names: cold tail, limber tail syndrome, broken tail, dead tail, and broken wag. They all refer to a condition in which the dog's tail hangs limp from the base or is held horizontal for three or four inches and then drops down. Painful but relatively harmless, cold tail can be associated with swimming, a bath in water that's too cold or too warm, or even after any activity that involves a lot of tail action. The tail usually returns to normal within a few days. To shorten recovery time, ask your veterinarian to prescribe an appropriate anti-inflammatory drug as soon as you notice the condition.

When to Seek Treatment

You'll probably know when your dog has been injured. Sometimes, though, dogs try to hide that something's wrong, either because they want to keep working to please us or from some ancestral imperative that tells them to hide any sign of weakness. That's when you have to learn to read your dog's body language. Limping is an obvious sign of pain or injury, but if you look closely you may see other indications that your dog isn't feeling her best. Get her checked out if she stands hunched over or holds her neck rigidly. Some dogs become unwilling to run or begin to refuse certain obstacles, change the way they approach certain jumps, or start knocking jumps over instead of clearing them cleanly. Any unexplained change in behavior or loss of condition is a clue that something's wrong. Make a habit of checking your dog over weekly so you learn what's normal and what's not.

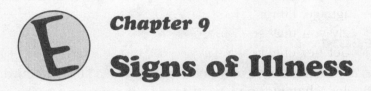

Chapter 9

Signs of Illness

As a dependent member of your family, your dog counts on you to recognize when he is ill and then provide help. At the same time, dogs retain enough of their "wild" characteristics to often cover up signs of illness or act very stoically. Your best defense against illness is good preventive health care, coupled with frequent observation and recognition of your dog's normal, healthy state.

Bleeding from Any Orifice

If you see blood coming from your dog, chances are 90 percent that the condition is abnormal and in need of attention. The only time a bloody discharge is normal is in unspayed female dogs at the proestrus stage of their heat cycle. Other than that, your dog should not have a bloody discharge.

Types of Bleeding

If you do notice blood, you may need to start with a little detective work to find its source. A bloody drip from the vulva of a spayed female or from the penis of a male may indicate a bladder infection. Blood from the vulva of an unspayed female dog who is not in her heat cycle could indicate an overgrowth of the uterine lining or a uterine infection—both potentially life-threatening.

A bloody discharge from the mouth could be as simple as a small cut on the gums or tongue or as silly as a lost baby tooth on a puppy. Coughing up blood is a bad sign and requires immediate veterinary attention.

Blood in stool can be black with digested blood from a problem such as a stomach ulcer, or bright red from a bleeding problem in the intestines. Bloody discharges from any part of your dog's body may indicate cancer or a bleeding disorder such as autoimmune hemolytic anemia or von Willebrand's disease.

FACT

Von Willebrand's disease is a blood-clotting disorder caused by a genetic deficiency. There is currently a genetic test that can be done to screen breeding animals for this disease. Doberman pinschers and Scottish terriers are two of the breeds that are prone to von Willebrand's disease.

What to Do for Bleeding

A bloody nose may need pressure and/or a cold compress, either of which is applied to the top of the nose. Bleeding from the mouth is also easy to care for if it is just a baby tooth; you can put a cold compress on the spot or just wait it out. The bleeding should stop fairly quickly on its own. Under most circumstances, blood is a good indicator that you need to have your dog checked out. If you see blood in your dog's urine or stool, you must get her to a veterinarian. If possible, scoop up a sample of the urine or stool. Any bleeding associated with a growth or tumor should get veterinary attention as well.

ALERT!

A bloody discharge can be an emergency in certain situations—spurting blood from an artery, coughing up blood, or blood from the vulva of an unspayed bitch that is not in heat. Apply pressure to any spurting areas, and head for your veterinarian's office!

Difficulty Breathing

Normally dogs take ten to thirty breaths per minute. This varies with temperature, activity, and size of the dog. In hot weather, a normal dog may pant up to 200 times per minute. A dog that is breathing faster than normal may be taking shallow breaths that aren't as efficient at moving oxygen into the lungs. If your dog seems to be working to breathe, not just breathing naturally, something is wrong.

Difficulty in breathing can have a number of causes that may or may not be related to the respiratory tract. A dog in pain often has quick, shallow breathing. Any abdominal problem that puts pressure on the diaphragm can cause respiratory difficulty as well. A dog that has been hit by a car or had other trauma might have broken ribs or what is called a pneumothorax (free air in the chest, putting pressure on the lungs). Pneumothorax is a serious, potentially life-threatening problem that requires immediate veterinary care.

Respiratory Problems

There are many respiratory causes of difficulty in breathing, starting at the nose and working down to the lungs. A dog with a respiratory infection may have purulent (pus-filled) discharge from the nose that blocks his airways. Any obstruction in the nose—blood clots from banging the nose on something hard, inhaled foreign objects, or tumors—can reduce the amount of air going into the lungs.

The same holds true for all the airways down to the lungs. Dogs can also inhale foreign objects into the trachea. Certain dogs, such as many toy and brachycephalic breeds, may have a collapsing trachea, which decreases the open airway of the trachea or windpipe. These dogs may cough, gag, or struggle to breathe deeply.

Pneumonia and Other Lung Problems

Once air gets down to the lungs, other problems can arise. Pneumonia is an infection of the lungs by either viruses or bacteria. It can be quite serious, especially in puppies or dogs with poor immune systems. Dogs with pneumonia may cough, gag, retch, or just have painful breathing. These dogs usually show other signs of illness such as a fever or poor appetite, and they may cough up greenish mucus.

Pneumonia can also be caused by parasite migrations, such as with roundworms, or if the dog aspirates, or inhales, bits of food into the lungs. If your dog has pneumonia, your veterinarian may perform a process known as a tracheal aspirate. This involves injecting sterile fluid into the trachea, then sucking it back out into a syringe so it can be cultured and examined. X rays are also very important in diagnosing pneumonia.

FACT

It is common for cancer to spread or metastasize to the lungs. The cancer cells block or overwhelm healthy lung tissue, making it harder for your dog to get enough oxygen. Radiographs or ultrasound examinations of the chest are very important for all canine cancer patients.

Excessive Drinking

Dogs may drink more than usual for a number of reasons. Certainly in hot weather your dog will consume more water, especially if she has been active or out in the hot sun. However, some health problems can cause an increase in drinking too.

What's Making My Dog So Thirsty?

Any situation that might dehydrate your dog will lead to increased drinking. Diarrhea and vomiting take a lot of fluid from your dog that must be replaced. Fever or mild heat stroke can stimulate dogs to drink more than usual, as can bladder infections and mild kidney problems. More serious problems like kidney failure can also lead to increased drinking and urinating, or sometimes to a drop in drinking and little urine production.

Dogs need about 10 ml of water per pound of body weight daily for maintenance. Activity, environment, or health problems can all increase the amount needed. Ideally this will come from fresh water, but if your dog is ill, she may need fluid replacement by intravenous injections.

Certain hormonal diseases directly influence the amount your dog drinks. With diabetes mellitus, for instance, either the pancreas doesn't produce enough insulin or the insulin present isn't working properly to remove extra glucose from the blood. A diabetic dog therefore drinks more water to flush out the extra glucose.

Dogs that suffer from Cushing's disease (excessive adrenal secretions) or from Addison's (not enough adrenal secretions) may show increased thirst. Female dogs with pyometra (uterine infections) will often be very thirsty, and dogs with increased calcium in the blood are also very thirsty.

Monitoring and Treating Increased Thirst

Before you can notice an increase in drinking, you need to have a rough idea of how much your dog normally drinks in a day. Make sure water bowls are always available and refill them with fresh water at least twice daily. Just like humans, dogs prefer fresh, cool water. Pay attention to whether you need to fill the bowl up more often than usual.

If you are concerned about changes in drinking habits, be sure to let your veterinarian know. He may need to do some blood work, including special blood tests requiring a short hospital stay, to carefully measure exactly how much your dog is drinking and how much urine is being produced.

Unexplained Weight Loss

It's important for dogs to stay fit and trim, but if your dog starts to lose weight without a diet change or increase in exercise, something may be wrong. Weight loss occurs in one of two ways—either insufficient calories are being taken in, or extra calories are being burned. If your dog's appetite and eating habits are still normal, the extra energy must be being used somehow, if not with exercise then possibly with a great metabolic use of calories.

Diabetes mellitus is one example of a disease in which a dog may have a good (if not voracious) appetite but still lose weight. This disease affects the production of insulin so the dog can't use all the calories consumed.

FACT

Dogs with cancer may have a loss of appetite that results in weight loss, or they may be quite hungry but still lose weight as the cancer cells consume lots of energy.

Because the causes of weight loss can be so serious, be sure to get it checked out. Certainly an unexplained weight loss of 10 percent of your dog's body weight is cause for a veterinary visit. Your veterinarian will want to check a fecal sample for parasites that can drain nutrition, then possibly do some blood work or check for abnormalities with X rays or an ultrasound.

Coughing and Sneezing

Coughing and sneezing happens in similar ways to dogs and people. Both are the body's way of removing an irritant from an airway. Sneezing helps the body deal with problems in the nose, such as inhaled pollen or irritation from something spicy like pepper. Coughing is usually caused by a problem further down the respiratory tract, such as mucus or fluid that goes down the wrong way.

When to Be Concerned

An occasional cough or sneeze is not cause for alarm. However, if your dog is sneezing repeatedly, possibly even to the point of sneezing a few blood droplets, you need to investigate the cause. A sneeze with a thick or discolored discharge should also be looked into. Your dog may need to visit the veterinarian, who will carefully look into the dog's nose with a special scope. Dogs can snort up grass or bugs, or they may develop cancerous growths that block nasal passages and cause repeated sneezing.

Coughing may be the result of something simple like inhaling water, or it could be a sign of a serious problem, such as cancer or pneumonia. Heart problems that allow fluid to build up in the lungs may be accompanied by a cough as well. Some of the worst sounding coughs are actually caused by respiratory viruses known as canine cough or kennel cough that are usually not serious and are easy to treat.

Dogs with canine or kennel cough may actually sound like a honking goose! Despite the horrible sound, these dogs often feel fine, and they can recover completely with some nursing care at home. Your veterinarian may also give you some medications to speed up the process.

Diagnosing and Treating a Cough

Dogs with a chronic (ongoing) cough will need a full veterinary workup. This could include blood work, X rays, and possibly an ultrasound or an examination of the airways with an endoscope. The veterinarian may decide to perform a needle biopsy, which involves removing a small sample of cells for examination, or a tracheal wash, in which the trachea is washed with sterile fluid, which is then checked for any unusual cells. Treatment for coughing problems may include oxygen therapy, cough suppressants, antibiotics, or other treatments needed to treat the primary cause of the cough.

Discharge from Eyes, Ears, and Nose

Your dog's eyes, ears, and nose are all sensitive areas with plenty of specialized nerve endings to help with seeing, hearing, and sense of smell. Any discharges from these areas may interfere with your dog's keen senses and may indicate a deeper problem.

Recognizing Eye Problems

Normally, your dog's eyes should be bright and clear with no discharge. A clear discharge may mean a mild irritant (dust or pollen in the eye) or a hair rubbing against the sensitive cornea. Any discolored or thick discharge such as pus or heavy mucus is abnormal and cause for alarm. Eye problems can go from minor to serious very quickly. If your dog has a discharge and is squinting, he needs to see a veterinarian!

Some breeds are prone to entropion, a condition that causes eyelids to turn in so that hairs rub on the cornea. This is most common in dogs with shortened faces and long facial hair such as Shih Tzus and breeds with wrinkled skin like bulldogs and Shar-Peis. These breeds may need special surgery to prevent eye problems.

Recognizing Ear Problems

Your dog's ears should normally have a reasonable odor. Dogs with ears that hang down and prevent air circulation may have a slightly musty odor, but there should never be a foul odor. A small amount of yellowish wax is normal, but dark brown wax and unusual or bloody discharge are all abnormal. Dark wax resembling coffee grounds may indicate ear mites, while green or yellow discharge can be a sign of a bad infection. Dogs with yeast infections of the ear often have clear discharge along with very red and inflamed ear tissue. If your dog is rubbing her ear, cries when you touch it, or holds her head cocked to one side, you need to check out the ear. Remember—she does have two, so you have one for comparison if you aren't sure whether something is normal. Many ear infections only affect one ear, most commonly the left.

Sniffing Out Nose Health

The old saying that a healthy dog has a cold nose is true part of the time. Normally a dog's nose feels cooler than the rest of the body and is moist, but on a hot, dry day, your dog's nose will feel warm and dry. If there is discharge coming from the nose, something is not quite right. A purulent, pus-like discharge indicates infection—it may be bacterial, or caused by cancer, or possibly a foreign object is stuck up there. Believe it or not, some dogs even inhale grass, which gets stuck and causes an infection! A blood-tinged discharge could be from trauma, such as hitting the nose on something hard, or could be from cancer or a bleeding disorder. A dog that sneezes frequently may get nosebleeds just as people do.

Do not clean your dog's nose off before heading to the veterinary hospital. Your veterinarian will want to see the discharge and may need to put some on a slide or culture it to see exactly what the problem is and plan the best possible treatment.

Scratching and Biting the Skin

A dog that is itching, rubbing, and scratching is an uncomfortable dog. Along with the discomfort, the pruritus (itchiness) may be a sign of underlying problems, such as allergies. The skin itself is an important first-line barrier against bacteria and parasites. Skin that is scratched with tiny cuts is ripe ground for infections. Anything more than an occasional scratch or rub (such as many dogs do right after they eat) is worth investigating.

The most common cause of itching and scratching is the presence of parasites. Fleas, ticks, and various mites can all make a dog extremely uncomfortable. These pests may also carry serious, even life-threatening, diseases, which they pass on to their host dog. (See Chapter 12 for more information on parasites.)

Allergies are another notorious source of itching. With many dogs, food allergies show up as skin problems rather than stomach or intestinal complaints. Inhaled allergies may stimulate a skin reaction as well. Basically, if your dog is itching and scratching, has open sores or inflamed skin areas, you should contact your veterinarian. Once parasites are ruled out, your veterinarian may do skin tests or blood work to find the cause of that itch.

FACT

Where your dog starts scratching can be significant. A dog with a mild ear infection may rub his ear or even come over and try to get you to rub it. Dogs with allergies often rub their faces and scratch their armpits. Licking or sucking of flank areas may indicate a behavioral problem.

Listlessness, Lameness, and Collapsing

One of the important things to notice every day about your dog is his level of activity. If your dog is normally bouncing around, begging someone to throw a toy or go for a walk, you should be concerned if one day he is just lying quietly in the kitchen. Any time your dog holds up a paw, is walking awkwardly, or is reluctant to move, you should investigate the cause. Lethargy, lameness, and collapse can all be signs of serious problems.

Normal and Abnormal Lethargy

If your dog is very quiet and less active than normal, think over the activities of the last day or so. Perhaps you were at dog camp and he swam all day for the first time this year. In that case, he is understandably tired and perhaps even a bit sore. If you've simply had a normal day or two at home, however, you need to keep thinking.

Muscle soreness, a fever, even an upset stomach can all make your dog less active. Check gums for pink color (that returns quickly after pressure) to rule out any major internal bleeding. Check your dog's respiratory rate and heart rate—you can check a pulse on the inside of the thigh if you can't feel the heart itself. If gum color, heart rate, or respiratory rate are abnormal, contact your veterinarian.

Investigating Lameness

Lameness can vary a great deal. A stoic dog may walk despite severe arthritis while a puppy may cry and hold a paw up for minutes after having a toe stepped on. As always, it is important to know what's normal for your dog.

If your dog is lame on one foot, carefully examine that leg from the toenails on up. A cracked or broken nail can be very painful. Gently feel between toes for any thorns or cuts. Carefully bend each joint as you move up the leg. Even if your dog is tough and doesn't cry or pull away, his breathing will change as you reach the area that hurts. Any redness, unusual swelling, or tender areas should be considered unusual. Your veterinarian will help you decide on appropriate treatment. For minor muscle pulls, a cold soak with the hose for five minutes and an anti-inflammatory prescribed by your veterinarian may do the trick!

ALERT!

If your dog won't walk on the leg at all, or the lower limb is hanging loosely, you may be dealing with a broken bone. Use extreme care to try to keep the leg from moving and get your dog directly to the veterinarian.

When a Dog Collapses

A dog that has collapsed has a serious problem. It could be heatstroke, serious internal bleeding, or a heart problem. Cancer, the aftermath of a seizure, or bloat can also cause a dog to collapse suddenly. Quickly make sure nothing is blocking your dog's airway and head for your veterinarian. If you suspect heatstroke, apply cold compresses to the dog's head and groin while someone else drives.

Swelling or Bloating

A healthy dog normally has a trim figure with a waist that can be clearly seen when you look from above and a tuck-up right before the hind legs when you look from the side. If your dog's figure is round, she may just be overweight, or she may have a medical problem. A sudden increase in width is a definite cause for alarm. Bloat, or gastrointestinal volvulus, is a life-threatening condition that happens when a dog's stomach has twisted. Your dog needs to go to the veterinarian immediately, even if it's the middle of the night.

Distended Abdomen

Some owners believe their dog is overweight when actually the abdomen is distended with fluid. Fluid can build up in the abdomen over weeks or days. This may be secondary to a heart condition, cancer, or severe inflammation. Your veterinarian will want to tap your dog's abdomen and take a fluid sample for analysis and possible culture.

Other Reasons for Swelling

Other areas of your dog's body may show swelling as well. Swollen joints can be caused by chronic arthritis or acute infections such as Lyme disease. Cancer may show up as a lump or swelling almost anywhere. These swellings could be benign such as a lipoma or serious such as osteosarcoma, or bone cancer. A swollen nose or muzzle could be caused by a bee sting. As always, it is important to know what's normal for your dog so you can immediately identify any changes. If you're concerned about an unusual swelling, ask your veterinarian to check it out.

Diarrhea and Vomiting

Vomiting and diarrhea may come together as a pair of gastrointestinal problems, or they may show up separately. These problems can be mild and minor or serious and life-threatening.

QUESTION?

Do dogs eat grass to vomit?
Dogs with an upset stomach do sometimes eat grass. Other dogs graze for a "salad." See what type of grass your dog is chewing. Salad-lovers prefer new grass, while older, tougher grass is more likely to help the dog vomit.

What Is Diarrhea?

Diarrhea occurs when food and fluid pass through your dog's intestinal system faster than normal. The cells lining the intestinal tract don't have time to resorb the water and other fluid they routinely would. Your dog passes what would be a normal stool except for the extra fluid. Diarrhea can occur after eating unusual foods—think of yourself when you eat an unusually spicy meal—or from an infection that disrupts the cells lining the intestines. Parasites such as hookworms may also interfere with the normal digestive process and cause diarrhea. A mild case of diarrhea should clear in a day or so.

Diagnosing the Problem

Diarrhea may smell and look different depending on the cause. For example, puppies with parvo may pass some digested blood, which gives their diarrhea a distinctive odor. A dog with a pancreatic problem that is not digesting fats well may have grayish, smelly diarrhea. No matter how gross and disgusting the stuff is, you should save a sample for your veterinarian. A fecal sample can help your veterinarian identify parasites, test for diseases such as parvovirus, and check for blood in the stool. A small amount is all that is needed—about a tablespoon at most.

Chronic diarrhea (lasting more than a week) can be a sign of a metabolic disease such as pancreatic insufficiency or can be related to cancer. Work-up for a chronic diarrhea problem can require blood work, special X rays, and possibly biopsies and endoscopy (examination of the stomach and intestines with a special scope).

Causes of Vomiting

Some vomiting is triggered in the brain centers where nausea originates. Dogs that get carsick have this type of vomiting—they aren't truly sick, but their bodies aren't happy, either. Most vomiting originates in the gastrointestinal tract—usually the stomach. If your dog eats something bitter or irritating, his body may want to get rid of it, causing him to vomit. Illnesses that disrupt the tract, such as parvo, will also cause vomiting. Vomiting can also occur as part of a generalized problem such as a neuromuscular disease. Dogs may vomit occasionally just from a mild upset stomach.

Some medications are designed to stimulate vomiting when your dog has eaten a foreign object or something unhealthy such as chocolate or certain poisons. *Always* check with your veterinarian before making your dog throw up. There are certain poisons that do more damage if they are vomited back up, such as petroleum distillates and certain acids and alkalis.

Retching without throwing up anything may be a sign of bloat or gastrointestinal volvulus. Bloat is a medical emergency, and if your dog shows the classic symptoms (described in Chapter 17), you should head for your veterinarian right away.

Treatment for Vomiting and Diarrhea

If your dog vomits once or twice but can keep water down and feels fine otherwise, you can keep an eye on him at home. Holding off on food for a day or so may help your dog recover from vomiting and diarrhea. He needs fluids, though, so if he can't keep water down, you need to contact your veterinarian. This is even more crucial in puppies and older dogs. After a day with no food, you should start back with a bland diet and gradually work over to your dog's regular diet. Your veterinarian can provide special prescription bland foods or guide you to homemade substitutes.

A dog that is vomiting only or has diarrhea only will be slower to dehydrate than a dog who is dealing with both at the same time. Along with fluid loss, your dog will lose important electrolytes and minerals that are important for normal body functions. Your veterinarian will be able to help you decide what treatment is necessary, and will guide you if he feels home care is all that you need.

Chapter 10

E **Recognizing
and Managing Pain**

As uncomfortable and unpleasant as it is, pain has a purpose. It's what tells a creature that it's been injured, and it can prevent further injury by signaling danger. Amazingly, people used to think that dogs didn't feel pain, but we know better now. The past decade has seen advances in recognition of pain in animals, the ability to assess their pain, and the understanding of how they respond to various types of pain-relief drugs.

What Is Pain?

According to one definition, pain is a usually localized physical suffering associated with a disease or an injury. It's also described as an unpleasant sensation that occurs when nerve endings are stimulated. Whether in humans or animals, pain is a complex phenomenon with physical and psychological components. Pain is often difficult to recognize and interpret in dogs, but in no way does that imply they don't feel it.

Whether pain is short-term or long-term, it can make your dog's life very unpleasant if it's not managed properly. Pain may certainly have a protective role in minimizing injury and preventing further damage, but unrelieved pain can make a dog's condition worse and has no beneficial effects. Any time you believe your dog is in pain, ask your veterinarian what can be done to help.

How Dogs Feel Pain

The sensation of pain is transmitted by way of the nervous system, a network of billions of nerve cells, or neurons. (See Chapter 6 for more information about the nervous system.) One of the jobs of this system is to interpret sensory information acquired through smell, hearing, sight, taste, and touch. When your dog cuts himself on a barbed-wire fence, for example, the sensation stimulates numerous nerve endings beneath the skin. These nociceptors transmit a pain signal through sensory neurons in the spinal cord. This reaction releases a neurotransmitter that relays the pain signal from one neuron to another until it reaches the part of the brain where pain perception occurs. The signal then travels to the cerebrum, at which point your dog realizes that he's in pain and yelps.

The perception of pain is unique to each individual, human or dog. (That's one of the reasons pain is difficult to manage.) Factors that affect each dog's individual response to pain include age, gender, health status, and breed differences. For instance, young dogs have a lower tolerance for sudden pain, but they're less sensitive to the emotional stress or anxiety that accompanies anticipated pain (such as having the anal glands expressed). Healthy dogs tend to tolerate pain better than sick dogs, but sick dogs may be less likely to respond obviously to pain because they don't feel like making the effort. A stoic working or herding breed may show less response to pain than an excitable or sensitive breed.

FACT

Nociceptors are the free nerve endings of neurons that have their cell bodies outside the spinal column. They look like the branches of small bushes. Different nerves transmit information about different sensations, such as pain, cold, heat, and pressure.

The response to pain can be involuntary or voluntary. For instance, when a groomer's nail clippers cut into the quick, the painfully sensitive blood vessel that feeds the nail, the dog reflexively jerks his paw back. That's an involuntary response. A voluntary response is based on experience. A dog who's had his nails clipped too short in the past remembers the pain and jerks his paw back before the clippers even touch the nail.

Types of Pain

The sensation of pain can originate in the skin, bones, joints, muscles, or internal organs. Each causes a different type of pain. For instance, pain caused by injury to the skin or superficial tissues is called cutaneous pain. Minor cuts, burns, and lacerations are examples of cutaneous pain. A broken bone or sprained joint produces somatic pain, which originates from ligaments, tendons, bones, blood vessels, and nerves. Nociceptors located within body organs or body cavities produce visceral pain, such as a stomachache.

Recognizing Pain

When humans are in pain, they usually don't hesitate to let other people know about it. A person may yell, shake the affected limb, limp, or otherwise express the feeling of injury. Dogs are a bit more subtle. A few individual canines don't mind letting you know that they've been hurt or don't feel well, but most dogs try to hide pain. It's an evolutionary response dictated by thousands of years of predatory knowledge: The weak don't survive. (Or maybe they secretly pass it on that pain means a trip to the veterinarian.) While they're generally not as secretive as cats, dogs will make a pretty good effort to keep you from knowing that they're not in tip-top condition. You have to be alert and observant to figure out that your dog isn't feeling his best.

Signs of Pain

Recognizing and finding the source of pain in dogs is a challenge. Dogs can't say where it hurts or how much it hurts, so you and your veterinarian must rely on your knowledge and observations of your dog's normal behavior.

Knowing what's normal is one of the most important ways you can recognize and assess pain in your dog. Once you really start to pay attention to your dog's regular actions and habits, anything that's abnormal will jump out at you.

The early signs of pain are subtle. They might include eating less, failing to greet you at the door when you come home from work, or not wanting to be groomed when normally that's a pleasurable experience. More obvious signs of pain include limping, reluctance to move, squinting or pawing at the eyes, crying out or whining when touched, or even snapping when touched. Any unexplained abnormality in your dog's routine behavior or activity level is significant and warrants a visit to the veterinarian. Common signs of pain you should watch for include the following:

- Changes in personality or attitude, such as a normally quiet and docile dog becoming aggressive or an aggressive dog becoming quiet
- Abnormal vocalizations, such as whining or whimpering, especially when a painful area is touched or the dog is forced to move
- Licking, biting, scratching, or shaking of one area
- Piloerection, a reflex of the muscles at the base of the hair shafts that causes the hair to stand on end
- Changes in posture or movement, such as limping, holding a paw

up, or tensing the abdominal and back muscles to produce a tucked-up appearance

- Changes in activity level, including restlessness, pacing, lethargy, or reluctance to move
- Loss of appetite
- Changes in facial expression, such as dull eyes or pinned ears
- Changes in bowel movements or urination, such as straining

Your veterinarian will check your dog's heart rate, respiratory rate, and body temperature. All of these tend to increase in the presence of pain. The veterinarian may check a blood sample for elevations in glucose, cortico-steroid, and catecholamine concentrations.

Diagnosing the Pain

To find the source of the pain, your veterinarian will probably begin by palpating your dog's body, examining it by hand to check the condition of the organs and search for painful lumps or bumps. He may put pressure on the trigger points along the spine and check the range of motion of the legs by extending and flexing the joints to look for signs of discomfort. Once he knows where the pain is, your veterinarian can try to figure out what's causing it and how to treat it.

When there isn't an obvious cause for pain, such as a surgical wound, for instance, or a broken bone, sophisticated diagnostic techniques can help. These include analysis of the cerebrospinal fluid, radiographs of the spine using dye (myelography), measurements of the electrical activity in the muscles (electromyography), and brain imaging with computed tomography (CT) or magnetic resonance imaging (MRI) scans.

If your dog balks at taking a certain pain medication, ask if there's another way to give it. Some drugs can be made into syrups that are applied to the gums so the medication is absorbed through the mucous membranes. Others can be compounded into something tasty, such as peanut butter, to make them more palatable.

Acute Versus Chronic Pain

Often described as short-term pain or pain with an easily identifiable cause, acute pain is the body's way to warn of injury or disease. It usually starts out as a sudden, sharp pain that becomes an ache. Acute pain begins in a specific area and may then spread out. It can be mild or severe and may last for only a few days or for weeks, depending on the type of injury or disease. Pain is most intense within the first twenty-four to seventy-two hours of injury.

Veterinarians commonly treat acute pain that is the result of either trauma or surgery. Causes of acute pain include fractures, bowel obstructions, bladder stones, and gastroenteritis (stomachache). Depending on the cause, acute pain responds well to medication such as analgesic drugs (pain relievers). It may be also be relieved surgically.

The word "chronic" means always present, or significant for its long duration or frequent recurrence. Chronic pain is defined as pain that has lasted for six months or longer. It lasts far beyond the time needed for an injury to heal and no longer serves its purpose of preventing injury. Rather than performing its protective function, chronic pain is often associated with a disease that has a long duration, such as cancer. This is a debilitating type of pain that requires long-term specialized treatment. Unfortunately, chronic pain is more difficult to treat than acute pain. To deal with it effectively, your veterinarian may need to perform a number of diagnostic tests and try many different approaches to pain relief.

Surgical Pain

Pain resulting from surgery is one of the most obvious forms of acute pain. Unfortunately, while surgery helps to relieve an underlying problem, the pain it causes isn't always as easy to cure. Surgery (and some invasive diagnostic procedures) can cause significant pain in dogs, but because dogs can't communicate their level of discomfort, it's difficult to provide proper pain medication. If dogs don't get the necessary pain relief, they can lose their appetite and become stressed, both of which reduce the effectiveness of the surgery.

ALERT!

Some surgical procedures are more painful than others. These include orthopedic procedures, which involve trauma to large muscle masses; chest surgery; and surgery of the eyes, ears, nose, or teeth. Dogs undergoing these types of surgeries are more likely to have a high degree of pain and to need a certain level of pain relief. Spay/neuter surgery on young, healthy dogs tends to generate less pain.

Treating Surgical Pain

Veterinarians have learned that the best way to prevent surgical pain is to provide presurgical pain relief. Anesthesia blocks the knowledge of pain during surgery, but now veterinarians can give dogs a combination of pain-relief and anesthetic drugs. Why is this helpful? The anesthetic drugs that veterinarians use today provide quick recovery from anesthesia, which is a benefit. However, that same quick recovery can bring on intense acute pain unless the anesthetic drug is paired with a pain-reliever.

Presurgical pain relief means less anesthesia can be used, as well as less postsurgical pain relief. The improved safety of anesthetic drugs, combined with this ability to provide presurgical pain relief, also allows surgeons to perform more invasive procedures than they could in the past.

Non-Medical Pain Relief for Surgery

Good surgical techniques can also reduce the pain experienced from surgery. These include minimizing tissue trauma by making smaller incisions and preventing tension on suture lines. Bandages to pad and protect the traumatized area are also essential. After surgery, making the dog comfortable on warm bedding as he comes out of the anesthetic haze can also help.

Post-Surgical Pain Relief

Many advances have been made in pain relief for animals, but managing post-surgical and chronic pain is still difficult. That's because not all drugs are effective in every situation. Some cause side effects when used over a long period, and some aren't convenient for owners to give at home.

Researchers have hope, however, that a new slow-release narcotic drug will be able to provide convenient, safe, and long-lasting pain relief for dogs and improve the treatment of chronic and postsurgical pain. Currently, no medications are licensed for use in dogs to treat postoperative pain, although some veterinarians, with the informed consent of the dog's owner, may choose to use certain medications to help the dog feel more comfortable after surgery.

Managing Pain

Pain management is important for any condition that interferes with your dog's normal activity, appetite, interaction with you, and ability to have a good day. How pain is managed depends on the type and cause of the pain. Some pain can be cured, while other types of pain can only be managed. In any case, preventing and relieving pain is an important goal that you and your veterinarian can work toward together.

Effective Pain Relief

Because different animals have different responses to pain, different signs of pain, and different reactions to treatment, finding the most effective form of pain relief can be a complex and difficult task. There's no one-size-fits-all solution. Cost can also be a factor; pain relief isn't always cheap.

When they enter the profession, veterinarians take an oath that includes the promise to use their scientific knowledge and skills for the benefit of society through the protection of animal health and the relief of animal suffering.

The first thing to realize is that complete elimination of pain isn't necessarily possible or desirable. The main goal is to help your dog cope with pain so he doesn't suffer. Successful pain management allows a dog to continue to engage in normal activities, such as eating, sleeping, moving around, and interacting with people or other animals. Factors your veterinarian will take into account in approaching pain relief are your dog's breed, age, health status, personality, the drugs and techniques available, and the type, cause, and degree of pain.

Traditional Therapies

Medication is probably the first form of pain relief that most people think of, and most veterinarians use drugs with pain-relieving properties as the first line of defense against pain. Opioids, for instance, usually have the effects of dulling the senses, relieving pain, or inducing sleep. Opioid patches placed on a dog's skin can provide long-lasting and steady pain relief, unlike shorter-acting medications that can wear off before the next dose is given.

ALERT!

Dogs process drugs differently than people. Never give your dog any kind of pain-relief medication without first checking with your veterinarian. Tylenol and ibuprofen, for example, are toxic to dogs even in very small amounts.

Some analgesic drugs include local anesthetics, which numb only a particular area. Certain medications known as nonsteroidal anti-inflammatory drugs (NSAIDs) are often used to treat the chronic pain of arthritis or cancer. NSAIDs don't directly eliminate pain, but they can decrease it by treating inflammation. Several NSAIDs have been developed specifically for use in dogs, including carprofen, etodolac, meloxicam, and deracoxib.

Different types of drugs have a sedative effect. They work to decrease anxiety and can enhance the effectiveness of analgesic drugs, but they don't necessarily relieve pain in and of themselves. Never assume that a sedative or tranquilizer by itself will be enough to relieve your dog's pain. Acepromazine, or "ace," is a commonly used sedative that does not provide much in the way of pain relief.

Remember that your veterinarian is tailoring the type of drug, dose, and frequency of administration to your dog's individual needs. Just because your neighbor's dog is getting good pain relief from a certain medication doesn't mean that your dog will respond the same way. The dose and duration of effect of analgesic drugs varies greatly from dog to dog. Your veterinarian may also choose to use a combination of analgesic drugs from different drug classes to achieve the best pain relief and reduce the risk of side effects. As your dog's needs change, your veterinarian may modify the dose or frequency of administration. He may also require periodic blood work to make sure the drug isn't affecting liver function, which is a common side effect.

Non-Medical Pain Management

Effective pain management goes beyond drugs. Keeping your dog comfortable will also help him feel better more quickly. If he's recovering at home, place his bed in a quiet, well-ventilated area. Take steps to limit any stress on him. Your dog may love your kids and the neighbors' kids, but he's not up to dealing with them right now. Keep visits short and quiet. Your dog will probably enjoy some gentle petting for a brief time, but high-pitched shrieks and kids running around are likely to put him on edge, and rough play is not appropriate.

Your dog needs to eat well to recover, so diet is important too. He may be in so much pain he doesn't feel like eating, but he needs nutrition in order to heal. Tempt your dog's appetite with canned food. If that doesn't work, try warming his food in the microwave. The heat will improve his ability to smell the food, which should help his appetite. Test it with your finger before giving it to him to make sure there aren't any hot spots.

Osteoarthritis of the hip joint is a major cause of lameness in dogs of all ages. It occurs when degradation of cartilage surrounding the bone causes a gradual development of joint pain, stiffness, and reduced range of motion. It most often develops secondary to hip dysplasia in dogs.

Weight loss is another aspect of diet that can help relieve your dog's pain, especially if he suffers from an orthopedic condition such as arthritis or hip dysplasia. (See Chapter 15.) Veterinarians now believe that overweight dogs with painful hips and lameness caused by osteoarthritis may improve through weight reduction alone. While there's no cure for osteoarthritis or hip dysplasia, a weight-reduction plan may delay the need for surgery. This is especially important for large-breed dogs, whose size puts more stress on the joints, or active dogs such as sporting breeds, who enjoy lots of running or hunting.

Alternative Therapies for Pain Relief

So many people have found pain relief through alternative therapies such as acupuncture and chiropractic methods that they want their dogs to experience the same benefits. These types of alternative and complementary therapies are no longer unusual for animals; many traditionally trained veterinarians now offer their clients a full range of services by joining forces with or making referrals to practitioners that offer these treatments. Among the therapies that may benefit dogs are acupuncture, chiropractic therapy, magnetic field therapy, massage, and nutraceuticals. (If you're interested in learning more about the options, turn to Chapter 18.)

ALERT!

Steroids can be used for pain relief, but they're a drug of last resort. Over the long term, steroids have a detrimental effect on the health of joint tissues, particularly cartilage. Long-term use of steroids can lead to diabetes and adrenal gland problems.

Few studies have been done to prove the effectiveness of these treatments. Much of what's known has been extrapolated from studies in humans. Nonetheless, many dog owners believe alternative therapies have made a difference in their pets' quality of life. Because not much is known about how or why certain treatments or techniques work in animals, always go to an experienced practitioner. Just because something is natural doesn't mean it's harmless.

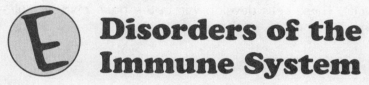

Chapter 11

Disorders of the Immune System

Your dog is surrounded by potential enemies in the form of bacteria, viruses, parasites, and other health-destroying invaders. Dogs rely on their immune system to fight off these potential invaders and help to keep them fit. While the immune system will save your dog's health many times over her lifetime, sometimes it goes haywire and starts to make mistakes. Here's a look at both sides of your dog's immune system—the friend and the foe.

Your Dog's Immune System

Your dog has a wonderful defense against diseases and health problems—the immune system, which constantly goes to battle to fight off invaders. The immune system uses several types of cells in the bloodstream to fight off bacterial and viral invaders, including lymphocytes, neutrophils, and macrophages. These cells develop within the bone marrow, spleen, and lymph nodes.

Defender Cells

There are two main groups of defender cells, or lymphocytes—B cells and T cells. The B cells produce antibodies against bacteria. B cells can be exposed to antigens through plasma cells or on their own, and they then develop specific antibodies against those antigens. T cells often work via the thymus (tissue in the chest that helps these lymphocytes develop) and are active against viruses and delayed hypersensitivity.

The immune system also includes secretions known as immunoglobulins that act as antibodies and respond to infections. The primary immunoglobulins are Ig A, which acts near mucosal surfaces such as the moist linings of the mouth and the nose to prevent bacteria and viruses from entering the body; Ig E, which acts along the lining of the respiratory and intestinal tracts to keep invaders out; and Ig G, which can be found throughout the body fighting infections. These immunoglobulins can cause problems, too—they can become sensitized to your dog's own tissues or react against foreign tissue such as a kidney transplant.

Fighter Cells

Your dog also has cells that actively attack and ideally consume and destroy bacteria and viruses. These cells include the neutrophils (in the category of white blood cells), the macrophages, and the mast cells. Neutrophils and macrophages may actually eat bacteria and viruses. Mast cells release many immune mediators such as histamine. These mediator substances can make your dog miserable even while her body is trying to help. Think of the symptoms that lead you to take antihistamine medications!

FACT

When your veterinarian checks a complete blood count on your dog, she is looking at white blood cell counts and a differential. The white blood cell count tells her how many infection-fighting cells are in your dog's bloodstream. The differential, determined by looking at the cells on a microscope slide, gives her an idea of how many cells there are of each type of white blood cell—for example, how many neutrophils, how many lymphocytes, etc. These measurements can guide your veterinarian in diagnosing the cause of your dog's illness and planning an effective treatment.

Autoimmune problems such as autoimmune hemolytic anemia and certain skin problems develop when the immune system cells fail to recognize your dog's own cells. The immune cells attack the dog's other cells because they appear to be foreign invaders. These can be difficult conditions to treat.

Your Dog's Natural Defenses

Your dog has a number of defense mechanisms in addition to the immune system itself. Virtually all of your dog's systems have some built-in safeguards and alarms. Together with the immune system, they work to keep your dog healthy and happy.

Your dog's skin is a barrier to bacteria, viruses, fungal infections, and parasites. Many of these disease agents can only get a foothold on your dog if the skin has been broken through trauma or internal disease reactions, such as allergies. Even your dog's coat acts as protection from these outside invaders.

Along the respiratory tract are cells that trap and catch dust and other debris, including bacteria and viruses that are trying to make their way into the lungs. Coughing and sneezing remove many of those infectious agents and irritants. Eyes produce tears that wash invaders away. Problems that reach the stomach may be actively removed by vomiting. The gastrointestinal tract secretes mucus to help protect it from caustic substances and may speed up passage to remove toxic wastes quickly via diarrhea.

Immune Reactions

There are a few different types of immune reactions. Some reactions can be immediate, such as anaphylaxis. Other reactions are delayed and require multiple exposures to the offending substance.

What Is Anaphylaxis?

Anaphylaxis is a dreaded reaction by a dog to a sensitizing substance, such as snake or bee venom or proteins in certain vaccines. Sometimes this occurs on the first exposure, but it may take a second exposure to get a really severe reaction. In anaphylaxis, your dog produces the immunoglobulin Ig E, which starts a reaction among the body's cells resulting in a release of histamine. Your dog will have an intense inflammatory reaction with edema, often pruritus (itchiness), and possibly liver or breathing problems. He can even go into shock and die.

What to Do for Anaphylaxis

Anaphylaxis is not common, but can be scary and is life-threatening. If you suspect your dog is having a reaction, get to your veterinarian immediately. Your dog will need treatment for shock and possibly epinephrine to reverse the histamine response.

If your dog has had an anaphylactic reaction to a vaccine, your veterinarian will discuss other ways to keep him safe from infectious disease. If he has a reaction to bee stings, you should discuss having an Epi Pen kit for your dog and what dosage to give in case of future problems.

Allergies

Allergies are sometimes a case of your dog's immune system and defenses getting the wrong signals. They represent a reaction of your dog's body against foreign substances that may or may not actually be a real threat to your dog's health. Allergic reactions can be immediate or delayed. Some reactions only occur after multiple exposures to the offending substance. Along with food and inhalant allergies, many dogs show allergic reactions to insect bites. This includes the arch nemesis the flea as well as other bugs such as mosquitoes and black flies. Check out Chapter 12 for information on parasite problems.

Food Allergies

Some dogs have food allergies. These allergies can be to unusual foods or to foods that most people would consider normal dog food. Remember that although they are classified as carnivores, dogs are omnivorous in their eating habits, generally eating a wide range of food types with no problems. Still, some dogs may have allergies to normal dietary proteins. For example, some dogs are allergic to beef. For these dogs, the proteins in the meat stimulate allergic skin reactions. Up to 15 percent of all allergic skin disease in dogs may be caused by food allergies, the third most common itchy skin disorder.

FACT

Dogs that are less than six months of age and dogs older than six are the most likely to develop food allergies. Young dogs become sensitive quickly, while with older dogs it takes many exposures. The most common food allergies are to wheat, corn, beef, chicken, dairy products, and fish.

Most dogs with food allergies will show skin signs, such as inflamed ears and skin problems in the groin area. You may see them rubbing their faces or chewing their feet. It is now believed that at least some cases of inflammatory bowel disease (manifested by primarily by diarrhea) are also caused by food allergies.

Treating Food Allergies

A dog with food allergies will need a period of limited protein-and-carbohydrate diet to determine what foods are safe and must then be kept on that diet very strictly. (That means treats have to be considered, too.) There are special diets with very limited and unusual sources of protein and carbohydrates that can be used for testing and possibly for lifelong maintenance of your dog. Some dogs will eventually become allergic to these new sources of nutrition as well and require more dietary changes.

A novel approach to food allergies is to reduce proteins to very small components. These components are very easily absorbed and utilized and appear less problematic for dogs. This type of protein-reduced food can only be prescribed by a veterinarian.

Inhaled Allergies

Inhalant allergy, sometimes called atopy, is a reaction to substances in the environment like dust or pollen. Humans with inhalant allergies tend to sneeze, wheeze, and have a runny nose. Dogs most commonly show their inhaled allergies by breaking out with skin problems. These allergies tend to start out as seasonal problems. When the pollen counts are high, you sneeze and your dog scratches. Wiping your dog off in the evening with an unscented dryer sheet may remove some of the offending pollens. Following the guidelines for human sufferers helps as well—these include using air conditioning and staying indoors with the windows closed on days when mold and pollen counts are high.

Treating Inhaled Allergies

Mild cases may be controlled by short-term medications such as antihistamines or corticosteroids, but in the long run your dog may do best with a desensitization program. With this therapy, your veterinarian will do a skin test on your dog by injecting small amounts of allergens under the skin. Offending allergens cause red bumps or wheals. Once the problem allergens have been identified, small amounts of those allergens will be specially mixed for your dog. A schedule of allergen injections will gradually accustom her body to these substances. The strength of the injections increases with time, and the time between injections also increases. Many dogs do very well on this type of program.

Autoimmune Skin Problems

Another set of skin problems in dogs comes under the heading of autoimmune problems. In these cases, the dog's immune system reacts against his own skin cells. There are a number of skin-related autoimmune diseases in dogs. Some of these diseases just affect the skin, while others are generalized immune problems, with skin troubles just one of the possible symptoms. All of them require close cooperation between you and your veterinarian to keep your dog in the best possible condition. Topical or oral corticosteroids or other immunosuppressive drugs may be needed along with occasional antibiotics or special baths and diets.

The Pemphigus Complex

Pemphigus is a skin disorder that has a variety of forms. Pemphigus foliaceous is the most common form. Dogs with this disorder often develop scabs and pustules on the head and feet that gradually spread over more areas of the body. Blisters are also present, but they rupture easily and aren't seen very often. With the open skin sores, dogs often develop secondary bacterial infections. Breeds such as akitas, chows, bearded collies, and Doberman pinschers are prone to this.

Pemphigus vulgaris is the most severe form of pemphigus. Dogs with this condition develop severe ulceration at areas where hairy skin joins mucous membranes, such as near the mouth, nose, and anus. It may also affect the feet and can even cause nails to fall out. It is common for other serious immune problems to occur as side effects of pemphigus vulgaris. A skin biopsy may be required to get a clear-cut diagnosis of this disorder.

Dogs with pemphigus of any type will almost always require prednisone therapy along with other immunosuppressive drugs such as azathioprine or even chemotherapy drugs.

Chemotherapy drugs often work as immunosuppressives to slow down or shut off the reaction of the body against its own tissues. For this reason, these drugs may be used to help dogs with autoimmune problems. Cyclosporine is an example of one of these medications. Unfortunately many such drugs have side effects, so careful and consistent monitoring of your dog's health is important.

Systemic Lupus Erythematosus

Systemic lupus erythematosus, or SLE, is an immune disorder that affects a wide range of body systems, from neurologic to skin to blood components. In a dog with SLE, the immune system has two defective actions. Immune complexes (clumps of cells formed when antigens and antibodies interact) can be deposited in organs and interfere with their function (as described for glomerulonephritis, on page 153). This disease also stimulates the formation of autoantibodies—antibodies that react against the body's own normal tissues. Dogs with SLE will show skin reactions, ulcers on oral tissues, possibly behavior changes, and even additional autoimmune problems with blood cells and platelets. (Refer to the description of AIHA and autoimmune thrombocytopenia on pages 158 and 159.)

How can I figure out what all those complicated disease names mean?
Sometimes there are clues to what a disease name means. For instance, the suffix "itis" means inflammation. So arthritis is an inflammation of the joints, *arthro* being the Greek word for joint. The suffix "osis" or "osus" simply means that the condition is abnormal.

Dogs with SLE are diagnosed by a combination of biopsies of affected areas and blood tests. Treatment for SLE usually starts off with corticosteroids, but immunosuppressive drugs may also be required. Immunosuppressive drugs act to limit the body's response to infection and inflammation. This group of drugs includes some medications such as aziathioprine and cyclopsorine.

Autoimmune Kidney Disease

The kidney is an organ that is quite sensitive to immune diseases. Any deposits of cells or proteins will interfere with the efficiency of its intricate filtering and reabsorption system. While some breeds such as Shih Tzu, Lhasa apsos, Doberman pinschers, soft-coated wheaten terriers, and Samoyeds may have genetic based renal disease, immune problems can strike any dog. (See Chapter 15 for more on genetic diseases.)

Glomerulonephritis

In glomerulonephritis, part of the kidney's filtration system (the glomerulus) is inflamed. This might be the result of a bacterial infection or even cancer, but it can also be caused by deposits of antigen and antibody from immune diseases. These immune deposits interfere with the kidneys' function of filtering out and resorbing protein. This problem is indicated by the presence of protein in the urine.

Amyloidosis

Amyloidosis is another type of kidney disease. In this case, the protein amyloid is deposited along the kidney's tubules. The amyloid interferes with the kidney function and leads to renal disease. This protein may get deposited in other tissues as well. Amyloidosis is most common in Shar-Peis. Dogs with the disease suffer from swollen, painful joints, cyclic fevers, and kidney disease. Blood work, urinalyses, and biopsies might be required to definitely diagnose amyloidosis. Dogs with this problem are treated with anti-inflammatory drugs and immunosuppressives.

End-Stage Renal Disease

The kidneys are so efficient that symptoms of kidney problems can be hidden for a long time. More than 75 percent of the working tissue must be damaged before routine testing will show any sign of kidney disease and before your dog will show any clinical signs of illness. Dogs with end-stage renal disease (ERD) often have had a long course of chronic kidney problems. Blood tests, a thorough clinical history, and urinalyses are important for diagnosing kidney disease. In some cases, your veterinarian may need to do a biopsy and/or an ultrasound exam.

ALERT!

New testing for end-stage renal disease (ERD) looks for tiny amounts of a protein called albumin in the urine. This test is extremely sensitive and may catch kidney failure early on, when intervention is most likely to succeed. Many veterinarians recommend screening middle-aged and senior dogs for kidney problems.

Signs of Kidney Failure

Dogs with kidney failure may drink large amounts of water and pass a large amount of diluted urine. They may also go to the opposite extreme and stop drinking much and therefore pass little urine. It is important to push fluid therapy for dogs with renal problems to stimulate urine production. If you can't encourage your dog to drink, your veterinarian may need to give subcutaneous fluids under the skin or use an intravenous catheter to push fluids directly into your dog's system.

Treating Kidney Problems

Along with fluids to flush out the kidney system, your dog may need antibiotics to fight infection, extra vitamins to make up for those lost in the fluid flush, and medications to encourage red blood cell production and to fight anemia. The kidney is an important source of erythropoietin, which stimulates red blood cell production. That's why secondary anemia is often a by-product of kidney damage. Dialysis is only available at a few veterinary schools and specialty practices. It is primarily used for acute renal crises, not long-term maintenance.

FACT

Some veterinary schools and specialty practices are working on kidney transplants for dogs with nonresponsive kidney failure. Rejection is a problem, just as it is in people, and families are required to adopt the donor dog—usually a healthy shelter dog.

Immune Diseases of the Gastrointestinal Tract

Along with attacking skin and kidneys, immune diseases may interfere with digestion and the gastrointestinal tract as well. The formation of immune complexes may block cells that are important for absorbing and transporting fluids and nutrients into the body. Other immune problems can damage the cells directly.

Inflammatory Bowel Disease

Inflammatory bowel disease (IBD) in dogs is characterized by large numbers of lymphocytes collecting along the intestinal tract and in the stomach. A number of different versions of this problem are seen in dogs, depending on which areas of the intestines are affected. Dogs with IBD will have vomiting and diarrhea, often with accompanying weight loss. This is a chronic problem and may be cyclic, which means your dog may experience periods of normalcy. IBD may be caused by a hypersensitivity reaction to drugs, bacteria, viruses, or parasites. It may also have a genetic component. Most dogs are diagnosed as adults, but sometimes even young dogs will show signs of this problem, especially if there is a genetic predisposition. Basenjis and German shepherd dogs are two breeds that seem predisposed to IBD.

Diagnosing and Treating IBD

Diagnosis of IBD may require blood work, an endoscopic exam, and a biopsy. Treatment varies with the cause and the severity of the signs. It is important in all cases to eliminate any parasites. Your dog may need medications to cut down on bacteria in the intestines and steroid or immunosuppressive drugs to reduce the inflammation. Increasing fiber in the diet may help. If your dog has a sensitivity to certain foods, a bland food can also be helpful.

Because the drugs used to treat autoimmune disease have the potential for side effects and are usually administered for the lifetime of your dog, it is important to have regular checkups to catch any complications early on. A close partnership with your veterinarian is extremely important!

Autoimmune Blood Disorders

When the immune system reacts against cells in the blood, your dog's life could be in danger. These threats may be acute and short term, or they may become chronic problems that require life-long care. These reactions may be triggered by drugs, vaccines, or viral infections, or the dogs involved may have a genetic predisposition.

Autoimmune Hemolytic Anemia

Autoimmune hemolytic anemia (AIHA) is a well-recognized syndrome that occurs when a dog's body no longer recognizes its own blood cells and attacks them. There are two versions of AIHA. The first is more rare and more serious. It generally involves middle-aged, larger-breed dogs. The disease comes on very quickly. The dogs show profound anemia, often have blood in their urine, and may appear yellow (jaundiced) on their light skin areas or by their eyes or gums. These dogs need immediate veterinary care, and the prognosis is not good.

The more common version of AIHA syndrome is acute but not quite so severe. In this case, signs may develop over a couple of days. Cocker spaniels have a genetic predisposition to developing this version of AIHA. Affected dogs become weak or fatigued easily. These dogs' gums will appear pale in color, and you may notice a yellowish cast to the gums and eyes. Astute families may notice that their dog's abdomen is a bit distended, as the liver and spleen are often enlarged. Luckily, dogs with acute AIHA generally respond well to therapy with corticosteroids such as prednisone that limit the body's immune responses.

Autoimmune Thrombocytopenia

Another autoimmune condition involving cells of the blood is autoimmune thrombocytopenia. Female dogs suffer from this syndrome more often than males. Thrombocytes are the cells that yield platelets, the components of blood that are so important in blood clotting. In this case, the cells that are attacked are the thrombocytes, so platelet numbers drop dramatically. Dogs with a very low platelet count develop reddish discolored areas on their skin. They may have nosebleeds, blood in the stool, and blood in their urine. Due to the bleeding, these dogs may become anemic as well! Dogs with autoimmune thrombocytopenia need treatment with corticosteroids and possibly immunosuppressive drugs as well. A blood transfusion may also be needed for short-term treatment. This should be done with typed blood that matches your dog's.

Dogs have different blood types, just as people do. DEA 1.1 is the most common type, occurring in 40 percent of all dogs. This is also the most reactive blood type, so dogs with DEA 1.1 positive blood should only donate to other DEA 1.1 positive dogs. Dogs with DEA 1.1 negative or DEA 1.2 negative blood are considered to be universal donors. Your veterinary clinic may keep donor dogs on call to help in emergencies.

Autoimmune Arthritis Conditions

Certainly most of us know friends or relatives with rheumatoid arthritis. This painful condition can affect dogs as well. As with the other autoimmune disorders, the body incorrectly reacts against its own normal tissues. In this case, the joints are the target—both the joint fluid and the joint cartilage.

Rheumatoid Arthritis

Dogs with rheumatoid arthritis show a shifting leg lameness, which means they may be lame on one leg one day and a different leg two days later. They may also have very swollen, tender joints. Because the cartilage is being targeted by the immune system, it will erode, leading to joint deformities and bones that pop out of joint. An offshoot of rheumatoid arthritis is plasmacytic-lymphocytic synovitis, seen in medium- to large-breed dogs but primarily only involving the stifle (knee) joint. Both conditions are treated with steroids and immunosuppressive drugs along with pain medications as needed.

ALERT!

Newer treatments for these autoimmune conditions are always being researched. Depositions of gold salts and new anti-inflammatory drugs look hopeful, as do nontraditional treatments such as acupuncture. Ask your veterinarian about physical therapy techniques to help keep your dog mobile as well.

Idiopathic Polyarthritis

Idiopathic polyarthritis is another autoimmune problem that affects joints in dogs. This disease syndrome tends to strike certain breeds. German shepherds, Doberman pinschers, retrievers, spaniels, and pointers are among the larger breeds it is found in. Even toy breeds may show this problem however, especially toy poodles, Yorkshire terriers, and Chihuahuas. Dogs with this disorder have joint problems along with cyclic fevers, lethargy, and loss of appetite. They may be stiff and lame. Steroids are the first line of treatment for idiopathic polyarthritis.

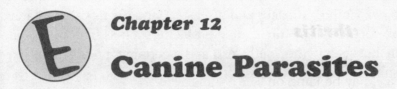

Chapter 12

Canine Parasites

By definition, parasites are beings that can only exist through the help, willing or not, of another living being. In dogs, this category includes internal and external pests such as worms, ticks, and fleas. These creatures must be associated with a dog or other animal for at least part of their lifetime. Not only do they drain nutrients from dogs, they cause a wide variety of health problems and may even transmit diseases. Your goal as a responsible dog owner should be to keep your dog as parasite-free as possible for a long, healthy life.

Fleas—Tough Enemies

On a list of athletes of the parasite world, fleas would jump to the top (literally). These parasites can leap many times their own height, run very swiftly, and have become resistant to many anti-flea medications. They not only cause healthy dogs to itch but can stimulate severe allergic reactions and can also carry other parasites and diseases. Tapeworms can be transmitted by the bite of a flea. Life-threatening problems such as bubonic plague (not common, but seen in the Southwest) and a certain type of typhus may also be transmitted through flea bites.

A heavy load of fleas on a small puppy can cause serious anemia. Fleas will even enjoy a meal of your blood if they get the chance, along with any furry pets such as rabbits and cats. Dealing with fleas is like planning to fight a war!

Where Do They Come From?

Fleas are found in many areas, living for short periods of time on the ground or in houses, though they must be on their hosts to feed and breed. Fleas can jump from one dog to another and can be shared with cats, rabbits, squirrels, and other wildlife. Most of the fleas we see on our dogs are actually the cat flea—*Ctenocephalides felis*. Once adult fleas find a suitable host, they feed by taking blood meals. Then the females lay eggs, which may stick to the hair of your dog or fall off in the areas where he sleeps, lies, or walks in your house. Larvae hatch and go into a pupa where the adult fleas will develop. Adult fleas can remain safely in the pupa for long periods of time (months) until hosts show up. They can detect movement, warm temperatures, and even carbon dioxide, so they definitely know when a living being passes close by.

QUESTION?

How can I tell if my dog has fleas?
Part the hair and look for tiny running bodies. It may be easiest to roll him over and look in the relatively hairless area of the groin. If you see or feel dark grit in your dog's coat, take some off and put it on a white paper towel. Add a drop of water. If the grit dissolves and turns red, you know it is flea feces—the red is from the blood meals.

How to Win the War

Fighting fleas requires a concerted effort. *All* your pets need to be treated—even the cat and dogs that may not show any itching. You need to get rid of the adult fleas, stop reproduction, and with any luck prevent new fleas from joining the family.

When you're treating fleas, remember that a flea bath will only get rid of the eggs and adult fleas on your pet at that moment. Once he jumps out of the tub all clean and flea-free, new fleas will immediately jump on from the carpet or ground. You need to follow up the bath with a dip, spray, powder, collar, or topical treatment to deter new fleas or even kill them if they try to jump on your dog. The rugs need to be thoroughly cleaned, as well as areas along walls and behind doors. You can also set off "flea bombs" to catch any fleas that are left. Outside you can try planting chrysanthemums, spreading borax or diatomaceous earth, and discouraging rodents (who may serve as hosts) from living near your home.

Prevention

Preventing flea infestations is easier than getting rid of them once they have moved in. This means the best plan for fighting fleas is to take action before you see evidence of them. When warm weather approaches, start thinking about flea control, which is often combined with tick control. There are new medications that act as flea birth control by interfering with the development of the flea's protective chitin covering. Insect growth regulators stop any fleas that get on your dog from successfully reproducing. Finally, you can also find drugs that act to kill fleas. Many of these medications now come in topical forms that can be applied to your dog once monthly. Pyrethrins (from chrysanthemums) are found in many flea-control products.

Flea-control products that are safe for use on your dog are often *not* safe for use on your cat or house bunny! Some sprays may be dangerous for birds as well. While you need to treat all the furry animals in your household if you have a flea infestation, realize that you may need special medications for each species.

Ticks—Another Tough Customer

Ticks are another external parasite that seem to battle back. These are tough arachnids (eight-legged creatures) that not only eat blood meals but may carry many serious, life-threatening diseases. They come in a variety of sizes (all small, though), and the primary species vary from region to region. Ticks can be differentiated from fleas in that they are rounder and they either walk or are firmly fixed to your dog's body. Most are brown, but some, such as deer ticks, are very small and whitish in color. Female ticks get very large after a blood meal and their color changes from brown to a grayish shade.

The Life of the Tick

The ticks most often found on dogs are the dog ticks, Dermacenter and Rhipicephalus, and the deer tick Ixodes. These ticks go through four life stages. Female ticks lay eggs after they engorge with a blood meal. The eggs may be deposited in cracks and crevices or on the ground. The eggs hatch into larvae that climb up on grass, hitch a ride on a host, and take a big blood meal themselves. The next stage is a nymph and another cycle of hitching a ride on a host, a blood meal, and on to the next stage—the adult.

FACT

Some ticks, such as Rhipicephalus, may spend their entire lives feeding off only one species—the dog. Other ticks feed off many types of hosts. For example, deer ticks may feed off mice, other rodents, lizards, dogs, coyotes, or people who happen along before they get to their definitive host, the deer. Some ticks use birds as an intermediate host as well.

The Heavy Load They May Bear

Unfortunately ticks aren't only a threat for the blood-sucking damage they can do. Many ticks can carry one or more deadly diseases. The list includes Lyme disease, canine ehrlichiosis and babesiosis, even Rocky

Mountain spotted fever (which isn't confined to the Rocky Mountain area anymore). These diseases may show up as problems in the blood with immunity deficits or anemia; swollen, painful joints; rashes; fevers; and damage to the heart. These sidekicks have the potential to kill your dog. You are susceptible to many of these diseases as well, if a tick feeds off you.

More Battle Plans

Like fighting fleas, fighting ticks is a two-stage battle—removal and prevention. If you find ticks on your dog, they need to be carefully removed. There are special tweezers made to remove them, and you should wear gloves to prevent infection. Do not use a lighted match or pour gasoline on the tick. It doesn't work and is dangerous to your dog. If the head is left in your dog's skin, a localized infection may result. Your veterinarian can help you treat those spots.

The best plan as always is to prevent tick infestations to begin with. Many of the topical agents and collars used for flea control will also work against ticks. You want something that will kill the ticks almost immediately—they must feed for twenty-four to forty-eight hours to pass on most diseases. Better yet, some products will repel them from your dog to begin with. If you live in an area with ticks or plan to travel where ticks are common, you need to discuss with your veterinarian the best and safest method to protect your dog, as this may vary with different dogs.

Mites and Lice

Mites are a group of small parasites that may attack dogs. There are three main mites that might be found on dogs: the ear mite, Otodectes; the sarcoptic mange mite, Sarcoptes; and the demodectic or red mange mite, Demodex. Skin problems caused by mites are often referred to as mange. Demodex is not contagious, though ear mites and sarcoptic mites are. They will spread among dogs, from cats to dogs, and (rarely) even to people! If one pet in your household is found to have mites, it is a good idea to check them all carefully. Lice are also parasites that attack dogs via their skin, though they aren't very common in dogs.

Ear Mites

Ear mites tend to be found in dogs that live with cats. You might notice dark, coffee-ground type buildup in your dog's ears, and she may be scratching a bit. Your veterinarian can diagnose a mite infestation by examining a swab of the discharge under a microscope. Most cases can be treated with topical ear medications, though severe cases may need a parasiticide.

Sarcoptic Mange

A dog with sarcoptic mange is usually very unhappy and uncomfortable. These mites burrow into the top layers of the skin, where even a few of them can stimulate a very strong itch response. Dogs with sarcoptic mange can barely walk, as they keep stopping to scratch. With all the scratching, they have open skin areas, which are then in danger of infection. Sarcoptic mange mites are contagious, and dogs with these parasites often have picked them up from local wildlife, including foxes and squirrels.

Diagnosing sarcoptic mange can be tricky. Skin scrapes are the best method, but it can be hard to find mites. If your veterinarian suspects sarcoptic mange, he may start treatment even with a negative skin scrape.

FACT

Skin scrapes are used to diagnose cases of mange. Your veterinarian will choose a couple itchy areas of skin and pucker it to scratch a sharp blade across the top. The thin skin layers are then examined under a microscope. It may take many skin scrapes to find a sarcoptic mite, but Demodex are usually easy to find.

Sarcoptic mange is often treated with a combination of drugs along with baths or dips. Any related infections must also be treated, and your veterinarian will try to make your dog comfortable and relieve some of the itching.

Demodex—Mite of the Red Mange

Demodex is a tiny mite that can be found in normal dogs. Most dogs get along quite well with their demodectic mites and have no problems.

Unfortunately, some dogs have immune problems that are either temporary, as may be seen in puppies or debilitated dogs, or permanent from immune defects. In these dogs, the mites overgrow and cause skin reactions. A few red spots on a puppy may be treated topically or may clear by themselves with no treatment. Dogs that have more than five spots or large areas of reddened, sore skin have generalized Demodex. As mentioned, this is a marker for immune problems.

Demodex is usually easily diagnosed by a skin scraping. Dogs with generalized Demodex will need serious treatment, often with both drugs and dips combined. Since this condition is associated with a genetic defect, dogs that suffer from it should be spayed or neutered and not bred.

Cheyletiella—Walking Dandruff

Cheyletiella is a short-lived mite most often seen on puppies. It shows up as a line of dandruff down their backs. This mite is not usually a serious threat to your dog's health and can be treated by medicated baths.

Lice

Lice come in two main types—biting and sucking. Biting lice tend to be smaller and can move quickly. Lice tend to be host-specific, which means they rarely move from people to dogs or vice versa. Neither type is very common in dogs. Puppies may sometimes have lice from a dirty environment and may spread to them from their mother. A large number of lice could make a puppy anemic, but normally the effects are just poor coats and nits or eggs attached to hair shafts. In most cases, medicated baths or dips will take care of this parasite.

The Most Common Internal Parasites

The most common internal parasites in dogs are roundworms (especially the *Toxocara* species), hookworms (primarily *Ancylostoma*) and whipworms (*Oxyuris*). Reports suggest that more than 80 percent of all puppies will be born with, or quickly acquire, roundworms. These parasites live in the intestines and drain vital nutrients that growing puppies need. On rare occasions a puppy will vomit up roundworms, but worms are normally diagnosed when your veterinarian checks a fecal sample. Whipworms do not pass as many eggs as roundworms or hookworms, so repeated fecal checks may be necessary. Your veterinarian may elect to treat for them anyway based on clinical signs. Picking up after your dog is very important to reduce the chances of internal parasites being spread.

Roundworms

Roundworms can infect puppies before they are born and can also be transmitted via the dam's milk. Adult dogs get roundworms by accidentally ingesting eggs deposited on the ground. The immature larvae migrate through your dog's body and can cause damage to the liver and lungs. Puppies with roundworms often show a bloated abdomen, dull coat, diarrhea, and possibly intestinal blockages. Adult dogs develop some resistance, but even they can show the effects of roundworms.

It is very important that all puppies be checked for roundworms and dewormed. These parasites can also infect people. While they don't reproduce in humans, they can cause serious damage, even blindness, while migrating through tissues. Young children who play in dirt are at greatest risk.

Hookworms

Hookworms are nasty parasites. They are smaller than roundworms but with a set of mouth hooks that dig into the intestines and drain nutrients and blood. Again, puppies can be infected in utero or via their dam's milk. Hookworms can be ingested and can also penetrate the skin, and they cause skin lesions in people as they migrate through the body. Because of their voracious nature, hookworms can actually kill a puppy by making it severely anemic. Dogs with hookworms will show anemia, possibly bloody diarrhea, weight loss, and poor coats.

Whipworms

Luckily whipworms are not as prevalent as roundworms or hookworms. These are small intestinal parasites with a whiplike, tapering tail (hence the name). The eggs need to be ingested to complete their life cycle, but they can survive in the ground for long periods of time. Whipworms cause diarrhea, often with mucus and blood. Dogs with whipworms may defecate frequently and strain to do so. A large number of whipworms can be a serious drain on an adult dog, let alone a puppy. Whipworms are resistant to treatment, so repeated treatments may be necessary. It is also important to clean up the environment, or your dog can easily become reinfected. Cement runs may be bleached, while dirt runs may need to be dug up and replaced with fresh soil.

Tapeworms

While the internal parasites mentioned above do more damage to our beloved dogs, tapeworms have the highest level of owner recognition and horror factor. This may come from finding dried rice-like segments around your dog's tail or, heaven forbid, freshly passed wiggling tapeworm segments on your furniture or rug. Tapeworms are more often discovered at home, when segments are passed out of the anus, than by fecal checks. There are two common species of tapeworms found in dogs and a few unusual ones.

The Common Tapeworms

The most common tapeworms are *Dipylidium caninum* and *Taenia pisiformis*. These two tapeworms have different life cycles, and differentiating them is important for treating your dog and preventing future cases of tapeworm infestation. Dipylidium use fleas as their intermediate host. Dogs that have fleas often accidentally eat one while grooming and scratching. Taenia use rodents as their intermediate host, and dogs that hunt mice or rabbits can pick them up while hunting if they eat their prey. Clearly it is important to keep your dog flea-free and minimize hunting opportunities if you want to stay free of tapeworms.

The Less Common Tapeworms

There are other tapeworms that are seen in dogs. *Echinococcus* species can use northern rodents or sheep as intermediate hosts. While these tapeworms are not usually serious in dogs, they can lead to life-threatening cysts in the lungs and liver of people. Dogs that work sheep or that live in the northern part of North America should have periodic fecal checks for these parasites. (Fecal checks work better for this type.)

FACT

A fecal sample from your dog is often the best way to diagnose intestinal parasites. You need to bring a small amount of stool (about a tablespoon, preferably fresh) to your veterinarian. This will be mixed with a special salt solution and either run through a centrifuge or allowed to sit. The final solution will be examined under a microscope to see if it contains eggs passed by adult parasites living inside your dog.

Diphyllobothrium is a large tapeworm seen in dogs from the northern half of the United States and Canada. This parasite uses fish as an intermediate stage and does not cause serious problems in dogs, but it can lead to serious anemia in people. This is another tapeworm species best diagnosed by fecal checks.

The Less Common Parasites

Some parasites that are not commonly found in our dogs can still cause serious health problems. Some of these parasites have geographical limitations, and others require certain hosts. While small in numbers, their effects can be big.

Lungworms

Capillaria is a roundworm that prefers lungs to intestines. This parasite affects dogs and foxes. Larvae head right to the lungs, where they develop and remain as adults. Dogs with this parasite may cough and have chronic bronchial irritation. This parasite is diagnosed when eggs are found in the feces. (Eggs are passed into airways by the adult roundworm. Dogs cough them up and sometimes swallow them.)

Fluke Infestation

In northern areas of the Midwest and north central Canada, dogs may come in contact with the fluke parasite known as Paragonimus. This fluke is passed into fresh water through mink feces. The larvae then get into freshwater snails and crustaceans. Dogs that eat snails or freshwater crustaceans (even by accident) may pick up this parasite. If the fluke migrates to the brain, it is virtually impossible to treat, but most often this parasite causes no problem. Normally it ends up elsewhere and dies on its own without causing a great deal of trouble. Still, it is best to keep your dog from snail hunting!

The Salmon Fluke

Another fluke, this one aiming for the intestines, is *Nanophyetus salminocola*. This disease is seen in dogs that live in the Northwest and eat raw salmon. While the fluke itself is not especially harmful, it may carry a rickettsia that causes something called salmon poisoning. Dogs with this problem will have a fever, vomiting, and diarrhea and may even die. Treatment is intensive and usually requires hospitalization. Certainly, it makes sense to avoid feeding raw fish.

QUESTION?

What are rickettsia?
Rickettsia are a group of microorganisms that fit somewhere in between bacteria and viruses. These tiny particles of trouble often cause diseases. Many of them are transmitted through the bites of arthropods such as fleas, but even parasites such as flukes may carry harmful rickettsia.

The Protozoan Problems

Protozoal parasites are small single-cell organisms that can't exist very well outside their given host or a specialized environment. Many of the common protozoa we may find in our dogs can also affect people. Good hygiene is very important in dealing with these and any parasites. Sharing love with our dogs is one thing—sharing parasites of any kind is another!

The best way to diagnose protozoal infections is with a fresh fecal sample. In this case, your veterinarian will take a small sample directly from your dog's rectum. The sample will be mixed with saline and examined under a microscope for protozoa actively moving around. A regular fecal test would kill the protozoa and make them virtually impossible to detect.

Giardia

Giardia is sometimes called beaver fever, but beavers shouldn't bear the blame for this one. This protozoal parasite is quite hardy and can exist for long periods of time in a wet environment. Streams and ponds are its favorite sites. Drinking infected water may lead to severe diarrhea, sometimes with blood or mucus. The cysts are then passed into the feces and may contaminate other bodies of water. There are treatments for Giardia, but it can be difficult to diagnose. Your veterinarian may need to check multiple fecal samples, including some fresh ones taken on a rectal exam. This parasite can be spread to people as well, so you and your dog should both avoid drinking water from streams or ponds in areas where this parasite is known to exist. There is now a vaccine for dogs in epidemic areas.

Coccidia

Coccidia are well-known intestinal protozoa that can infect dogs. There are many species, but virtually all work the same way. Dogs that live in a less-than-clean environment, especially puppies, may ingest cysts through contaminated food or fecal material. Dogs with Coccidia may show diarrhea, sometimes with blood. In puppies this can be a debilitating disease. People are resistant, but kennel areas still need to be kept immaculately clean to prevent puppies picking up this protozoa. Diagnosis is fairly easy with fecal checks.

Treating Intestinal Parasites

As always, one of the best treatments for disease problems is prevention. Keeping your dog's play area clean, picking up after your dog on walks, yearly or even twice-yearly fecal checks, and helping your dog to stay in the best condition possible all reduce parasite problems or at least keep them to a minimum. Still, it is possible for your dog to pick up parasites just by walking where a dog deposited eggs days before. So even the best-cared-for dog may have parasites at some time.

Traditional Treatments and Prevention

Yearly or even twice-yearly fecal checks are a quick, easy, and relatively inexpensive way to make sure your dog never gets a serious parasite load. Always pick up after your dog, and encourage others to do so as well. If you are adding a new dog to your family, do a fecal check as soon as possible so you don't contaminate your yard with parasite eggs or larvae. If your dog still manages to pick up some intestinal parasites, there are many safe medications that will kill the parasites and leave your dog in good health. Some of these include pyrantel pamoate, ivermectin, and febendazole. Different medications are used for different parasites, and some parasites may develop drug resistance, requiring you to try a second, different medication. If you see worms or suspect a parasite problem, check with your veterinarian. Many over-the-counter dewormers are not very effective.

Certain parasites, such as whipworms, may require repeated treatments on a set schedule to totally clear your dog. It makes sense to do a follow-up fecal check after finishing a course of treatment to be sure it was effective.

FACT

Some heartworm and flea and tick preventives also guard against selected intestinal parasites. You might want to check with your veterinarian to see if one of these makes sense for your dog.

The Nontraditional Way

There are some herbal and homeopathic medications that are believed to be effective for dewormings. Remember, just because something is natural or organic does *not* mean it is safe! Do not try any of these remedies without consulting a veterinarian experienced in their use. Black walnut is often touted for dewormings, along with garlic, but used incorrectly these could be toxic to your dog (as could many traditional dewormers if used incorrectly). Follow-up fecal checks are important to determine that treatment was successful.

Heartworm

Once you finally remove the parasites from the intestines, you need to address another internal parasite. Heartworms, *Dirofilaria immitus,* are potentially life-threatening parasites in dogs. Originally seen only in the Deep South and isolated pockets around the country, heartworm has now spread to most of the United States. It is spread by many types of mosquitoes and is a threat all year round in warm areas.

Heartworm Life Cycle

Adult heartworms live and thrive in the heart and pulmonary arteries of dogs. Some may also be in the lungs in large blood vessels. These are long-lived parasites, some living as long as five years! During this time, if there are both males and females present, they produce many tiny young, called microfilaria. The microfilaria get into the bloodstream and are picked up when a mosquito bites your dog. These microfilaria develop in the mosquito and then move to its mouth so that they can be injected into another dog when the mosquito feeds. In other words, this parasite can only be spread from dog to dog with the help of a mosquito.

Heartworm Damage

Heartworms can be deadly! Dogs with a mild case of heartworm will cough, lose some of their stamina, and may be weak or short of breath. The worms block the blood supply of fresh oxygen to other tissues, including the lungs, heart, kidneys, and liver. By the time these clinical signs show up, some of the damage is irreparable. Dogs may die from a heavy load of heartworms.

Heartworm Diagnosis

Heartworm diagnosis may involve multiple specialized tests. There are a few simple and easy tests your veterinarian can run right in the clinic. The first is to check a blood sample for antigens. This test picks up protein in the blood shed by adult heartworms. This test will pick up infections early—with luck before the adults are even reproducing. This test specifically looks for proteins from female worms. If your dog only has one or two worms, there may not be enough antigen to detect. A second test screens a blood sample for actual microfilaria. While microfilaria found in a blood sample are almost always from heartworms, they do need to be clearly identified before any treatment is started.

Your veterinarian may also want to do X rays or even an echocardiogram (special ultrasound of the heart) to look for worms or the damage they cause. Enlargement of the heart and the large blood vessels that go to the lungs are highly suggestive of heartworm infection. A complete blood panel may be done before any treatment is started to see if your dog already has liver or kidney damage.

Preventing and Treating Heartworm Disease

Certainly, the ideal situation is to prevent heartworms from infecting your dog to begin with. There are numerous preventive medications. These range from daily pills to monthly medications. Work is also being done on even longer-range products. Some of these medications require that your dog test negative for heartworm first, as a rapid die-off of the parasites could cause shock reactions. These products may be effective against some of the intestinal parasites your dog is susceptible to as well. Some practitioners use black walnut herbal preparations and homeopathic remedies along with twice-yearly blood tests to catch early infections. Check with your veterinarian about a safe product for your dog. Some breeds are sensitive to ivermectin, a common ingredient in heartworm preventives, and should use other medications.

ALERT!

Many dogs of certain breeds, such as collies, Border collies, Shetland sheepdogs, and Australian shepherds, have a genetic susceptibility that allows medications like ivermectin to pass into the brain. There are dogs of these breeds that have no problem with these medications, but it is wise to discuss with your veterinarian which medications to use and check with your dog's breeder to see if a particular line is known to be susceptible.

Dogs that are diagnosed with heartworm infections will need treatments to kill both the adults and the microfilaria. Currently the only approved treatment for the adults is an organic arsenic compound—obviously a drug to be used with care, as you want to poison the worms but not your dog! This medication requires intravenous administration and your dog may need to be hospitalized for care and observation. Dogs must be kept quiet after this treatment. While the adult heartworms are now dead, your dog's body must absorb the remains and keep any pieces from shedding off and causing trouble. Some veterinarians have been successful using ivermectin at higher than preventive dosages as well.

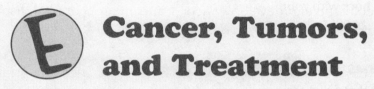

Chapter 13

Cancer, Tumors, and Treatment

Unless you're into astrology, the very word "cancer" sends shivers up your spine. A dictionary definition of cancer is "a malignant tumor or neoplasm"—"neo" for new, "plasm" for tissue. With many of the infectious diseases that previously shortened the lives of our dogs under control, with better parasite management and better nutrition, many of our dogs are living longer and healthier lives than ever before. Longer life spans, however, come with an increase in cancer. Cancer is the leading cause of death in dogs over ten years of age.

What Is Cancer?

Cancer is uncontrolled growth of cells. The word "tumor" is used interchangeably, but officially tumor simply means swelling. A cancerous growth may be caused by a mutation of the genetic material in just one cell and grow to be a very large life-threatening mass. Almost any tissue or cell type can develop cancer. Cancer can be a fatal disease or a mere nuisance.

Benign Versus Malignant

In speaking of cancers, the terms "benign" and malignant" are often used. A benign cancer is one that is generally not life threatening. It does not usually spread or metastasize to tissues far away in the body. In general, benign tumors grow slowly and have more specialized cells. Even a benign tumor can kill your dog, though, by putting pressure on tissues such as the brain or eroding locally through large blood vessels.

The many varied cells that make up your dog's body all start from basic cell types. As these basic "stem cells" divide and grow, many of them go on to become very specialized. Think of the many different cell types your dog's body has—they all come from one egg cell and one sperm cell! Each cell has a set life span and number of reproductions it can undergo. But these controls can be lost, and that's when cancer moves in.

Malignant cancers tend to grow very quickly and aggressively. They wipe out normal cells, drain exorbitant amounts of nutrients, and interfere with normal vital functions such as breathing. These cancers often spread to other tissues, sometimes even quite far away in the body. For example, mammary tumors tend to spread, or metastasize, to the lungs.

What Causes Cancer?

The causes of cancer are as varied as the cancers themselves. Environmental factors, genetic predispositions, even viruses have all been implicated in the development of certain cancers. Anything that can influence or change the genetic material in cells that regulates their growth and function is capable of causing a cancer. Cells are mutating all the time in your dog's body, but the immune system normally cleans them up right away. Any dog with a lowered or damaged immune system is more vulnerable to cancer.

ALERT!

A recent study determined that exposure to certain pesticides is a factor in the development of bladder cancer in Scottish terriers. This breed probably has a genetic weakness or predisposition, which the pesticides act upon to cause the cancer. Most cancers have similar multiple influencing factors.

In some cases the cancer agent is well established, such as feline leukemia virus for cats or cigarette smoke for lung cancer in people. Even so, there will still be cats with leukemia virus who don't get cancer and people who chain smoke who don't get lung cancer. So for cancer, there seem to be genetic predispositions that are important as well. Certainly, different breeds of dogs have become associated with different cancers. Giant-breed dogs have a much higher risk of osteosarcoma (bone cancer) than the toy breeds. Boxers are on the list for a relatively high incidence of lymphoma, while it is not a common cancer for cocker spaniels.

What Are the Types of Cancer?

Each cancer is based on a certain type of cell from your dog's body. Your dog could develop liver cancer from some of her liver cells or brain tumors from mutated nerve cells. Carcinomas are malignant tumors rising from epithelial cells—skin cells and cells that line or cover different organs. Sarcomas tend to develop out of underlying tissues such as bone, liver, and spleen. Adenomas are cancer of glandular tissues like the thyroid.

As mentioned above, cancers are labeled malignant or benign. Each individual type of cancer acts differently and will have a different prognosis and treatment plan.

Diagnosing Cancer

Cancers can cause a wide variety of signs in your dog and mimic other disease processes. They are often accompanied by other health problems and may have very nonspecific symptoms. There are many changes you may notice in your dog that push you to schedule a veterinary visit. Once you arrive at your veterinarian's, there are a wide variety of tests that can help diagnose cancer and guide the treatment plan for specific cancer. Remember, "cancer" is really a catchall word that doesn't describe a specific disease.

Signs You Might See

The problems your dog might experience depend greatly on the type and location of her cancer. In general, dogs with any type of cancer will show some weight loss. This may be related to a decrease in appetite or perhaps to the draining of nutrients by the cancer as it grows. Many dogs show a decrease in activity and stamina. Instead of a mile walk, your dog may want to turn back early.

Depending on the specific cancer, your dog could have vomiting or diarrhea. She could be lame or act pained when touched in certain areas. Dogs with cancers of nerve tissue may have an uncoordinated gait. You may notice an actual lump on your dog, such as a large fatty tumor or lipoma on the rib-cage area. It could be a small lump—mast cell tumors as tiny as a small bug might be noticed on a shorthaired dog. A dog may have a sore that fails to heal or a discolored area on the skin. Dogs with growths in their mouths often drool or pant more than usual.

Diagnostic Testing

Testing for cancer usually starts with a complete blood panel. Your veterinarian will check that all the main body systems are fine. All areas of the body will be examined for cancer and to determine whether your dog is healthy enough to handle treatment if a cancer is found. Any obvious lumps or bumps may have a needle aspirate taken, be surgically biopsied, or even be totally removed.

Your veterinarian may try to examine some cells right in the office, but often tissue samples need to be sent out to a veterinary pathologist. Veterinary pathologists are specialists in examining tissues for any abnormalities. They will process the sample, maybe using special stains, and examine the cells under a microscope.

FACT

An FNA is a fine needle aspirate. Your veterinarian will put a needle into a suspicious growth and draw out some cells. These cells are then checked under a microscope for any indications of cancer. You can get "false negatives"—when you feel there is no cancer, but in truth, the needle sample simply missed the area of cancer cells and only sampled normal cells. Still, a positive result gives you a quick diagnosis.

Along with these laboratory tests, many dogs will need X rays or ultrasound examinations. It is traditional to check chest X rays for any sign of cancer spread. Three views are best; left side, right side, and with the dog on his back. Ultrasound can also be used to carefully locate any unusual growths or even to guide a biopsy attempt.

Sometimes, despite all this information, the best way to get a definitive diagnosis is to do an exploratory surgery. Your veterinarian can then take biopsy samples, possibly remove any growths, and check to see that other tissues and organs all appear healthy.

Treating Cancers

Once again, the actual treatment plan for cancer in your dog will be influenced by many factors. First, how old is your dog? Is he in good physical shape otherwise? Aggressive treatment that makes sense in an athletic six-year-old dog might not be appropriate for a fifteen-year-old with a bad heart. The type of cancer—both its location and the likelihood of its being benign or malignant—needs to be considered. Different types of cancer respond to different therapies. Distance from facilities that offer specialized treatments, such as radiation, could be another limiting factor. Sadly, economics may play a part in your treatment plan as well. Chemotherapy costs are dropping, but they can still be quite expensive, as can other treatments. Sometimes the best treatment for quality of life issues can be hospice-style care, which provides pain relief and nursing care while your dog simply lives out his life in comfort. The cancer treatment goal is not always a cure. Often, the goal is to achieve a remission and gain quality time for your dog.

ALERT!

Your veterinarian may want to "stage" your dog's cancer. Staging involves looking at the cells in your dog's cancer, plus checking for spread to lymph nodes or other tissues. The cancer is then graded according to its stage of development, from stage one (mild) to stage four (most serious). Prognosis and treatment may vary with the exact stage your dog is in.

Traditional Therapy Plans

Once you have a definitive diagnosis of cancer, you can start to plan your treatments. You need to coordinate this closely with your veterinarian as both of you will need to be committed for any therapy to work. Depending on the exact type of cancer your dog has, possible courses of action include surgery alone; surgery with follow-up chemotherapy; a combination of surgery and radiation; chemotherapy alone; or chemotherapy plus radiation. Expect your veterinarian to discuss your case with, or refer you to, a veterinary oncologist (a cancer specialist). With new developments coming along frequently, it is difficult for your regular veterinarian to stay on top of all the latest information.

Surgery

Before your veterinarian does surgery, she will check your dog for any obvious metastasis of the cancer. If your dog has mammary cancer and it has already spread to the lungs, it may not make sense to put her through a big surgery. Your dog's overall health will also be assessed to be sure she can handle the treatment regimen.

When it comes to cancer surgeries, bigger (or longer) is better! Your veterinarian will be trying to get all your dog's cancer, plus a margin of cancer-free tissue around the edges, known as clean margins. Microscopic cancer cells may escape this surgery, but sometimes a surgery can be a cure. Be aware that if radiation or chemotherapy is to follow surgery, your dog may not grow back all his shaved hair—or it may grow back a different color!

Very Specialized Surgery

Some cancers require the skills of a board-certified veterinary surgeon. A cancer in the mouth that requires removal of half a jaw will actually leave your dog looking fairly normal, but it requires skill to leave her with the capability to eat and drink. Dogs with bone cancer may sometimes have bone-sparing surgery. Normally, a dog with bone cancer faces the amputation of the affected leg. Sometimes it is possible for veterinary surgeons to remove the cancerous bone, put in a bone graft with metal plates and screws, and leave your dog all her limbs. Surgeries that remove large areas of skin, such as with some mammary tumors, may require skin-grafting procedures.

Radiation

Radiation therapy uses very focused X rays to kill cancer cells. Most veterinary hospitals don't have the technology for radiation therapy, so you will probably be referred to a veterinary school or specialty referral practice. Your dog will need anesthesia so that he lies perfectly still and doesn't disrupt the radiation beam or cause it to miss the desired site. Radiation therapy schedules can vary from daily for a short period of time to long-term weekly for palliative care. Expect some reddened, sore "radiation burn" areas on your dog's skin. Some dogs will also get nauseous.

Radiation therapy maybe used not only to destroy cancer cells but also to help relieve pain. Radiation therapy used for pain control is called palliative therapy. This will not destroy the cancer cells but may prolong your dog's quality of life. Bone-cancer patients may respond to palliative radiation therapy.

Chemotherapy

Chemotherapy is the use of drugs to kill cancer cells. The ideal chemotherapy drug kills only cancer cells and has no side effects. Unfortunately, we don't have a drug of that caliber yet. Still, dogs often fare better on chemotherapy than people. If your dog needs chemotherapy, your veterinarian is likely trying to reduce the cancer or remove it temporarily (a remission). It is unusual to achieve a cure in dogs with chemotherapy. With their shorter life spans, it makes more sense to try to gain quality time while not making them seriously ill from side effects.

Depending on the exact protocol used for your dog, he may need to be hospitalized for intravenous administration of his medication. If he can take pills at home, you will need to wear gloves to protect you when you give them. Many dogs do best on a combination of medications. The most common side effects are nausea and loss of appetite. There are excellent medications to help control vomiting. For the appetite loss, here is your chance to develop your canine culinary skills. There are many excellent home-cooking recipes for nutritious snacks to keep your dog's strength up. Dogs on chemotherapy often wipe out many of their immune system defenders. As a result, they may need periodic breaks from treatment to recoup and/or antibiotics to help keep infectious agents at bay.

Less Common Therapies

There are always new developments in cancer treatment. These range from high-technology treatments to bolstering your dog's own immune system to fight off the cancer. Beware of any treatment touted as a complete cure. Always verify your dog's health before starting any new treatments, and establish a plan for rechecks to make sure his blood counts and blood panel stay within reasonable limits.

High-Tech Cancer Fighters

Some of the high-tech cancer-fighting strategies involve temperature changes or light. Cancerous tissue may be frozen off with cryotherapy or burnt off with hyperthermia. Lasers are becoming more popular for surgeries of all types. Phototherapy uses light-sensitive drugs and focused light to kill cancer cells. Your dog is given a light-sensitive medication that preferentially goes to the cancer cells. Then a light source is shone on that area, bombarding the light-sensitive cells.

Making up customized vaccines against a cancer is another new technology that may help your dog. Cells from your dog's cancer are processed into a vaccine, then administered to try and stimulate your dog's own immune system to fight off the cancer cells more efficiently.

Nutrition and Herbs

Recent studies have shown us that diet can be an important part of your dog's fight against cancer. Cancer cells seem to prefer carbohydrates as their energy source. So a diet with limited carbohydrates, but some added fat to provide energy for the normal cells makes sense. Both cancer cells and normal cells need high-quality protein, so no skimping there! "Cancer cachexia" is a term used to describe thin dogs battling cancer. It is important to provide enough calories for your dog to maintain a functioning condition.

In addition, supplements such as vitamin A and vitamin C may help your dog. Antioxidants are also important.

Along with the traditional supplements, veterinarians who are comfortable with herbal use may add echinacea and goldenseal to the diets of dogs with cancer. Other herbs may be used as well. If you choose to go with a home-cooked diet for your dog at this time, consult your veterinarian or a veterinary nutritionist to be sure the diet is balanced and provides the nutrients he needs. Wheatgrass and flax seed oil both have anecdotal support as cancer therapies and certainly should be safe.

Preventing Cancer

As with so many health problems, the ideal way to deal with cancer is to prevent it ever getting started in your dog's body. This may be easier said than done. If your dog has a genetic predisposition to a certain cancer, the disease may get a foothold no matter what you do. Still, there are ways we can help to keep cancer at bay.

A Healthy Environment

The knowledge we have from human medicine on the effects of environmental hazards can be applied to your canine companions. Being exposed to secondhand smoke is as dangerous for dogs as it is for children, so your dog's health is another good reason for you to quit. Being exposed for long periods of time to other noxious fumes, such as gasoline or industrial solvents, is bad for your dog too. If something makes you feel ill or woozy, it undoubtedly makes your dog feel that way as well.

Pesticides are sometimes a necessity, such as on farms or ranches, but the more we can avoid exposing our dogs to them, the better. Always follow guidelines about pesticide exposure carefully. If the directions suggest waiting two hours before letting your dog on the lawn, why not wait a whole day just to be extra safe? Better yet, remember that crab grass will look green and healthy when regular turf is dried up from drought, so why not leave it!

What Your Dog Eats

In general, dogs eat healthier, better-balanced meals than most people. Some preservatives are necessary in packaged foods to keep them from going rancid, which can also cause health problems. Still, it makes sense to avoid foods with extra preservatives or added dyes. Fresh foods and balanced plain dry kibble are better alternatives than the fake stews that appeal to people more than dogs. Extra vitamins and antioxidants such as coenzyme Q10 may help to keep your dog healthy over a long life. Always check with your veterinarian before adding supplements, as too many vitamins can be as harmful as too few.

The Genetic Factor

At this time, the capability to fix most genetic defects is beyond us. In the future (and even in a few isolated cases right now) genetic defects may be correctable and treatable. Certainly, if a breed of dog is prone to a certain cancer, it would be nice if the defective gene could be changed in utero or after birth to help your puppy avoid that fate. For now, it is important to research the background of your puppy as thoroughly as possible. Ask about health problems seen on both sides of her family—the dam's and the sire's. Knowing the cause of death of related dogs could help you to choose a healthier pup.

General Health

Your dog's immune system is known to be a factor in guarding her against cancer. Precancerous or cancerous cells show up in all of us over time. Luckily, a healthy immune system can often deal with these threats on its own, so keeping your dog in excellent health is important. A fit dog is a healthy weight and is getting plenty of exercise. That, along with good food and preventive care against parasites and infectious diseases, gives any dog a better chance of fighting off any cancer or handling treatment if a cancer should manage to become established.

The Less-Than-Scary Cancers

Luckily there are some cancers that are less than scary. These include at least one cancer known to often spontaneously regress and some cancers that usually do next to no harm to their canine hosts. Two of these are usually seen in young dogs and one in older dogs.

The "Good" Young Dog Tumors

One of the cancers that is sometimes seen in young dogs is a histiocytoma. These are also called button tumors, as they look like raised, round, reddish buttons. These growths usually appear alone and on dogs under three years of age, and they often occur on the ears or muzzle. While surgery can be done to remove these tumors, they usually regress spontaneously.

Papillomas are wartlike growths caused by a papillomavirus. These small growths tend to show up around the mouth, usually in groups. Again, these growths tend to regress on their own.

Lipomas

Lipomas are fatty tumors that tend to show up on middle-aged to senior dogs. These growths aren't necessarily associated with excess weight, and even thin dogs might have lipomas. The masses are usually round, smooth, and slightly movable. They tend to be found on the rib cage and body wall. Sometimes lipomas can grow large enough to interfere with your dog's movement. They very rarely grow large enough to outgrow their blood supply and get infected. Doberman pinschers and Labrador retrievers seem to be at risk more than other breeds. Surgery can be curative, but in many dogs the masses will recur.

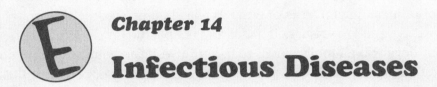

Chapter 14

Infectious Diseases

An infectious disease is one caused by an agent from outside the body showing up and creating trouble. Most often this means bacteria and viruses, though fungi, rickettsia, parasites, and protozoa are outside agents as well. The following sections focus on bacteria and viruses, especially the major varieties that can infect dogs, along with a discussion of treatment and prevention.

How Diseases Spread

Tiny organisms like bacteria and viruses don't do very well on their own. While some may be able to survive for a time, they need host species in order to thrive and reproduce in great numbers. These tiny invaders may be spread through the air, on dishes, or other surfaces in our homes or outdoors, including on feces or urine. While children eventually learn (at least we can hope!) to wash their hands and not put their fingers in their mouths, our dogs will naturally smell, sniff, and investigate with nose and tongue. You know how colds can spread through classrooms or on airline flights—dogs can be exposed at dog parks, in training class, kennels, or shows.

Respiratory Spread

The canine body is designed to keep invaders out of the respiratory tract. Along with its fabulous scenting cells, the nose has cells with cilia (thin strand-like projections) that line most of the respiratory tract. The cilia act to nab any debris—from dust to bacteria—that floats by them on the air currents. A thin mucus coating helps to trap anything that comes by. These cilia then use a concerted wavelike action to move that debris back up and out. When your dog coughs or sneezes, he is removing debris that the cilia caught.

Unfortunately, the cilia are very sensitive to the environment. They can be damaged in air that is very dry or conversely very humid, by secondhand smoke, or by other fumes in the air that passes over them. Some viruses and bacteria attack these cells directly and lower their defensive capabilities.

When a dog with a respiratory infection coughs or sneezes, she sends tiny droplets of infectious material into the air. If your dog breathes those in and they manage to get by her cilia, she has a good chance of being infected herself. Cells that fight infection, such as neutrophils and lymphocytes will then try to capture the infectious material and destroy it or at least neutralize it by wrapping it up in a defender cell.

Oral Spread

As you know, when your dog sniffs something interesting, he will usually lick it or even take a small taste. If he steps in something smelly, he will carefully lick his feet clean afterward. This practice can lead to the oral spread of diseases. For example, if he licks some material containing parvo virus (such as stool passed by a sick dog), he then takes the virus directly into his system. Many viruses try to get integrated into cells that divide rapidly as this helps them to spread quickly. Intestinal cells, with their very short turnover time, are ideal hosts for viruses.

Dogs may also drink in infectious agents from contaminated water. Giardia is a parasite that can be picked up from water.

FACT

Some diseases can be spread in a number of ways. Rabies can go directly into the body via a bite wound, or virus-infected saliva might be licked off from one animal to another animal. Vampire bats can spread rabies when they feed.

Spreading via the Blood

Just like in the horror shows, some diseases can be spread by direct injection into the bloodstream. It is not space aliens doing the injecting, however, but insects such as mosquitoes, along with parasites like fleas and ticks that put diseases into our dogs as they take their blood meals out. When a mosquito bites a dog that is infected with heartworm, the infectious larvae may be passed into the next dog the mosquito bites. Deer ticks are renowned for spreading Lyme disease. Open sores or wounds can admit diseases into the body as well. Once the infectious agent is in the blood, it can travel throughout the body to the desired final location.

Rabies

Rabies has a scary reputation, thanks to its part in classic stories like *Old Yeller* and *To Kill a Mockingbird*. Visions of slobbery, crazed dogs chasing people are closely associated with this disease. While rabies is a very serious disease that is virtually always fatal, it is controllable. Most of us will never encounter it. Rabies is a viral disease and has a preference for nerve tissues. It is spread through the bite or saliva of an infected animal and has been found in virtually all mammals. Most epidemics in the United States are in fox, raccoons, and skunks. Bats are one of the rare species that may carry rabies without ill effects—at least for a while.

Signs You Will See

Rabies virus goes for nerve tissue. It travels from the point of entry (such as a bite wound on a leg) up along nerves. There are two forms of the disease. In dumb or paralytic rabies, the victim is quiet, minimally responsive, and drools extensively. In the furious form, the infected animal is highly aggressive. A maxim for most animal caretakers is that a change in behavior (with no obvious cause and in an unimmunized animal) could signal rabies, so precautions should be taken.

Treatment and Prevention

Sadly, not even extensive supportive treatment can help with rabies. An infected dog will die. Therefore, prevention is by far the best way to handle rabies. Dogs that are current on their rabies vaccine are considered to be well protected, but if your dog has a known exposure to a rabid animal (a fight with a raccoon, for example), your veterinarian will suggest a booster vaccine. Dogs without current vaccinations that bite someone must be quarantined to see if they develop the disease or may even be euthanized. Rabies vaccination is required by law in most areas, and this is one vaccine you can't afford to skip.

Distemper

Distemper is a very nasty canine disease caused by a paramyxovirus. This virus usually gets into a dog through the respiratory tract. It then moves into the lymphatic tissues and spreads throughout the body. Puppies are especially susceptible. While distemper used to be fairly widespread and caused many serious epidemics among dog populations, the disease is now well controlled by vaccination programs.

The canine distemper virus is very similar to human measles virus. Early on, your puppy may receive a measles vaccine, as this will cross-protect her against distemper while not interfering with the maternal antibodies she may still have.

Signs You Will See

Dogs with distemper often start out with a fever and a cough, starting from three to twenty days after exposure. At this time, many dogs will have a very thick, greenish discharge from the eyes and nose. Pneumonia may follow, and some dogs will also show stomach and intestinal signs—vomiting and diarrhea. For some lucky dogs, this will be the end of the disease, and with careful nursing care they go on to recover. If a puppy is infected while the teeth are developing, some teeth may show a lack of enamel, as the illness interferes with normal body growth.

Other dogs will continue with the pneumonia and possibly develop hardpad disease, in which the pads on their feet grow thick and hard. About half of dogs with distemper start to show nerve damage about four weeks after the start of the illness. These dogs may show twitching and develop a funny gait with progression to full-blown seizures. Many of these dogs end up being euthanized.

Treatment and Prevention

Viral diseases do not have antidotes, in the way we think of antibiotics and their power over bacteria. There are very few medications that actually directly kill viruses, and those are very specific—a couple of eye medications, for example, work against herpes viruses. Treatment of viral diseases therefore consists of doing everything you can to support your dog's basic health and keep her strength up while her own body defenses fight off the virus. Your veterinarian may prescribe antibiotics for your dog to help fight off bacteria that might take advantage of her lowered body defenses. Your dog may also need additional vitamins, fluids, and special foods. Good nursing care—keeping her warm, cleaning off discharges, encouraging her to eat—may all help your dog to recover faster. Despite all efforts, some dogs will die, and others will end up euthanized due to debilitating neurologic disease.

As with so many diseases, it is much easier and makes much more sense to try to prevent distemper in the first place. This is easily accomplished by vaccinations. Most puppies receive distemper in their initial series of vaccinations with a booster a year later. The frequency of boosters after that is currently a matter of much debate. Discuss a vaccination schedule with your veterinarian, and come up with a customized schedule that makes sense for your dog and her lifestyle.

Parvovirus

Parvovirus is the other well-known canine viral disease. Parvo initially appeared in dogs in the 1980s and is thought to be a mutation of a feline virus. At first, many dogs became ill in epidemics because none had natural immunity. Now, with vaccination programs and exposures, more dogs recover from the disease or never even get ill. Still, this is a disease that can kill up to 30 percent of the dogs it infects. It is especially dangerous to Doberman pinschers, rottweilers, and German shepherd dogs. Parvo is spread through infected stool and dogs taking in the virus by mouth (licking or sniffing).

ALERT!

A less common version of parvo is seen in newborn puppies whose mother did not have adequate immunity against the disease. These puppies may be born with severe damage to the heart (myocarditis— inflammation of the heart muscle), and most of them die.

Signs You Will See

Parvo tends to show up as an explosive vomiting and diarrhea disease. The virus enters through the mouth and then travels to the rapidly dividing cells of the intestines. As it destroys those cells, the intestinal lining is now open to invading bacteria. In addition, the dog loses nutrients and fluids. Bacterial toxins add to the illness. Most dogs have a bloody, runny diarrhea with a very distinctive odor. Vomiting and diarrhea may be so severe that the dog becomes seriously dehydrated.

Treatment and Prevention

Dogs with parvo almost always require hospitalization for at least a few days. During this time, they are fed intravenous fluids (as their stomachs can't handle anything at all, even water!), and they may even get a blood transfusion to boost their immunity. Medications will be given to try and reduce the vomiting, keep inflammation to a minimum, and fight off bacteria taking advantage of the disruption in intestinal defenses.

This virus is quite tough and can survive in the environment for up to a year in the right conditions. It is important to be very thorough in cleaning and disinfecting any surfaces, crates, blankets, bowls, and toys that come in contact with a dog infected with parvo.

Once again, proper vaccinations can be lifesavers in the fight against this disease. Puppies should receive parvo vaccine in their initial puppy series with a booster at one year. The subsequent booster schedule depends on the customized vaccine regimen that your veterinarian draws up for your dog.

Infectious Canine Hepatitis

Canine hepatitis is caused by an adenovirus. It is normally shed into saliva, stool, and urine, and infection is spread orally—the common "sniff and lick" method. This is another disease that tends to strike young dogs and puppies. While dogs can recover from infectious hepatitis, some do not, and many of them need extensive medical care.

Signs You Will See

Infectious hepatitis often starts with vomiting and a fever. Most dogs have a very painful abdomen. Areas of hemorrhage are sometimes notice-able—including discolored areas under the skin or jaundice (a yellow tinge to the skin). Some dogs build up fluid in the abdomen and chest. Hepatitis means inflammation of the liver, and this virus attacks the liver with gusto. There may be some permanent damage to the liver in dogs that survive. In some dogs, immune complexes are deposited in the kidneys, causing kidney failure, or in the cornea of the eye, turning eyes a bluish color.

Treatment and Prevention

Dogs with infectious hepatitis almost always need veterinary hospital-ization, where they are put on an intravenous drip for fluids and may receive a blood transfusion. Vitamins and amino acid supplements are given intra-venously as well, as it is important to keep up your dog's strength without taxing the intestines or liver. Supportive antibiotics may be needed to pre-vent bacteria from flowing into the damaged tissues. Realize though, this is a viral disease, and no medication can specifically kill this virus. The dog's own body has to fight off the virus, so you and your veterinarian should work to help keep her body in the battle.

Once again, vaccination is the ideal way to prevent this disease. Hepa-titis is usually covered in the initial puppy vaccinations, with a booster at about one year of age. The frequency of subsequent boosters depends on your dog, her lifestyle, and her likelihood of exposure.

Infectious Canine Cough

Infectious canine cough has a number of different names, including kennel cough, canine cough, and infectious respiratory disease. It also has a num-ber of different causes. Very often, the parainfluenza virus works together with the bacteria *Bordetella bronchiseptica* to cause this very contagious dis-ease syndrome. Other bacteria and viruses may be involved as well, but these are the two main culprits. Dogs are exposed in large groups such as at kennels, dog shows, or shelters. One coughing dog can shed virus that spreads rapidly through the group. If you add in secondhand smoke or other fumes, the damaged respiratory tract is even more susceptible to this disease.

Signs You Will See

A dog with kennel cough will do a wonderful imitation of a honking goose. The dry, racking cough truly sounds terrible, but often the dog feels quite fine. The cough may last for a week or more, and your dog should be isolated during that time to prevent spread of the organisms. In some cases, the damage to the respiratory tract and its defense mechanisms is quite severe, and a few dogs may go on to develop pneumonia. Dogs with pneumonia cough, run a fever, and may lose their appetite and have a discolored nasal discharge. They are clearly sick, as opposed to the dogs with uncomplicated kennel cough that sound terrible but feel fine.

Treatment and Prevention

Dogs with uncomplicated kennel cough only need minimal treatment. A veterinarian may suggest a cough suppressant and possibly a vaporizer. Dogs with this cough need to be kept quiet and must not be allowed to exercise hard or bark as these activities will irritate the respiratory tract even more. If the dog progresses to pneumonia, more drastic measures are needed. In these cases, the dog will definitely need antibiotics. A few dogs get ill enough to need hospitalization and an oxygen cage. Special treats to encourage eating may be important, too, and extra vitamins are always beneficial. Again, a vaporizer may make the dog more comfortable.

FACT

The intranasal vaccine for kennel cough works by stimulating local immunity in the nasal passages. This makes sense, as infectious agents first try to enter the dog's body through these passages. If her defenses can catch and kill them right there, she will not get sick at all. The intranasal vaccine is administered through small amounts that are dripped into the nostrils. Some dogs may sneeze for a day or so after getting an intranasal vaccine.

There are a couple of different vaccination protocols that can be used for kennel cough. The parainfluenza virus is often included in routine combination vaccines. There are also separate vaccines for the bacteria *Bordetella bronchiseptica*. One is an intramuscular vaccine, and the other is an intranasal vaccine. You should discuss with your veterinarian whether and how often your dog needs these vaccines.

Leptospirosis

Leptospirosis is a dangerous bacterial disease that comes in a variety of forms (caused by a number of serotypes, such as grippotyphosa, pomona, icterohaemorrhagiae, and canicola). Leptospirosis is spread through the infected urine of a wide variety of wildlife species, such as raccoons, skunks, and rats. Dogs that encounter the infected urine (remember that sniff and lick pattern!) can take in this infectious agent. Leptospires can even penetrate skin and mucous membranes. In recent years, there has been an increase in the number of leptospirosis cases among pet dogs. People can also pick up this infection.

Signs You Will See

Dogs that pick up leptospirosis are often very ill. You may notice that your dog loses his appetite, is very lethargic, vomits, and has diarrhea. He might run a fever and have a painful abdomen, as this bacteria often attacks the liver and/or the kidneys. Hemorrhaging may be noticeable under the skin or internally. This illness can come on fairly quickly and escalate quickly into a serious problem. A few dogs even die before any treatment or diagnostic work is done. Unfortunately, many of the signs from leptospirosis are nonspecific and could have a number of causes. Your veterinarian may check urine samples looking for signs of this bacteria and take a very careful clinical history, including where your dog has traveled recently.

Treatment and Prevention

Since leptospirosis is a bacteria, it does respond to antibiotics. The commonly used medications are tetracycline and doxycycline. It is important that treatment be started right away to avoid permanent liver or kidney damage. Your veterinarian may prescribe a fairly long course of antibiotics to try and prevent a chronic carrier state. Your dog will also need supportive care. If he is very ill, he may be hospitalized with intravenous fluids, vitamins, and medications. Depending on the possibility of liver or kidney damage, specific medications will be administered to assist in healing those organs. Very ill dogs need warmth and treatment for shock with fluids and medications.

Because leptospirosis has become so widespread, it can be difficult to avoid coming in contact with this bacteria. Many new housing developments have flourishing wildlife populations that adapt well to being near people and their pets. There is a new vaccine or bacterin out for preventing leptospirosis. While previous vaccines had a fairly high risk of allergic responses, the new vaccines are much better. You need to discuss with your veterinarian if your dog needs this vaccine and if so, how often. The vaccine should cover all the forms of the disease, as vaccine protection and immunity are very specific. In epidemic areas, dogs may require twice-yearly boosters.

QUESTION?

What is the difference between a bacterin and a vaccine?
The term *vaccine* is generally used for any product given to induce immunity to a specific disease. Technically, however, it refers to products that stimulate immunity against a virus. *Bacterin* is the appropriate name for a product that stimulates immunity against bacteria. *Vaccine* has become the generally accepted term these days.

Lyme Disease

Lyme disease is a disease caused by the bacteria *Borrelia burgdorferi*. This disease is named after the town in Connecticut where the disease was first characterized. Lyme disease is spread through the bites of infected ticks. While the common deer tick is the tick we associate with Lyme disease, other tick species may carry it as well. Intermediate stages might involve nymphal stages of the tick feeding on mice and/or deer. People are also susceptible to Lyme disease.

Signs You Will See

Often families will find engorged ticks on their dogs, and so they know to watch for any problems. On people, this disease causes a classic rash and ring on the skin, but this may not be noticed on a dog.

Many dogs that test positive for exposure to Lyme disease on blood tests show no clinical signs. Dogs that actually develop the disease often start out with very acute onset painful lameness. Joints may become very swollen, red, and warm, and they are extremely painful. The accompanying fever and loss of appetite add to the impression of a depressed dog. Some dogs also go on to develop kidney problems from the deposit of immune complexes in the tissues. This syndrome can be fatal, as can rare heart problems.

While most dogs respond well to medications, some suffer from recurring bouts of arthritis and joint pain.

Treatment and Prevention

Luckily, most cases of Lyme disease are responsive to antibiotics. Tetracycline and doxycycline are favorites at this time. Your dog may need a long period of medication—up to four weeks or more. This is important to break that cycle of possible recurring arthritis, leading to permanent joint damage. Dogs in greater pain may need medications to keep them comfortable while the antibiotics are working.

Preventing Lyme disease can be difficult. Obviously, avoiding ticks should be a goal, but in some areas, that is almost impossible if you and your dog go outside for walks. There are many new and excellent topical tick preventives and repellants, so you can ask your veterinarian what products make the most sense for your situation. Certain collars and sprays, especially ones using DEET, are helpful, but don't combine products without checking with your veterinarian to make sure they are compatible.

It is believed that ticks need to feed on a dog for twenty-four to forty-eight hours before the infective organism can establish itself, so checking carefully for ticks after walks is a good idea. Use gloves or a tick puller to avoid contact with the potentially infected blood.

There is now a vaccine (that is, a bacterin) available that offers some protection against Lyme disease. Talk with your veterinarian about whether it makes sense for your dog to have this vaccine and, if so, how often.

Remember, if you plan to travel to an area known for ticks, you want a preventive plan in place *before* you get there!

Vaccines—The Ins and Outs

As you may have noticed in this discussion about infectious diseases, many of them are best controlled by preventive vaccinations. This is especially true for viral diseases, as there are very few medications that specifically kill viruses. And even with bacterial diseases, we see more and more drug resistance to antibiotics. Mother Nature clearly still knows best, however, for developing your dog's own natural immunity through vaccination is often her most effective defense.

How They Work

The simplest explanation for a vaccine is that it delivers a tiny amount of the disease-causing organism, known as an antigen, into your dog's body. This is usually via subcutaneous injection, but it can also be delivered via intramuscular injection or intranasal drops. This small stimulus activates the immune system (as described in Chapter 11). The lymphocytes, whose job it is to make antibodies, study this antigen and create customized antibodies to fight it. The cells whose job it is to engulf invaders gear up and go out to search for this antigen. The goal is of course, to provide just enough and just the right type of stimulus so that your dog does not get sick.

Types of Vaccines

Most vaccines come in one of three types: modified live, killed, and genetically modified. The modified live vaccines use a weakened form of the disease and tend to provide plenty of stimulus for an immune response. They may, however, cause your dog to shed virus (thereby potentially contaminating the environment or infecting other dogs), and have the potential to cause some illness in your pet. Still, the response is generally safe and very strong, leading to less need for boosters. Killed vaccines deliver the antigen substance in a totally safe (killed) form. The problem here is getting enough stimulus for your dog's immune system to react. For this reason other substances, called adjuvants, may be added to elicit a stronger response.

Some of the newest vaccines are genetically modified. A modified live vaccine has a slightly weakened form of a disease agent, but here the goal is to provide the smallest part of the disease-causing substance that is needed to provoke an immune response. A disease agent may have genes removed, or the vaccine may just be based on a small particle of the disease agent. An ideal genetically modified vaccine provides superb immune response but minimal reactions.

FACT

Adjuvants are substances added to killed vaccines to increase the immune response. These are agents that stimulate an immune reaction on their own. In a vaccine, the idea is that this increased immune response will lead to better protection against the disease as well. Unfortunately, some dogs will have reactions to the adjuvants.

What Vaccines Does My Dog Need?

The latest trend in vaccination plans for dogs is to customize the plan specifically for each dog. Virtually all dogs need the core vaccines. These vaccines protect your dog against the most virulent and dangerous diseases: rabies, distemper, parvo, and adenovirus (for hepatitis).

There are many other vaccines that are non-core. These include the vaccines for kennel cough, leptospirosis, Lyme disease, and Giardia. If your dog is boarded frequently, he may need a kennel cough vaccine of some sort. If you live in an area where leptospirosis is widespread, he may need the vaccine for that. You will need to sit down with your veterinarian and decide on the vaccines that are necessary for your dog based on his age, health, activities, and so on. Remember, this may vary from what a friend's dog needs.

Your veterinarian will also work out a schedule with you for boosters as needed based on your individual dog. Dogs that are homebodies may need less frequent boosters for many diseases. Plus, new research is ongoing that looks at the length of immunity stimulated by different vaccines. Recommendations may very well change from year to year.

Rabies vaccination is required by law in virtually all states and many countries. This disease is fatal and can also be spread to people. Your dog needs proof of a current rabies status for travel, boarding, and participation in dog events.

When Vaccines Cause Problems

While vaccines have been miracle workers when it comes to preventing serious disease such as rabies and distemper, they have the potential to cause problems in some dogs, too. Individual dogs may have allergic reactions, even immediate serious anaphylactic reactions, to certain vaccines. Other dogs may show delayed health reactions to vaccines. Some researchers feel this is related to overvaccinating—giving too many vaccines and/or giving them too often. This is why it is important to figure out just what vaccines your dog truly needs and how often.

Sharing Disease—Zoonoses

While we think of our canine companions as sharing our lives, possibly even our beds, we need to remember that they might just share some health problems as well. This is no reason to banish your dog from the house; instead, it's a way to stress the importance of good care to keep both you and your dog healthy. Illnesses that people share with animals are called zoonoses, and they range from parasites to bacteria and viruses. Remember, too, that many of these diseases can be passed back and forth both ways.

Common Zoonoses

Some of the most common zoonoses are parasites (as described in Chapter 12). These can be external parasites, such as fleas, or internal parasites, such as roundworms. Both you and your dog can be innocent hosts for fleas and ticks. While the fleas might prefer your nice furry dog, they will enjoy a human blood meal if it is available. Clearly, keeping your dog parasite-free is in your best interest as well.

Roundworms are the intestinal parasite most often seen in puppies. Good hygiene can prevent the spread of this parasite to people, along with the potential serious complications it can cause, such as blindness. Again, cleanliness and keeping your dog healthy by preventive medications and doing regular fecal checks will be beneficial to the whole family.

A few bacterial diseases can be shared too. If children keep getting strep throat, their pediatrician may recommend a throat culture of your dog. Sometimes children and dogs (or cats) will share strep bacteria back and forth, so just when you get your child cured, she picks it up again from the dog. Putting everyone on a course of antibiotics together may end this cycle of zoonotic disease.

The More Exotic Zoonoses

Some of the most serious zoonotic diseases are generally quite uncommon. Rabies is high on the list here. Rabies is almost universally fatal, and a dog with rabies could easily bite a family member and spread the disease. Due to the serious nature of this disease, rabies vaccination is required by law in most areas.

The tapeworms that cause hydatid cysts and life-threatening liver disease in people are not very common, but herding dogs imported from endemic areas do need screening.

None of these examples is meant to scare you. You are much more likely to share disease organisms with a friend or coworker than with your dog.

Chapter 15

Genetics and Inherited Disease

Learning that a dog has a genetic disorder is devastating. It's also costly. Hereditary heart malfunctions or orthopedic disorders can often be corrected surgically, but the expense can run into the thousands of dollars. With more than 350 hereditary diseases found in dogs, it's good news that scientists are slowly but surely working toward an understanding of the canine genome, the set of chromosomes found in every cell that contain the heritable genetic material that directs the dog's development.

Basic Genetics

Heredity is the genetic transmission of qualities and potentialities, called traits, from parent to offspring. Hereditary traits are numerous and include eye color, coat color, and size. Health and temperament traits are also hereditary. Among the many undesirable hereditary traits that can be passed on are deafness, eye disease, epilepsy, undescended testicles, and temperament flaws such as shyness or aggression. Traits are passed from parents to puppies by means of genetic material: genes, chromosomes, and DNA.

Genetic Material

Genes are bits of hereditary information. Passed from parent to offspring, their job is to control the transmission of a hereditary characteristic by specifying the structure of a particular protein or by controlling the function of other genetic material. Dogs may have as many as 200,000 genes. Over time, genes can mutate, or change. Sometimes a mutation is beneficial, but other times it results in genetic diseases.

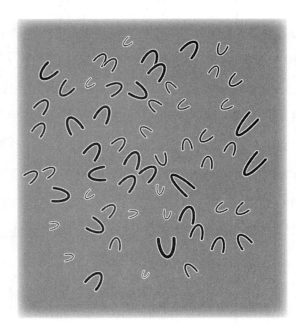

◄ Chromosome pairs resemble each other in length and shape. The exception is the pair of male chromosomes, with one having an X-shape and a smaller one having a Y-shape.

Proteins control a dog's developmental stages from egg and sperm through adulthood. They're also necessary to maintain all the different body functions. Each gene codes for different proteins.

Each gene resides at a fixed position on a chromosome. Chromosomes are large, complex molecules that are found at the center (nucleus) of every cell. They contain the genetic blueprint for an individual dog. Each chromosome contains a sequence of genes. Dogs have thirty-nine chromosome pairs (humans have twenty-three pairs), for a total of seventy-eight chromosomes. Of the thirty-nine pairs of chromosomes, thirty-eight are similar to each other. These matched chromosomes each contain matching types of genes, although the actual information on the two genes may vary. The sex chromosomes make up the last pair: an X and a Y (male) or two Xs (female).

Each parent contributes half of a dog's chromosomes. This occurs at the moment of fertilization, when the egg and sperm meet. Like a deck of cards being shuffled and dealt, some chromosomes are kept and others are discarded. It's purely chance that determines which chromosomes a puppy will receive. That's why puppies in one litter can all look or behave differently.

The genetic material that makes up chromosomes is called DNA, or deoxyribonucleic acid. DNA is the molecular basis of heredity and is constructed in the form of a double helix, which looks something like a spiral staircase. The purpose of DNA is to code genetic information for the transmission of inherited traits.

Genetic Transmission

Genes are paired on a chromosome and come in two types: dominant and recessive. A dominant gene can cause a trait to be expressed all by itself. A recessive gene, on the other hand, must pair up with another recessive gene before the trait it controls can be expressed. Coat color is one of the best examples of how this works. Let's say that you breed two black Labrador retrievers. The resulting litter contains black puppies and yellow puppies. That's because each parent carried a yellow allele, an alternative form of the gene that carries the black color. The yellow allele is recessive to the black allele, but since each parent contributed a yellow allele, and those yellow alleles were paired on a chromosome, the two were able to combine to produce yellow puppies. If a chromosome pair consists of a black allele and a yellow allele, then the black allele will be dominant, producing black puppies. So a dominant gene paired with another dominant gene or a dominant gene paired with a recessive gene will always produce, or express, a dominant characteristic, such as black coat color. Only a recessive gene paired with another recessive gene will produce a recessive characteristic, such as yellow coat color.

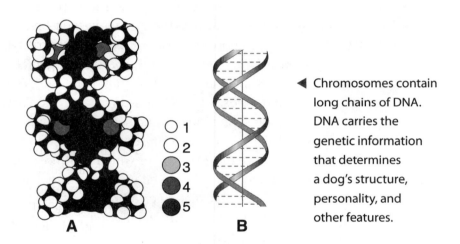

◀ Chromosomes contain long chains of DNA. DNA carries the genetic information that determines a dog's structure, personality, and other features.

How Diseases Are Inherited

Besides physical characteristics such as coat and eye color, diseases can also be inherited. They, too, are controlled by dominant and recessive genes. A disease or defect caused by a dominant gene is obvious, because the dogs that carry the gene develop that particular disease. When this happens, responsible breeders know not to repeat that breeding. A disease caused by a recessive gene is a little trickier to deal with. A disease-causing recessive gene can be passed on for generations without causing problems, but if it becomes paired with another recessive gene carrying the same disease, then the disease expresses itself, to the consternation of the breeder. Some diseases now have genetic tests to identify carriers of recessive genes, and researchers are working to develop more.

Besides helping breeders to identify carriers, genetic tests allow them to breed away from defective genes and ensure that defective genes aren't reintroduced in future breedings. For instance, von Willebrand's disease, a recessive bleeding disorder, is a problem in Doberman pinschers. Thanks to a genetic test and screening program, Doberman pinscher breeders can identify dogs that carry the disease or are affected by it. Using this knowledge, they can decrease the frequency of the defective gene by selecting normal-testing dogs for breeding. They can also breed carriers to normal-testing dogs and then use the normal-testing offspring in their breeding programs. That allows them to preserve the good qualities of the carriers without eliminating them from the gene pool, which is important for genetic diversity.

Known Breed Disorders

Dogs are subject to more than 350 genetic disorders that can affect the heart, eyes, skeletal structure, skin, hearing ability, and more. Some are single-gene diseases, meaning it takes only a single gene to turn them on, while others are polygenic, controlled by multiple genes. Environment and diet can sometimes play a role in the development of polygenic diseases, as in the case of hip dysplasia. Some of the most common hereditary diseases are various forms of heart disease, eye disease, orthopedic defects, deafness, epilepsy, bleeding disorders, and skin diseases. The following sections describe just a few of the hereditary diseases that can affect dogs.

Heart Disease

Forms of hereditary or probably hereditary heart disease in dogs include mitral valve disease (which is sometimes acquired and sometimes genetic) and dilated cardiomyopathy. While it's not known whether certain diseases have a hereditary basis (dilated cardiomyopathy, for example), the frequency of their occurrence in certain breeds is a pretty good clue that this is the case. Dogs can also be affected by congenital heart defects. A congenital defect is one that the dog is born with rather than one that develops later in life. Most congenital heart defects are hereditary.

Mitral Valve Disease

The heart has four chambers and four valves. Mitral valve disease (MVD), also known as mitral regurgitation or chronic valvular disease, occurs when the connective tissue making up the heart's mitral valve degenerates, causing it not to close all the way. Instead of flowing all the way out through the valve, some of the blood passing through it leaks back into one of the chambers, the left atrium, causing it to enlarge. MVD is diagnosed by the sound of the leakage, called a murmur. A chest X ray, electrocardiogram (ECG), and cardiac ultrasound (echocardiogram) can show how far along the disease has progressed and help the veterinarian decide whether it's time to start the dog on medication.

A normal heartbeat makes the sound "lub dub, lub dub." The sound made by a heart with a murmur depends on when in the cardiac cycle the murmur occurs. The noise it makes is either lub-shh-dub or lub-dub-shh.

MVD is common in toy and small breeds. One of the breeds in which it's most devastating is the cavalier King Charles spaniel. MVD usually develops in older dogs, but cavaliers have the highest rate of early-onset MVD of all breeds, and nearly 100 percent of these spaniels will develop MVD by the age of ten. It's the leading cause of death in the breed. Other breeds that are prone to MVD are miniature and toy poodles, Chihuahuas, Lhasa apsos, Yorkshire terriers, miniature schnauzers, and cocker spaniels.

Dogs with MVD can go for years without signs of heart failure, but eventually the disease progresses to the point that the body has a hard time getting enough oxygen. Fluid starts to build up in the lungs, a condition known as congestive heart failure. Medication can help prolong the dog's life for a time. MVD is polygenic, and environmental factors can affect its severity. It's important to keep a dog with MVD at a healthy weight, and plenty of exercise before the dog starts showing signs of heart failure can only help.

Dilated Cardiomyopathy

While MVD is a disease of small dogs, dilated cardiomyopathy is more likely to affect large- and giant-breed dogs. This disease of the heart muscle causes the heart chambers to enlarge and the walls of the ventricles (the muscular lower chambers of the heart that pump blood out) to become less able to contract. It's seen most frequently in Doberman pinschers but can also occur in boxers, Great Danes, Irish wolfhounds, Saint Bernards, German shepherd dogs, springer spaniels, and cocker spaniels.

Dogs with dilated cardiomyopathy show the signs of congestive heart failure. They may lose weight, seem lethargic, tire easily after only brief periods of exercise, or cough frequently. A chest X ray will show whether the heart is enlarged. The diagnosis is confirmed with an electrocardiogram to check for an abnormal heart rhythm (arrhythmia) and an echocardiogram to visualize the interior of the heart and assess its function by measuring the thickness of the heart walls and the heart's pumping ability.

Eye Disease

Cataracts, progressive retinal atrophy, glaucoma, and collie eye anomaly are some of the hereditary eye diseases found in dogs. These diseases and others can be tested for before a dog is bred. If you're buying a purebred puppy and the breed you're interested in is prone to eye disease, ask the breeder if the pup's sire and dam are registered with the Canine Eye Registry Foundation (CERF). CERF registers dogs that are free of heritable eye disease as certified by a veterinary ophthalmologist. Check the date on the CERF certificate. Dogs must be recertified annually to maintain their registration.

Juvenile Cataracts

The lens of a dog's eye is normally transparent. A cataract is an opaque spot on the lens. Dogs often acquire cataracts with age, but juvenile cataracts, which develop before six years of age, are hereditary. Juvenile cataracts may remain small, causing little interference with vision, or they can progressively grow larger, leading to blindness. They may start in only one eye but eventually affect both eyes. More than seventy-five breeds are prone to juvenile cataracts. Researchers are working to develop genetic tests to identify the carriers of cataracts in those breeds.

Progressive Retinal Atrophy

Progressive retinal atrophy (PRA) is an umbrella term for a group of hereditary eye diseases that affect more than eighty breeds. While PRA has the same general effect in all breeds, genetic mutations result in some differences among breeds as far as the age of onset and the speed at which the disease progresses. Types of PRA are early onset slow progression, early onset rapid progression, late onset, and sudden acquired retinal degeneration. The disease is inherited through a recessive gene.

ALERT!

Before you buy a purebred puppy, research the breed to find out what hereditary problems affect it. No breed is free of hereditary problems. Ask the breeder for proof that her dogs have tested clear of that breed's problems. Be aware that some problems, such as epilepsy, don't have tests or can show up later in life, after a dog has already produced offspring.

The first sign of PRA is night blindness, reluctance to go outside at night, or to move around in a dark room. Depending on the type of PRA, the dog may retain day vision for a while or become blind very quickly. There's no treatment for PRA, but researchers have identified a genetic marker that will help them develop a DNA test to identify normal, affected, or carrier dogs at an early age.

Glaucoma

The eye contains fluid that is slowly and continuously released from the eye. When the eye produces fluid faster than it can be released, pressure builds up within the eyeball. This condition, called glaucoma, damages the optic nerve and results in blindness if left untreated. Dogs can have primary glaucoma, which is hereditary, or secondary glaucoma, which occurs as a complication of some other eye disease.

Among the breeds that are prone to primary glaucoma are beagles, cocker spaniels, basset hounds, and Samoyeds. Any dog that has a hereditary predisposition to glaucoma should be examined annually by a veterinary ophthalmologist so the condition can be identified and treated as early as possible. Medication is available to help remove fluid from the eye or to reduce fluid production. When medication isn't effective, surgery can sometimes help.

Collie Eye Anomaly

Rough and smooth collies, Border collies, and Shetland sheepdogs may develop a condition called collie eye anomaly (CEA), which is a disease of the deep structures of the eye. Dogs are born with CEA, and it can be diagnosed by a veterinary ophthalmologist with the aid of an ophthalmoscope as early as four to eight weeks of age. CEA affects the development of the choroid, which provides the retina with oxygen and nutrients. Sometimes the choroid suffers only minor damage with little effect on a dog's vision, but in other cases retinal detachment results in blindness. CEA is inherited through a recessive gene, so make sure you purchase a puppy whose parents have up-to-date registrations with CERF and have never produced puppies with CEA.

Orthopedic Defects

Orthopedic diseases affect the bones, joints, and muscles. Common hereditary orthopedic problems in dogs are hip and elbow dysplasia, osteochondritis dissecans, and luxating patellas. All of these conditions are believed to be polygenic. Breeders can reduce the risk of producing puppies with orthopedic problems by having dogs X-rayed and evaluated by the Orthopedic Foundation for Animals (OFA) at two years of age (one year for patellar luxation) to make sure their hips, elbows, and knees are in good or excellent condition. If the breed you're interested in is prone to any of these diseases, ask to see the OFA hip, elbow, or knee clearances of both parents of any puppy you're considering buying.

Hip Dysplasia

This condition results when the head of the thigh bone (the femur) doesn't fit securely into the hip socket. Instead, the loose joint slips and slides around, causing inflammation, pain, and lameness. If your puppy or dog is limping for no apparent reason, he may have hip dysplasia. Your veterinarian will X-ray the dog's hips to see if there's a problem. Along with excess, and excessively rapid weight gain during puppyhood, high-impact exercise such as jumping at an early age can worsen the severity of hip dysplasia. Hip dysplasia is a multifactorial problem that's probably caused by multiple genes and influenced by environmental factors such as diet.

FACT

Breeds in which hip dysplasia is common include German shepherd dogs, Labrador retrievers, golden retrievers, Saint Bernards, Newfoundlands, and rottweilers. It can occur in any breed and is sometimes seen in small but stocky breeds such as pugs.

Mild cases of hip dysplasia can be treated with pain relievers (nonsteroidal anti-inflammatory drugs formulated for dogs) and nutraceuticals such as glucosamine and chondroitin. These particular nutraceuticals are food supplements that have a protective effect on cartilage (connective tissue that's important in the formation of joints) and can even help repair it. Severe cases of hip dysplasia may require a total hip replacement. If your veterinarian notices joint laxity while your puppy is still very young (less than four months of age), he may suggest a new surgical procedure to close the area between the two halves of the pelvis. The technique, called juvenile pubic symphysiodesis, forces the hip socket to rotate into a more normal alignment.

Elbow Dysplasia

Sometimes the elbow bones of one or both front legs fail to unite and move properly, a condition called elbow dysplasia. The most common sign of this disease is lameness. Your veterinarian can confirm the problem with

X rays. Like hip dysplasia, elbow dysplasia can sometimes be managed with medication and nutraceuticals. Low-impact exercise such as swimming and walks on leash can help preserve range of motion in the elbow joint and strengthen surrounding muscles. Dogs with severe elbow dysplasia may require surgery to fuse the joint, which helps relieve pain. Breeds that are commonly diagnosed with elbow dysplasia include golden and Labrador retrievers, English setters, English springer spaniels, rottweilers, German shepherd dogs, Bernese mountain dogs, Newfoundlands, and mastiffs.

Osteochondritis Dissecans

Rapidly growing puppies, especially those of large breeds, sometimes have shoulder cartilage that fails to calcify normally. Any stress on the joint then causes bits of cartilage to break into loose fragments. This condition, called osteochondritis dissecans (OCD), usually develops when a puppy is four to eight months old. It can also affect the elbow and sometimes the knee. Dogs with OCD may limp or show pain when the affected joint is flexed or extended. X rays can confirm the diagnosis. Rest and joint-protective nutraceuticals are the best medicine for OCD, but sometimes surgery is necessary to scrape away defective cartilage.

Patellar Luxation

Patellar luxation, or luxating patella, are fancy ways of saying that the kneecap slips out of place. You may also hear people refer to the condition as a slipped stifle. It's very common in toy and small breeds. If you notice that your puppy or dog sometimes has a hop to his gait, he probably has a luxating patella.

FACT

Dogs are considered to have one of the most "plastic" genetic compositions of any species. The same basic template produces dogs ranging from Chihuahuas to Irish wolfhounds and Mexican hairless dogs to Alaskan malamutes.

Patellar luxation can range from mild to severe. Your veterinarian will diagnose the problem by seeing how easy it is to push the patella out of the groove where it rests and whether it goes easily back into place. A grade one is mild, while a grade four is severe. Dogs with grade-one luxations usually don't need any treatment, but dogs with grade-two luxations or higher may require surgery to repair the knee.

The OFA certifies patellas of dogs one year or older, but a veterinarian can do a preliminary screening of puppies at six to eight weeks of age. If you're considering purchasing a breed that's prone to patellar luxation, ask if the breeder has his dogs' patellas registered with OFA and whether his puppies have been prescreened by his veterinarian.

Deafness

Deafness is hereditary in at least eighty dog breeds. The gene for deafness is often linked to genes for pigmentation patterns, especially those that involve white in the coat such as the merle gene (seen in collie-type breeds and harlequin Great Danes, among others) and the piebald gene (seen in such breeds as Dalmatians, bull terriers, and English setters). Blue eyes are often associated with deafness, although they're not a definite sign that a dog is deaf or may carry a gene for deafness. The genetics of deafness in dogs is not yet fully understood, so in breeds in which it's common, breeders must be especially careful.

Congenital hearing loss usually develops when a puppy is only a few weeks old, possibly because of the absence of pigment-producing cells, called melanocytes, in the ear's blood vessels. Needless to say, no deaf dog should be bred, and breeders are advised not to repeat any breeding that produces deaf puppies.

Epilepsy

Epilepsy, which is defined as repeated seizures, is one of the most common neurologic diseases in dogs. Dogs can have symptomatic epilepsy, meaning the disease has a specific cause such as a brain tumor or brain injury, or idiopathic epilepsy, meaning the cause is unknown. Often, idiopathic epilepsy is hereditary. It usually develops at one to three years of age but sometimes doesn't appear until later in life. No tests are yet available to identify carriers of epilepsy, so it's a good idea to ask breeders if any of the dogs they've bred have developed epilepsy. Work is ongoing to develop a DNA test for epilepsy.

Diagnosing epilepsy is a process of elimination. Since there's no way to predict when a seizure will occur, your veterinarian will usually have to rely on your description of the episode. It helps if you can videotape it so the veterinarian can see exactly what happens during the seizure. If that's not possible, take notes on what the seizure looks like. Knowing the type of seizure is important to a good diagnosis. A physical exam, blood work, and a neurologic exam to test behavior, coordination, reflexes, and nerve function can help rule out other conditions that might cause seizures.

FACT

Brain cells (neurons) communicate with each other through electrical and chemical signals. Sometimes the cells become overstimulated, causing an electrical storm in the brain. The result is a seizure. Seizures occur most often when a dog is relaxed or sleeping.

While there's no cure for epilepsy, medication can help control seizures. Treatment with medication is successful in more than two-thirds of dogs with epilepsy, but it can take time to get the type of medication and the dose right. Be aware that dogs can still have seizures while on medication; the important thing is to reduce the number and severity of seizures. Keeping a record of seizure occurrences will help your veterinarian judge the effectiveness of treatment. Take your dog to the veterinarian any time a seizure lasts longer than five to ten minutes or if he has three or more seizures in a day.

Always check with your veterinarian before changing or discontinuing antiseizure medication. Just because your dog isn't having seizures doesn't mean it's okay to take him off the medication. Sudden withdrawal of antiseizure medication can make the problem worse. Your dog will need to take it for the rest of his life.

Like any dog, dogs with epilepsy should be kept at a healthy weight. The stress that obesity puts on the body isn't good for them. Your dog's medication needs can also change throughout his life, so annual follow-up visits are important. Regular blood work may be necessary to ensure that liver function isn't affected by the medication. See Appendix A for information on the Canine Epilepsy Project.

Sebaceous Adenitis

This hereditary skin disease is common in standard poodles and can also affect Akitas, Samoyeds, and vizslas. As you might guess from the name, sebaceous adenitis (SA) is an inflammation of the sebaceous glands (small glands beneath the skin usually connected with hair follicles). Poodles or other longhaired breeds with SA develop symmetric hair loss on the muzzle, the top of the head, the ears, and along the top of the body. A shorthaired dog such as the vizsla develops circular areas of hair loss, mainly on the body. The skin becomes scaly and often develops bacterial infections. Sebaceous adenitis is diagnosed with a skin biopsy, sometimes referred to as a skin punch. There's no cure for the disease, but frequent baths with medicated shampoo can help, as can antiseborrhea drugs, corticosteroids, and antibiotics to ward off bacterial infections. Dogs with SA should not be bred.

Bleeding Disorders

When your dog gets a cut or scrape, the blood undergoes a sequence of chemical and physical reactions that causes it to thicken and eventually stop flowing out of the wound. This is called clotting or coagulation. Sometimes dogs develop bleeding disorders in which the blood doesn't clot properly. One of these bleeding disorders is von Willebrand's disease.

Dogs can inherit bleeding disorders, and von Willebrand's (vWD) disease is the most common of those conditions, having been identified in more than fifty breeds. It occurs when the body is deficient in a plasma protein called the von Willebrand factor, which is necessary for blood platelets to function normally. Fortunately, the bleeding associated with vWD is usually mild, but some dogs can have more severe problems, such as prolonged nosebleeds, bleeding beneath the skin, or blood in feces or urine. Among the breeds in which vWD is common are Doberman pinschers, German shepherd dogs, golden retrievers, Shetland sheepdogs, Scottish terriers, and miniature schnauzers.

ALERT!

Dogs with von Willebrand's disease or that carry the disease can be identified through a DNA test. The OFA maintains a vWD registry for breeds that are prone to the disease.

Health Registries

Health registries maintain databases of the results of health tests for various genetic diseases or disorders, including hip dysplasia, patellar luxation, eye problems, and more. The most well known of these registries are the Orthopedic Foundation for Animals (OFA), the Canine Eye Registration Foundation (CERF), and the Canine Health Information Center (CHIC). There's also the Institute for Genetic Disease Control (GDC), which has merged with OFA but still registers eye disease and tumors separately and helps breed clubs set up registries for diseases not covered by OFA. The Josephine Deubler Genetic Disease Testing Laboratory at the University of Pennsylvania, which offers a genetic testing and counseling program for many canine hereditary diseases, has developed a Canine Genetic Disease Information System to provide information to veterinarians, breeders, researchers, and dog owners. The Canine Genetics Laboratory, Baker Institute, at Cornell University has developed DNA tests for hereditary eye disorders. These are all multibreed registries or programs, but some breed clubs have their own health registries. Reputable breeders provide proof of the parents' health certifications from one or more of these registries. You can find contact information for health registries in Appendix A.

DNA Pawprinting

The availability of DNA analysis means that breeders and breed registries can positively identify dogs for registration and determine their relatedness to other dogs when planning breedings. Breeders can compare the genetics of the two dogs they're considering breeding to make sure they aren't carriers of certain diseases as well as to pinpoint desirable performance traits. This DNA fingerprinting—or pawprinting, if you will—is also useful in resolving identity and pedigree disputes. A microchip can migrate, a tattoo can fade, and fur can be dyed, but DNA doesn't change. DNA testing can provide definitive proof of the parents of a litter and is required for breedings using artificial insemination, such as with frozen semen.

A canine DNA profile is a series of markers from your dog's chromosomes. It comes printed out in color, making it simple to follow the identification. The American Kennel Club doesn't require DNA analysis to register a dog, but it does have a voluntary DNA certification program. If a dog registered with the AKC receives a certificate of DNA analysis, all future registration certificates and pedigrees issued for that dog will include his DNA profile number, plus DNA profile numbers for ancestors that have been profiled.

FACT

Not every disease has a genetic test yet, but the probability decreases that a puppy will develop a heritable disease when parents and other ancestors have tested normal, either through genetic tests or through diagnostic tests such as X rays.

DNA samples are collected by placing a small bristle brush inside a dog's mouth and swabbing it against the inside of the cheek to obtain cell samples. It's as easy as that. Many breed clubs conduct DNA profiling clinics at their national specialty shows.

Further Research

Scientists are developing maps of the canine genome. Once completed, this will guide researchers to an understanding of the underlying genetic causes of diseases in dogs, including a determination of the mutations that actually cause the disease. With this information, diagnostic tests can be developed so that breeders can reduce or eliminate the incidence of genetic disease in their lines. So far, researchers have located the genes that cause narcolepsy (sleeping sickness) in dogs as well as those for three inherited diseases that affect the retina. They have also developed more than thirty tests to identify heritable canine diseases. It's possible that the next ten to twenty years could bring tests for all known single-gene canine genetic diseases, allowing these diseases to be eliminated through genetic testing and selective breeding.

If you plan to breed your dog, plan the breeding carefully and perform all available tests to decrease the possibility that your dog will pass on a genetic defect.

As scientists work to decode the canine genome, their discoveries will allow breeders to use genetic information to prevent disease through more careful breeding. They will also allow veterinarians to provide new forms of treatment for genetic diseases, such as inserting a normal gene into the DNA of cells to compensate for a nonfunctioning or defective gene, a technique known as somatic gene therapy. In the not-too-distant future, if your veterinarian tells you that your dog has a hereditary disease, your options for treatment may go beyond surgery or chemotherapy or lifelong medication. Instead, your veterinarian may simply prescribe nose drops containing a retrovirus that will deliver a normal gene to correct the dog's problem.

Chapter 16

First Aid

First aid should be just that—the very first help you provide if your pet is injured. There are times when that quick bit of assistance totally takes care of the problem and other times when it is only the first step as you head for professional care. Luckily, there are a number of things you can to do help your dog in cases of minor accidents. One of the first rules is not to panic! If you panic, you won't be thinking clearly, and your dog will pick up on your tension. Stay calm, and you can be a positive influence for your dog.

Be Prepared—Have a First-Aid Kit

It is really nice to have a good first-aid kit available for any small emergencies you have with your dog. Most of these items are applicable for people too, so one kit can serve the entire family! Having one kit in the house and another in the car is also a good idea. Make sure everyone in the family knows where the kits are kept.

While you may add some items to customize a kit for your dog, virtually any dog first-aid kit should include the following items:

- *Activated charcoal:* This is to be used in some poisoning cases. Always check with your veterinarian and/or the National Animal Poison Control Center (NAPCC) before giving it to your dog.
- *Antihistamine:* Ask your veterinarian for the correct dose of an antihistamine, such as Benadryl, and keep some on hand for use after insect stings or other mild allergic reactions.
- *Artificial tears:* These are extremely useful for flushing materials such as dust or seeds out of your dog's eyes.
- *Bandage material:* This could include gauze rolls, gauze pads, and Telfa pads to cover wounds.
- *Diarrhea medication:* This can be as simple as Pepto-Bismol tablets or Kaopectate. Check with your veterinarian so you know the correct dose for your dog.
- *Disposable hot and cold packs:* These are handy for applying to sore areas.
- *Hydrogen peroxide:* This is an extremely effective way to make your dog vomit. Do *not* give this until you check with your veterinarian or NAPCC to see if this is the correct treatment for any poison your dog may have swallowed!
- *Ointments:* Tubes of antibiotic, corticosteroid, and aloe ointments are good for application to small wounds, cuts, and sores.
- *Pain medications:* Ask your veterinarian for some nonsteroidal pain medications to have on hand for emergencies.
- *Saline:* A small bottle of saline to flush out sore ears or wounds is helpful.

- *Scissors:* These make life easier if you ever have to cut bandage material or gauze.
- *Silver nitrate or styptic pencil:* These help to stop minor bleeding, such as when a toenail gets trimmed into the quick.
- *Tape:* Pack some adhesive tape for fastening bandages (leave a tab for quick removal!) and some duct tape to put over cut pads as a temporary bootie if you are hiking. Vetwrap or Elastikon are very useful for keeping bandages on—just don't make them too tight!
- *Thermometer:* Rectal ones are most accurate, but there are also ear and digital models for dogs.
- *Tweezers:* These are good for removing splinters and thorns. Some are specialized for removing ticks as well.

For the "natural pet," you might want to include Rescue Remedy for stress and trauma, arnica for trauma and wounds (use only the homeopathic version and give orally), plus a sterile needle for the acupuncture point under the nose that stimulates breathing. (Ask a veterinary acupuncturist to show you where this point is and teach you how to use the needle.) If your pet has special conditions, such as epilepsy or severe reactions to bee stings, you should ask your veterinarian about diazepam pills or enemas for seizures and an Epi Pen kit for anaphylaxis.

QUESTION?

How can I safely carry an injured dog?
A small dog may be easily tucked into a towel and safely carried in your arms. Always take extra care if you suspect any broken bones and try not to jostle them. For a larger dog, sliding the dog onto a blanket or board and then having two people pick it up works best. Remember to put a muzzle on before you try to pick up the dog!

Restraining Your Dog

If your dog is very frightened, hurt and in pain, he may not recognize you, and he certainly may not behave as his usual good-natured self. You need to assume that it is possible your dog will bite in those circumstances and take precautions. Some basic restraint techniques can help keep both of you safe.

Some people keep a quick muzzle on hand, one that slips over the dog's nose and snaps together behind the ears. Practice with one of these when you are not in a crisis situation—both to accustom your dog to the muzzle and to make sure it fits. For a less expensive version, take a strip of gauze, loop it around your dog's nose, then cross it under the chin and tie it behind the ears. Remember, your dog breathes through his nose. The bony tissue on top of the nose means you don't have to worry about shutting off airways.

CPR or Cardiopulmonary Resuscitation

CPR is a way of stimulating the heart and the lungs to function. The basics of CPR can be abbreviated as ABC: A for airway, B for breathe, and C for circulation. Any pet owner can learn these emergency basics.

Some Red Cross groups now offer CPR classes with a special practice dog! Many of them hold pet first-aid classes too. These classes are well worth your time. Check with your local Red Cross. Ask your veterinarian about pet CPR and first-aid courses too.

Performing CPR

Adult dogs may need full-blown CPR in some emergencies. Drowning, choking, electric shocks, or trauma may all cause your dog to stop breathing or his heart to stop beating. Luckily, dogs aren't as prone to heart attacks as people. First you need to have a clear airway. Your dog should be basically unresponsive, so you shouldn't be in any danger as you open her mouth and clear away any debris. (If your dog is fighting, she probably does not need CPR!) Close the muzzle and breathe into the nose. Try five or six quick breaths right away. If that doesn't work, you need to go into a routine of about fifteen or twenty breaths per minute. You should be able to see the chest wall expand as you breathe into the dog's nose.

CPR Compressions

To start circulation going, your dog will need chest compressions. Place her gently on her right side on a reasonably flat surface. Make sure there are no broken ribs you would be pushing on. (If ribs are broken, your dog's chest will move in an erratic pattern, not as a unified area.) For a big dog, put the heel of your hand against the chest, above and behind the dog's elbow, then put your other hand on top of the first. A small dog or puppy may just need one hand around the chest. Push quickly ten times. If you don't get any response, you need to do sixty to eighty compressions a minute.

If you have a partner to help work on your dog, one of you can breathe into the nose while the other person does chest compressions. If you have to work alone, alternate breathing and chest compressions.

Household Toxins and Poisonous Plants

The most important thing to realize about poisoning is that it is a problem best dealt with by prevention. Any household toxins should be shut away in cupboards that your dog can't reach or that are held shut by locks or child-proof catches. Better yet, put them in a cupboard in the basement or garage behind a closed door, placing multiple barriers between your dog and the toxin! Do *not* repackage products. If your dog chews on a bottle or consumes something, you need to know the ingredients and be able to read the label to the Poison Control Center to know what actions to take.

As for the plants, try to decide just how important that poisonous plant is to you and if it is worth risking your pet's health. This is especially true if you have a puppy around who may not always be under ideal supervision.

Actions to Take

If your dog has gotten into a substance that you think may be toxic, immediately call your veterinarian or emergency clinic. Have the container of the substance handy to read them the ingredients and to be able to guess-timate how much your dog may have consumed. Have your first-aid kit at hand to use if needed, and use it as directed.

It is important to remember that not all substances that are dangerous to dogs come with a skull and crossbones on the label. Chocolate, especially the dark baking chocolate, can be toxic to dogs, as can coffee, grapes, and alcohol. The same is true for many supplements. Even those labeled as "natural" or "organic" may be toxic to dogs.

Poisonous Plants

Unfortunately some dogs, especially puppies, like to chew on plants. They don't discriminate between the caustic lily and the safe spider plant. Even if your houseplants are all safe, odds are at least some of the trees, shrubs, or flowers in your yard are at least mildly poisonous. It pays to walk around your yard with a field guide and identify all the plants you find.

The easiest way to deal with poisonous plants that are large, such as shrubs and trees, may be to separate them from your dog. You could fence in a safe part of the yard for your dog to play in, or put small individual fences around the plants that might cause problems. Remember that fruits of certain trees, like chokecherries, may be poisonous. You need to pick up any fruits like these, as well as any rotting fruit that might attract bees along with your hungry hound!

Be very careful of any mushrooms that sprout up in your yard. If you find your dog chewing on one, grab a similar one for identification right away and be prepared to drive to your veterinarian. The same advice goes for any chewed-up plant. Look for leaves or blossoms so you can identify the plant and determine if it is poisonous.

Poison Control

Know the number for your local poison control center, or, even better, call directly to the National Animal Poison Control Center. This center has the special knowledge at their fingertips to tell if a drug or substance will be toxic to your dog based on your dog's size and the amount and type of poison consumed, and workers can guide you or your veterinarian through the actions to take and treatments to use. Normally there is a charge of $45 per case; however, many products are covered by the Animal Product Safety

Service. In these cases, the product manufacturer absorbs the cost of the call. Your veterinarian may have a membership and be able to place the call for free for you.

You can contact the Animal Poison Control Center at ☎1-888-4ANIHELP (426-4435) or ☎1-900-443-0000. The fee is $45 per case, with follow-up calls at no charge. (This can be paid by credit card.)

Wound Care

Sooner or later, it is likely your dog will get a cut or wound. Some of these injuries can be totally cared for at home, while others will need some veterinary attention. Try to check your dog over daily so that you catch any injuries soon after they happen. Treating injuries right away usually hastens healing time and reduces complications.

Small Cuts

Small cuts that only go through the skin and don't leave gaping wounds can often be treated at home. Flush the wound gently with saline solution, water, or a chlorhexidine wash. Tamed iodine solutions (like Betadine) can be used to clean small cuts as well. The antibacterial properties of iodine and chlorhexidine may help to prevent infections. In general, small wounds will heal fine if left open and kept clean. Applying a small amount of antibiotic ointment may help to keep the tissues moist. Too much ointment can interfere with healing however, so use a light touch! A gaping opening may need sutures to keep the tissues underneath hydrated and healthy.

A wound that has spraying blood usually means a cut artery. Apply pressure directly to the area. If the bleeding stops quickly, observe the wound for the next hour. Only small arteries will stop quickly with pressure. If bleeding starts again, you may need veterinary attention.

Punctures and Large Wounds

Punctures are dangerous wounds. What you can see on the surface may not give you an accurate idea of the damage to tissues underneath. Bleeding may be occurring inside and muscles may be ripped. These wounds tend to close over and allow bacteria to flourish inside. A puncture wound may need daily flushing to keep it open, prevent infections, and to encourage it to heal from the inside out. Large wounds may need suturing or daily wound care, including alternating wet and dry bandages to encourage healing and minimize the chances of infection. Your veterinarian can instruct you in the care needed for these types of injuries and may prescribe antibiotics.

A Broken or Bleeding Nail

Virtually every dog owner will face a broken or bleeding toenail at some point. You may accidentally make a cut that is too close to the quick while trimming your dog's nail. Or your dog might catch and tear a toenail on the carpet. Either way, this is very painful for your dog.

If your dog has totally torn the nail off a toe, there is usually very little bleeding. The foot is very painful, and the sensitive red tissue is easy to see. A nail that is cracked but not totally torn off may be even more painful as your dog will push the broken edge into sensitive areas with every step. It makes sense to remove that remaining bit of nail, so a trip to your veterinarian is a good idea. The sensitive tissues underneath will toughen up, and the nail will grow back, but your dog may be sore for a week or more. Try to avoid walking on rough surfaces during that time.

The most important thing to do for a bleeding nail (usually from a too-short trim job) is to stop the bleeding so that clotting can take place. The best way is to hold a silver nitrate stick on the area. This will sting, so you may need help holding your dog. If you don't have silver nitrate, there are other ways to stop the bleeding. Some people swear by sticking the offending toe into a bar of soap or a bowl of corn meal. Keep your dog quiet and don't let him lick the foot until blood has clotted. Also, don't be too afraid of the sight of your dog's blood. Just a teaspoon of blood or even less can look like a huge amount when it really isn't!

Lameness

A dog that is limping may simply need some quick first aid or may have a broken leg. Look at the leg gently and also consider the circumstances. If your puppy got a paw stepped on by your adult dog and is running around screeching and holding the leg up, simply catch her, calm her down, and wait five minutes. Most likely she will be fine. On the other hand, if you hear the squeal of brakes, look out, and see that your dog has escaped the yard and is running off on three legs, the odds are much greater you have a serious injury.

ALERT!

If a leg is dangling, there is obvious bone showing, or your instinct is that you have a serious injury, go to your veterinarian. Support the leg as carefully as you can, as motion will cause more damage. A quick splint made from a cardboard roll and a towel may help. Have someone help keep the dog quiet while you drive.

Wild Encounters

Occasionally your dog may have a run-in with local wildlife. While most of the time this simply means a wild chase after a swift rabbit, sometimes the encounters get a bit closer. Always keep your dog up-to-date on rabies vaccinations. Saliva from a wild animal, in bites or even on the coat, can carry this deadly virus. Still, many of our dogs' wildlife adventures are less threatening than rabies.

Skunked!!!

One of the worst nightmares for many suburban dog owners is letting the dog in on a spring night only to be overwhelmed by the musky odor of skunk! Don't panic, and don't reach for the tomato juice. First, you need to make sure your dog's eyes are okay. The spray from a scared skunk can be quite painful if it gets in the eyes. Flush your dog's eyes with the artificial tears you keep in your first-aid kit. Once that is done, you are ready to move on to clean up.

THE EVERYTHING DOG HEALTH BOOK

Tomato juice has fallen way out of favor as a deskunking agent. For one thing, to be at all effective, you need to do multiple rinses and that can get expensive, especially if you have a large dog. There are some excellent commercial preparations you can get at the local pet store, or you can try this excellent home recipe. Just be sure to wear rubber gloves, and keep the mixture out of the eyes (yours and your dog's).

1. In a bucket or other open container, combine 1 quart hydrogen peroxide, ¼ cup baking soda, and 1 tsp. liquid dish soap.
2. Sponge the mixture over your dog, working it into the coat.
3. Leave this on for 3 to 5 minutes, then rinse. The difference is amazing!

A Prickly Situation

Close behind the skunk encounters, and actually more serious, are encounters with porcupines. A curious dog that sticks his nose a bit too close may turn away with a mouth and nose full of quills! These quills have tiny scales at the sharp ends, which makes them difficult to pull out. If your dog is lucky enough to only have three or four, you may want to try to pull them yourself with a pair of pliers and a helper. Do not trim the ends of the quills; that only makes it more difficult to pull them out.

A dog with quills inside the mouth or more than just a couple will need a trip to the veterinarian, some sedation, and careful removal. Quills left behind (including those your dog may have chewed off to the skin level) can migrate into your dog's tissues and cause abscesses. Your veterinarian may give you antibiotics for your dog to prevent any infections.

Stopping a Dog Fight

The best way to deal with fights between dogs is to avoid them if at all possible. Keep your dog on leash unless you are in a very safe area and only dogs you know are around. With your dog on leash you can quickly pull her to you, scare off another dog, or even pick your dog up if you have to. Many aggressive dogs will back off at the united front of a dog and her person.

If a fight does break out, do *not* reach in to grab a collar. There is a very good chance that you will get badly bitten, even though it is by accident. Grab a tail or hind leg instead. There is still potential for a bite this way, though, as many dogs will whip around quickly to see who else is after them. If you have a bucket of water or a hose handy, start in with the water works. That usually startles the dogs enough to stop the fight. Swishing a broom or rake between combatants may work, or making a loud noise—even a whistle—can be a distraction.

Sadly, some of the worst fights may break out at home. Intact males and females tend to fight the most. And once two girls decide they don't like each other, they may try to fight to the death. In some of these cases, one of the dogs has to be rehomed.

Treating the Wounded

Very often when you get everyone calmed down, you will find that though there was a lot of nasty noise, there are very few actual injuries. Exceptions are two dogs that are not close in size or two very determined females. Check all the damp areas on your dog's coat—it may just be saliva, but be sure to part the hair carefully though to check for any bruises or bite wounds down in the skin. A puncture wound may look minor on the surface, but there could be muscle damage underneath.

If your dog is bleeding heavily, put pressure on the area and get to your veterinarian quickly. If your dog has open cuts, you need to clean them carefully and call your veterinarian. As bacteria would be moving from one dog's mouth to another dog's body, the chance of infection is high. Your dog may need some antibiotics.

Be aware that a dog who seems fine right after a fight may still be a bit stiff and sore the next day. As long as all body parts are working, the stiffness should wear off. A gentle massage may help!

Treating Burns

Having a burn injury is extremely painful to your dog, whether it is from a paw accidentally hitting a burner when jumping up in play or running through the embers of a bonfire. Burns can be quite serious, depending on how deep they go. You can help healing with some quick first aid.

Despite the old tales recommending putting butter or other greasy substances on burns, we now know better. The grease simply covers the area, hampering healing and sometimes even encouraging infection. For a mild burn, application of an aloe cream or, even better, a piece of an aloe plant brings some fast relief. Cold water is great for reducing inflammation.

One of the biggest problems with burns is that the defense barrier of the skin is gone. The tissues underneath the skin are exposed and very vulnerable to infectious agents. On top of that, fluid loss may lead to dehydration. A dog with a large or deep burn, may need to be hospitalized for fluid therapy. Special bandages will help keep fluids in and infection out. Antibiotics are often prescribed to help in fighting infection.

Temperature Problems

Getting too warm or too cold can both be problems for your dog. Heatstroke is more common than hypothermia, but both are possible problems for our canine friends. Common sense will help prevent these problems, and some thoughtful care can help dogs that suffer from these ailments.

Too Hot!

In very hot weather, you need to keep your dog quiet and cool, with plenty of fresh water and shade available. High humidity added to high temperatures is an even more deadly combination. This is no time to leave your dog in your car, which can become a fatal furnace in just a few minutes. This is also not a good time for those long games of fetch with your fanatic retriever. Your dog may not want to stop, so you have to judge and control his activity.

FACT

Normal body temperatures for dogs range from 100 to 102.5 degrees Fahrenheit, normal heart rates range between 60 to 160 beats per minute, and normal respiratory rates range between 10 to 30 breaths per minute. Heart rates vary greatly with the size, age, and activity level of your dog. Hot weather and exercise can increase the breathing rate. Know your dog's normals!

A dog suffering from heatstroke will pant, have trouble breathing, and may vomit or act disoriented. The heart rate may go up, and the dog could even go into seizures and die. Dogs sweat via their footpads and pant for temperature control. Putting ice cubes in the groin area, wiping pads with ice, and dribbling cool water in the dog's mouth may be all you need to do to help him cool off. A fan is also helpful, but don't submerge your dog in an ice bath. Going too cold too fast can be dangerous, too. Try not to lower your dog's temperature below 103.5 degrees. He is safe at that temperature, and the thermometer reading will soon drop even more. If your dog has heatstroke, be sure to contact your veterinarian, even if your dog seems totally recovered. Kidney problems may show up a day or so later and other metabolic abnormalities as well.

Frostbite and Hypothermia

A dog that has been out in the cold too long, especially one that has been wet as well, may suffer from hypothermia and even get frostbite. Dogs with hypothermia may shiver and act disoriented. Their heart rates drop, and they need to be warmed up. This should be done gradually with tepid water baths or warm towels.

Frostbite will show up days later—usually in extremities such as ears, toes, and tail. Because these body parts don't have the extra tissue to keep them protected against the cold, they are the most common areas for frostbite. These areas may feel extremely cold, and the skin might appear white. It could be days before you know if the tissues are truly dead. If they are, they will dry up and slough off. Dogs with frostbite may need antibiotics to prevent infection in the areas of damaged tissue.

Seizures

Epileptic seizures are discussed more in Chapter 17, but it is important to know what quick first aid you can apply to your dog in case of a seizure. Seizures are like short circuits in the electricity of your dog's brain. With no conscious control, your dog may stagger, twitch, vocalize, and even urinate or defecate. This is scary, but you need to stay calm and help your dog.

Old Myths about Seizures

Dogs can't swallow their tongues, so do *not* try to put your hand in the mouth of a seizuring dog and grab the tongue. What normally happens in those cases is that the person gets bitten and ends up dropping off their dog at the veterinary clinic while they drive on to the emergency room of the human hospital! The best way to help your dog is to guide her gently to a safe place, away from stairs she could fall down or other things she could bang into, and comfort her. Most dogs respond to being held in a blanket and to soothing touch and talk. Seizures generally last less than five minutes, even though it feels like forever to you!

The most common cause of seizures or epilepsy in dogs is genetic predisposition. Seizures may also be a result of metabolic problems like low blood sugar, cancer, infection, or trauma as well.

Recovery

As your dog comes out of the seizure, she may be disoriented. Do not get upset if she has urinated or defecated, but calmly help to clean her up. She may need to be gently restrained, as some dogs have vision problems right after a seizure. Dogs are usually back to 100 percent in an hour or two, and some are normal in minutes. If your dog has another seizure fairly quickly, say in less than an hour, you need to call your veterinarian. "Status seizures," seizures that repeat quickly or continue on for long periods, can do permanent damage to your dog's brain cells or even kill her.

Chapter 17

When to Seek Immediate Treatment

Sometimes when your dog is hurt you are sure she needs immediate veterinary attention, but other times you may not know. This chapter should help you make those decisions and also help make you comfortable with some of the treatments used for different health problems and why they are used. Whether you share your life with a beloved shelter special or a top purebred show dog, you want the best care possible for your companion.

Trauma

Being hit by a car, running and jumping and coming up lame, accidentally being banged by a door—all of these are examples of trauma that may afflict your dog. Trauma may lead to obvious wounds or injuries such as a broken leg or deep cut, but it can also cause internal damage that is harder to see. If you know your dog's normal state, you will be better at picking up any changes.

Fractures

Fractures are broken bones—in dogs, this most often means a leg. Fractures are usually associated with being hit by a car. A leg that dangles, that your dog will not put any weight on, that is obviously wounded, or where the bone is showing are all examples of broken bones. If your dog has been hit by a car, you must take her to a veterinarian even if no bones appear to be broken. Along with obvious leg fractures, she could have broken ribs. The chances of having internal damage are high—most dogs can't tangle with a motor vehicle and win. You need to stabilize the fracture if possible. If your dog will lie down, gently put a paper towel tube next to the leg. Use masking tape to hold it by the leg, and then tape a towel over the whole thing. Another option is gently sliding your dog onto a board or blanket and having two people pick it up. A small dog may be carefully scooped up into a blanket or large towel. Remember your first aid basics (described in Chapter 16), and be sure you don't get bitten! A broken leg will require a splint, cast, or surgery, using metal pins and plates to repair the damage. Do not allow a broken bone to dangle as this will cause more tissue damage.

Internal Damage

While broken bones are dramatic and catch our attention right away, internal damage may be more life-threatening to your dog. If she is having trouble breathing, is breathing very shallowly, or is coughing up blood, you know there is damage to the lungs and the chest. Open wounds directly into the chest are very serious. Again, these are emergencies, and you must take her directly to your veterinarian. Try to keep airways clear—wipe off the nose, clean anything in the mouth if you safely can. If the chest is flailing (ribs moving strangely in and out), put a wrap around the chest. Pneumothorax, the entrance of free air into the chest, can be deadly.

Abdominal Trauma

While broken bones and damage to the chest and lungs are usually apparent right away, trauma injuries to the abdomen may be subtler in appearance. If your dog is bleeding internally, she may look fine at first glance. A check of her gums or feeling her pulse may indicate otherwise.

To check for internal bleeding, first look at your dog's gums. If she has pink areas, touch them. The color should go away, then quickly come back. If the pink areas are already whitish or the color only returns slowly, she has problems. You can feel for a pulse in the groin area on the inside of a hind leg. Use your fingers (not your thumb) and you should feel a strong, steady beat.

Any distension, or expansion, of the abdomen could indicate free blood or urine pooling in the tissues. This is cause for alarm, as is blood in the urine or stool. If your dog is suddenly very touchy about having her abdomen touched or "splints" her abdomen (holding it very taut) you know she has pain there.

Treating Trauma

When a dog with obvious trauma arrives at the veterinary hospital or emergency clinic, the first actions are to guard against shock. Your dog's breathing, heart rate, and temperature will quickly be checked. Direct pressure is put on any bleeding areas. An intravenous line will be placed so that fluids can be quickly injected into her system to combat shock, along with any necessary medications. Many of these tasks are performed by skilled veterinary technicians. In the meantime, your veterinarian will do an overall evaluation of your dog. Most trauma cases will require a chest X ray. Even a small air leak can build up over time and cause death. If there is free air in your dog's chest, a special tube will be placed that allows air to escape but no air to go in. The chest itself may be wrapped.

If the heart and lungs are okay, the next step is checking the abdomen. Your veterinarian may take X rays of the abdomen as well as palpate (feel) it gently for any abnormalities. Sometimes a needle will be put into the abdomen to see if there is free fluid (urine, blood, or gastrointestinal leakage) present. If there is evidence of major problems in the abdomen, your dog will be stabilized and then go to surgery for repairs. If no major damage shows up, your dog will still probably at least stay overnight for careful observation.

Bloating and Swelling

Bloat is a word that strikes fear in the hearts of many dog lovers. Bloat is a simple term for gastric dilatation/volvulus. This condition causes the stomach to fill up with air and often to twist. Twisting shuts off the openings where the extra air could have escaped and also may tighten down on blood vessels, cutting off the free flow of blood to and from the stomach. This is a life-threatening, very serious emergency.

What Causes Bloat?

Research into the causes of bloat is quite extensive and continues even today. Researchers at Purdue University have looked at many aspects of dogs' daily lives for clues to this problem. Bloat tends to occur in large and medium-sized breeds such as Irish setters and Great Danes, with dachshunds being one of the smaller breeds in which it is seen. What many of these breeds have in common is a deep chest. That conformation may allow more room for the stomach to move.

Experienced dog people know that it is wise to rest your dog for at least an hour after a meal, letting food digest while your dog is quiet. It also helps to limit the amount your dog can drink right before and after a meal. Some research has looked into different types of diets as factors, such as dry food versus canned, and even certain ingredients, but there are currently no clear answers.

Signs You Will See

If your dog is bloating, you may notice a number of different signs. Your dog's abdomen may look distended. In the belly area, the skin is taut, and your dog may act as if he's in pain. Many dogs act like they are trying to vomit, but nothing comes up. Some dogs pace nervously refusing to lie down and in general acting uncomfortable. Eventually, your dog may show signs of shock and collapse due to the changes in blood flow. A dog in shock may be collapsed, have very pale gums, feel cold, and have a weak but rapid heart beat when you feel the heart or the pulse in the groin area. Any of those signs should be warnings that your dog is in shock or very close to it.

How to Handle Bloat

If you suspect your dog is bloating, you should call your veterinarian or emergency clinic right away. When you arrive, they will quickly evaluate your dog, palpating her abdomen and listening to her heart. The next step is to try and pass a stomach tube. If the tube goes in and gas is released, your dog will immediately feel much more comfortable. If the tube can't get into the stomach due to a twist, your veterinarian may stick a large needle right through the body wall into the distended stomach to relieve pressure and release some gas. Your dog will then head into surgery if her heart is stable.

ALERT!

If your dog's stomach has been twisted for a long time, or is twisted very tightly, some tissue will be necrotic (dead) due to the reduced blood flow. This is very dangerous, as untwisting the tissues will release some nasty bacteria and toxins. While your veterinarian will try to reduce the effects of those toxins with medications, some dogs do not survive. Other dogs will require removal of the dead tissues.

In surgery, the stomach is carefully untwisted, and the intestines and stomach are carefully evaluated for damage. The stomach is then fastened down to the body wall with sutures in an effort to prevent a recurrence of this problem. Most dogs end up staying in the hospital for a couple of days with intravenous fluids and careful observation.

The Seizuring Dog

Not many sights are as frightening to a dog lover as a dog in full-blown seizures. In simplest terms, seizures are a short circuit in the electrical pathways in the brain. Too many neurons fire at once, without the normal controls in place. Seizures can have many causes, ranging from genetic predispositions (epilepsy) to poisons to metabolic diseases to cancer or trauma. One of the most common causes in purebred dogs is a genetic predisposition.

Signs You Will See

Most dogs show distinct "pre-ictal" or preseizure behaviors. They may become very clingy, pacing and acting uncomfortable, and some go off to a safe hiding place. If your dog has epilepsy, you will usually be able to detect a pattern to the seizures. Once your dog starts into a seizure, she may stagger around, fall down, or lie with her feet moving. Many dogs howl, and often they urinate or defecate. After a seizure, your dog will be exhausted as seizures drain a lot of energy. Some dogs are disoriented after a seizure or may even be temporarily blind. Often dogs become upset when they see or smell the urine or stool as they are normally well housebroken.

It is now thought that some of the obsessive compulsive behaviors dogs may show, such as intense tail chasing, and some of the rage syndromes, when dogs suddenly act aggressive for no reason and then are normal minutes later, may actually be seizure disorders. If your dog shows these symptoms, you should see a veterinary behaviorist.

What You Need to Do

First, stay calm. You don't need to worry about your dog swallowing her tongue. She can't. Do not put your hand into the mouth of a seizuring dog.

While in a seizure, your dog is not aware of who or what is around her. She could easily bite you without consciously meaning to. Many dogs respond to gentle petting and careful restraint, such as holding them wrapped in your arms or a blanket. A soft voice may help as well. If you can tell a seizure is coming on, make sure you get your dog to a safe place where she won't fall down stairs or bang into things. When the seizure stops, move her to a clean resting place.

If your dog seizures for more than five minutes or has repeated seizures, call your veterinarian. Prolonged seizures can raise the body's temperature to dangerous levels.

If this is your dog's first seizure, you should also contact your veterinarian. Your veterinarian will do a thorough exam and look for causes of the seizures, by doing blood work to check out her liver function and look for any signs of poisoning, toxins, or infections. At some point X rays or an electroencephalogram may be needed. You will need to discuss with your veterinarian whether your dog needs to start treatments. All medications have side effects. If your dog only seizures once a year, she might be better off without daily medications.

You should mark on a calendar any time your dog has a seizure (or even if you suspect she may have had one while you were out). Eventually you may be able to predict when the seizures will come and give your dog extra medication.

Treating Seizures

Unless your dog has seizures from a well-known cause, such as a liver problem that can be treated, you need to assume your treatment goal will be to minimize the number and length of any seizures, not to cure your dog. Luckily, some dogs respond extremely well to seizure treatments. Part of the care for seizuring dogs involves being very careful about diet, exercise, and anything that might stimulate a seizure. You need to work with your veterinarian to design a lifestyle plan customized for your dog.

Medications are an important part of controlling seizures in epileptic dogs. Phenobarbital and potassium bromide are the best-known medications for dogs. Liver problems can be a side effect of these medications so your veterinarian may also prescribe herbal medications such as milk thistle to minimize liver reactions. Diazepam (valium) is often used to help stop a seizure, and your veterinarian may provide you with a diazepam enema to give at home if needed. Once your dog starts on seizure medications, you must be faithful, giving the medications daily and on a routine schedule. Suddenly stopping medications may precipitate more seizures.

Collapse

Few things are scarier than seeing your dog suddenly collapse. A few quick observations as you head for the veterinarian can help assure your dog gets the proper treatment as quickly as possible. There are multiple causes of collapse and these can vary with the age of your dog.

Problems of the Heart

While dogs do not normally suffer the classic heart attacks we see in people, there are canine heart conditions that may cause an acute collapse. Dilated cardiomyopathy is a disease with an inherited predisposition for some breeds such as Doberman pinschers and boxers. In this case, the heart ("cardio") muscle ("myo") is stretched and thinned out so much it can no longer efficiently pump the right amount of blood. The body receives less oxygenated blood than it needs, and areas get shut down, leading to collapse. Some dogs with this problem simply run across the yard and drop dead. If caught early, by noticing less stamina, perhaps labored breathing or on a routine exam by your veterinarian, this condition can be controlled for a while with medications. Unfortunately, the only real cure is a heart transplant, which isn't available for dogs.

Atrial and ventricular fibrillation, in which the small atrial or larger ventricular chambers of the heart beat so fast they don't actually move much blood, can also lead to acute collapse. This can be caused by damage to the heart muscle or the nerves controlling the heart rate or by stimulating toxins. This condition may be diagnosed in a routine exam, or you may notice a lack of energy and stamina in your dog, coupled often with panting or pacing.

Not Enough Oxygen

Along with the heart failing to pump enough oxygenated blood, your dog may actually not be getting enough oxygen into his lungs. Simply choking, such as with a tennis ball stuck in his mouth, blocking his airways, could cause an otherwise healthy dog to collapse. In this case, you must quickly pull that obstruction out.

Dogs with short faces—the brachycephalic breeds, such as English and French bulldogs—may suffer from brachycephalic syndrome, especially in hot, humid weather. These breeds often have small nasal openings and a long soft palate (flap on the roof of the mouth). When a dog breathes, air is pulled in, creating some negative pressure inside the palate. In these dogs, the palate may get sucked down and block off the airways. This could lead to a faint or collapse. If your short-faced dog labors to breathe in hot, humid weather, ask your veterinarian to do a thorough airway exam (possibly under anesthesia). Surgery may be required to help these dogs breathe easily.

Nerves Gone Astray

Neurologic problems may also lead to collapse. A dog with a sudden injury to the discs in the neck or back, or with chronic degeneration of these discs, may collapse and even be paralyzed. In these situations, the protective shock-absorbing disc in between two vertebrae has been squeezed and is putting pressure directly on the spinal cord. Depending on exactly where this happens, your dog may be in great pain, lose control of his hind end, or even lose control of most of his body. Disc disease is seen in long-backed dogs such as dachshunds and Bassets, but also in Great Danes and Doberman pinschers, which have neck disc problems.

Wobbler's is a common name for a disc problem seen in the necks of certain breeds such as Great Danes and Doberman pinschers. In these cases, the vertebrae of the neck are not stable. When they move, they put pressure on the spinal cord. Anti-inflammatory medications may help, along with management techniques, such as using harnesses instead of collars, but some dogs may require surgery.

Less Common Causes of Collapse

Less common causes of collapse in dogs may be cancer, metabolic problems like Addison's disease, or poisonings. Cancers such as hemangio-sarcoma create large tumors in the liver and spleen that are delicate and may easily rupture and bleed out into the abdomen. The sudden, severe blood loss can cause collapse, as can blood loss from a bad wound. In Addison's disease, minerals like sodium and potassium get out of sync and lead to heart problems. Addison's is diagnosed with extensive blood work and requires medical therapy.

An easy way to remember whether the adrenal problem Addison's causes is from too much or too little in the way of secretions is that with Addison's disease, you need to "add" steroids and mineralocorticoids.

Some poisons may lead your dog to collapse. Strychnine causes severe seizures and collapse simply by wearing your dog out from the stress of non-stop seizures. If you suspect poisoning, or if your dog is having multiple seizures, seek immediate veterinary attention.

In some areas, such as Florida, certain toads can release toxic substances through their skin. Small dogs may collapse after catching a toad. If you suspect your dog has ingested toad toxins, quickly washing out your dog's mouth will help.

The bottom line? Collapse of your dog should mean an immediate trip to your veterinarian or emergency clinic.

Shocking Situations

An electrical shock can be deadly or merely spine tingling, depending on just how much power coursed through your dog's body. It is important to remember that conditions capable of shocking your dog could give you a shock, too.

The Dangers of Cords

Most dogs get electrical shocks by chewing on electric cords. Puppy-proofing should include running wires through rubber or plastic hose or arranging wires where they can't be reached by curious canines. Even an older dog might grab a wire if it runs across his path. A quick bite might leave your dog with just a yelp and a slightly sore mouth. A definite grab could leave an electrical burn in the mouth (visible on the corners of the lips and on the tongue) or even disrupt the electrical patterns of the heart, leading to collapse.

How to Handle Electric Shocks

The first and most important thing to remember is that if you get shocked too, you won't be able to help your dog. Use a piece of wood, like a broomstick, to snatch the plug from the wall. If necessary, flip the circuit breakers to shut off power to the area.

Electric shocks can also happen outside the home. A sparking wire on the ground, especially if it is wet out, can present grave danger to both you and your dog. If your dog collapses near a downed wire, stay clear to keep yourself from being shocked as well. Use a tree branch or long wooden pole to slide the wire away from your dog or your dog away from the wire. If this is impossible or too dangerous, give your utility company an emergency alert call.

Once your dog is safely away from the electrical danger, check for a heartbeat and to see if she is breathing. If need be, administer CPR (see Chapter 16). Even if your dog comes around quickly, go to your veterinarian for a thorough exam. Sometimes problems show up a day or so later.

Chapter 18

Alternative Therapies and Treatments

Sometimes it takes more than medication or surgery to heal a dog's ills. When that's the case, people often turn to alternative therapies. While many people often turn to these options as a last resort, others are discovering that they can be more beneficial and effective if they're used from the beginning in addition to regular veterinary care. There's not much research to actually prove the benefits of alternative therapies, but based on clinical and anecdotal evidence they are often helpful and rarely harmful.

What Is Alternative Therapy?

Alternative therapies are those that are not mainstream forms of treatment. They are sometimes called complementary because they can be used in conjunction with traditional veterinary medicine for additional benefits. Alternative therapies can be physical or medicinal. Physical therapies are those that involve physically manipulating the dog's body in some way. They include acupuncture, chiropractic, massage, and TTouch. Medicinal treatments include herbal remedies and flower essences, homeopathic medications, and nutraceuticals. For the most part these remedies are safe, but certain herbal remedies are dangerous if misused. Remember, just because something is natural doesn't mean it's harmless.

Acupuncture Treatments

This ancient Chinese technique is based on the theory that the body contains channels, known as meridians, through which energy flows. As long as the channels remain open, the body is healthy. If they become blocked, the flow of energy becomes unbalanced, causing illness. To correct the imbalance, an acupuncturist stimulates certain acupuncture points (acupoints) on the body. Each acupoint is associated with different internal organs, joints, and regions of the body.

FACT

Laser acupuncture is painless and takes less time than traditional acupuncture, although its effects may not be as long-lasting. It's often used to treat spondylosis (spinal arthritis) in dogs and to speed wound healing after injury or surgery.

Acupuncture points are richly supplied with nerves and blood vessels, which is perhaps why stimulating them is so effective. Needles are traditionally used to stimulate these points, but modern veterinary acupuncturists may also use lasers, finger pressure (acupressure), injections of liquid solutions like drugs or vitamins, heat (moxibustion), or even surgical implantation of gold or stainless steel beads at pressure points. Acupuncture is believed to improve the normal flow of blood, energy, and nutrients by releasing constrictions of muscles and the surrounding tissue.

Conditions That Respond to Acupuncture

Acupuncture is perhaps best known for treating musculoskeletal problems such as arthritis or mild cases of hip dysplasia, but practitioners have used it to soothe a number of other conditions. These include hormonal disorders, neurological problems such as anxiety or epilepsy, allergies, digestive problems, and skin disease. In conjunction with pain-relief medications, acupuncture helps speed recovery after surgery.

What to Expect

If you decide to take your dog to a veterinary acupuncturist, expect the first visit to take thirty minutes to an hour. As with traditional medicine, the first goal is to determine the source of the problem. The veterinarian will need to take a full medical history and examine your dog. Once he knows what the problem is, he can discuss treatment options with you before performing the acupuncture itself.

QUESTION?

How does the veterinarian know where the acupoints are?
Dogs and humans have similar skeletal structures and organ placement, so canine acupressurists determine their procedures and positions based on those used for people.

The actual acupuncture is done by inserting thin, flexible needles at the appropriate acupoints. If a dog has a painful shoulder joint, the acupuncturist might stimulate acupuncture points that pass through the shoulder joint as well as points that affect joints in general. For an organ problem, the practitioner might stimulate points that are connected to that organ as well as points that influence infection or inflammation.

Acupuncture needles may be a half-inch to two and a half inches long and are left in place for fifteen to thirty minutes. Depending on the problem, the veterinarian may recommend a series of four to eight weekly treatments. After that, your dog may need only an occasional tune-up. Expect each treatment to cost $40 to $60 or more, depending on where you live.

Doesn't It Hurt?

Certainly your dog will feel some kind of sensation when acupuncture needles are placed. That sensation may or may not be painful, but it can be startling the first time it happens. An acupuncturist would suggest that the discomfort is related to the amount of blockage in the area. Most dogs, once they've been through an acupuncture treatment or two, relax for the treatment because they've learned that they feel better afterward. When a dog simply won't have anything to do with acupuncture, the veterinarian may substitute laser acupuncture or acupressure.

Chiropractic Treatments

According to this system of therapy, disease is believed to be the result of a lack of normal nerve function, which can be treated by manipulating or adjusting the body. Chiropractors believe that spinal misalignments affect all other areas of the body. In other words, when the spine is healthy, so is the rest of the body, and when the spine is out of whack, the normal flow of nerve impulses to organs and other body tissues is interrupted. As with acupuncture, it's believed that certain areas of the spine correspond to other areas in the body, and the area of the spine that's misaligned determines where problems may crop up.

How Chiropractic Can Help

Conditions that are commonly treated with chiropractic include arthritis, hip dysplasia, other causes of lameness, and intervertebral disc disease. Besides improving flexibility, it can reduce the amount of pain medication needed. Any time a dog has soreness from an injury, whether it's a major one such as being hit by a car or a minor one such as slipping and falling on a slick surface, chiropractic may help restore mobility and flexibility. Chiropractic can help aging dogs whose joints are becoming stiff to stay active and comfortable. Other conditions that sometimes respond to chiropractic adjustment include chronic gastrointestinal problems and skin lesions known as lick granulomas.

Chiropractic is also used as a preventive procedure. If your dog enjoys flying disc games, agility, flyball, and obedience trials, chiropractic can help maintain his flexibility and keep him in peak condition. Consider chiropractic if your normally fearless dog begins hesitating at jumps or your normally attentive dog stops looking at you while heeling. He may have an aching back or neck. Chiropractic may also be a solution for show dogs that have gait problems or don't stand properly. Rambunctious puppies can benefit from regular chiropractic care, as can dogs with long backs, such as basset hounds, corgis, dachshunds, and Lhasa apsos. These breeds often develop musculoskeletal problems, and chiropractic may be useful in decreasing the likelihood that back problems will occur.

Chiropractic Treatment

The chiropractor who works on your dog may or may not be a veterinarian. Some veterinarians are trained in chiropractic, and some chiropractors are trained in animal anatomy. In any case, the American Veterinary Medical Association guidelines on alternative therapies call for a licensed veterinarian to diagnose, prescribe, and monitor chiropractic treatment of animals.

FACT

If your veterinarian recommends chiropractic treatment but doesn't provide it himself, you can find a list of veterinarians and chiropractors trained to treat animals through the American Veterinary Chiropractic Association (listed in Appendix A).

The number of visits required will depend on the severity of the problem, as well as your dog's age and condition. Young, healthy dogs usually don't need as many adjustments as older dogs or dogs with a serious problem. Some dogs need a brief series of weekly adjustments, while others may need several visits per week.

Most dogs seem to enjoy the release provided by an adjustment and may even help by shifting their bodies as the chiropractor works on them. By the end of the session, they're often relaxed or sleepy. You will often see a distinct improvement in your dog's mobility after only one treatment.

Massage Therapy

Everyone loves a good massage, and not surprisingly dogs do too. Massage can be done by rubbing, stroking, kneading, or tapping with the hand. Besides feeling great, massage has real therapeutic benefits. It increases the circulation of blood to the skin and muscles—which improves the flow of oxygen and nutrients through the body and carries away fluids and toxins—helps relax, stretch, and tone tight muscles, reduces inflammation and swelling in the joints, increases range of motion, promotes healing, prevents injury by improving flexibility, and releases stress. (Yes, dogs can get stressed too!) Just about any dog can benefit from regular massage, whether it's strictly for relaxation or part of an injury rehabilitation program.

Trigger-Point Therapy

One specific aspect of massage is known as trigger-point therapy. Trigger points feel like hard nodules located within muscles or fascia (the connective tissues that cover or bind muscles). They often develop in response to disc disease, trauma, or other causes of lameness and can cause problems long after the original problem is dealt with. When a trigger point is touched, even the toughest dog may yelp in pain. Trigger points can occur anywhere in the body, but they're common in the heavy muscles of the neck, shoulders, and thighs. They are often found at the same sites as acupuncture points.

When a trigger point develops, the muscle tightens, becoming shorter and weaker because the dog tries not to use it. This affects the joints and, eventually, movement. Signs of trigger points include acute or chronic pain, muscle spasms or weakness, and stiffness. To relieve the pain, trigger points must be released. Deep tissue massage is one of the ways of releasing them. (Acupuncture and chiropractic can also help.) Once the therapist identifies the trigger point, she applies steady pressure to the area, followed by massage of the surrounding area to help relax it.

QUESTION?

Are there any times a dog should not receive massage?
Massage is not helpful and can actually be harmful for dogs with broken bones or joint sprains, ruptured vertebral discs, cancer, fever, or shock.

Finding a Therapist

Your dog's massage therapist may be a veterinarian trained in massage techniques or a licensed massage therapist trained in animal anatomy. You can also take classes to learn animal massage techniques yourself. Check at a local massage school to see if this type of class is offered.

TTouch

While it may seem similar to massage, TTouch is a different kind of therapy. Developed by animal expert Linda Tellington-Jones, it uses simple, circular movements of the hands over a dog's body with the purpose of activating cellular function. These touches cause changes in brain wave patterns that are different from those evoked by massage or petting. The effect of TTouch has been described as "turning on the electric lights of the body."

Benefits of TTouch include improved circulation, coordination, and general health. It has also been used to help restore function in dogs with both acute and chronic problems such as hip dysplasia, spondylosis, cruciate ligament damage, and arthritis. For dogs with emotional or behavioral problems, or that have suffered a physical trauma, TTouch can help reduce tension and induce calm. Anyone can learn to perform TTouch, and it's a great way to build a bond with your dog and help him with any health problems he may have. See Appendix A for more information on finding a TTouch practitioner or learning TTouch techniques.

Herbal Remedies

People have been using herbs and other plants for their healing properties for thousands of years. Many of today's drugs are derived from herbs, but some people believe the plant itself can be a more effective medicine than its pharmaceutical cousin. Herbs can act to tone or invigorate the body or to remove toxins from it. Among other things, certain herbal remedies have been found to hasten the healing process, build up the immune system, and inhibit tumor growth.

Types of Herbs

Traditions of herbal treatment are divided. Chinese herbal practitioners tend to use combinations of herbs to treat problems. Western herbal practitioners are more likely to use a single herb. Both methods can be effective. Among the herbs a holistic veterinarian may use are cranberry for urinary tract infections; garlic, which helps fight bacteria; ginger for nausea or motion sickness; milk thistle for liver disease; and raspberry tea or raspberry tablets to help ease delivery of puppies. Certain herbal preparations have a relaxing or tranquilizing effect. These include kava kava, Saint John's wort, and valerian root.

Using Herbs Safely

Although they might seem like gentle and harmless remedies, herbs are powerful stuff. Just like pharmaceutical drugs, they can have side effects. Used incorrectly, they can be toxic. Among the herbs or herbal oils that can be toxic to dogs are pennyroyal oil, tea tree oil, comfrey, and hops.

ALERT!

Because no quality control standards exist for herbal preparations, it's important to choose herbal products carefully. Buy from a manufacturer whose label states how the formula was prepared, the exact dose of herbs included, and provides an expiration date.

Give your dog herbal remedies only on the advice of your veterinarian. If he's not familiar with herbs, seek out a veterinary herbalist. Working with your veterinarian, the herbalist can determine whether the remedy you want to try is appropriate for your dog's condition and how it will interact with other medications your dog may be taking. For instance, some herbal remedies and cortisone drugs tend to counteract each other's effects.

Bach Flower Essences

Floral extracts known as Bach flower essences were developed for human use by an English doctor in the early twentieth century to help heal emotional imbalances. Today, they are often used to help dogs as well. The best known of these is called Rescue Remedy, which is frequently used to soothe dogs that have suffered a trauma or feel anxiety in certain situations such as riding in the car, staying at a boarding kennel, or visiting the veterinarian. Other flower essences that can benefit dogs include crab apple, which helps to purify wounds and is useful for dogs that lick themselves frequently; mimulus, for shy dogs or dogs that are fearful of loud noises; olive, for dogs that seem tired or lethargic; and walnut, for dogs that need help adjusting to a new place or situation.

Flower essences are among the herbal remedies that are safe and gentle, and they may certainly be an effective adjunct to your dog's health care. However, they should never be substituted for a proper veterinary diagnosis or necessary behavior modification. If your dog is lethargic for more than a day or two, you need to find out why, and if he's afraid of the noise made by thunderstorms or the vacuum cleaner, you can seek help from a behaviorist.

Homeopathy

The theory behind homeopathy is the belief that "like cures like." In other words, homeopaths believe that the substance that produces certain signs of illness can also be used in extremely diluted form to treat those same signs of illness. A substance that in a normal dose would cause vomiting, then, would be the basis for a homeopathic remedy to treat vomiting.

When they diagnose an illness, homeopathic veterinarians take into account not only a dog's physical symptoms but also the dog's personality or mental state. For instance, two dogs might have kidney disease, but one is thirsty all the time, has begun having accidents in the house, and seems withdrawn. The other has stopped drinking much water, urinates very little, and seems irritable. Although they have the same disease, each would receive a different homeopathic remedy based on their differing symptoms.

One well-known homeopathic remedy is arnica, which is useful for relieving pain from any kind of injury or surgery. It helps speed healing and reduces bruising. Look for arnica at health-food or pet-supply stores that carry natural products. Make sure you use the homeopathic version and not the herbal, which can be toxic. Use it as directed until you begin to see improvement.

Hypericum is another homeopathic remedy that can help with pain relief. It's usually prescribed for injuries that affect the nerves, such as contusions, lacerations, or punctures. As with arnica, use as directed and under the advice of a veterinarian. Also let your veterinarian know if you don't see any improvement after three doses.

Nutraceuticals

Nutraceuticals are foods or food products that are believed to positively affect health. These supplements have become popular with dog owners and veterinarians in recent years because of their usefulness in treating joint pain and skin problems as well as their general lack of side effects. Nutraceuticals are derived from plants and animals and include such substances as amino acids, antioxidants, essential fatty acids (EFAs), herbs, minerals, and vitamins. They're available in health-food stores, grocery stores, and pet-supply stores and are even found as ingredients in some dog foods and treats.

Nutraceuticals for Joint Pain

Translucent, elastic cartilage is a specialized connective tissue that's important in bone growth and joint formation. As dogs age, their cartilage starts to wear down. When this happens, exposed bones can rub together, causing pain. The result is osteoarthritis, which can affect any joint. Heavy use of the joints, such as in running, jumping, and twisting to catch a flying disc, as well as obesity, can all increase the risk that osteoarthritis will develop.

ALERT!

Nutraceuticals rarely have side effects, but occasionally a dog may vomit or have diarrhea. Other dogs may drink more water than usual or bleed longer than normal if they get a cut. If you see any of these side effects, simply reduce the amount you're giving and you should see an improvement.

It used to be thought that broken-down cartilage couldn't be repaired, but studies have shown that certain nutraceuticals can indeed help synthesize cartilage. This helps reduce the pain of arthritis and increases an arthritic dog's mobility. Nutraceuticals that have this function include glucosamine, chondroitin, and methyl sulfonyl methane (MSM).

- **Glucosamine** is an amino sugar that helps promote the formation and repair of cartilage. Shellfish such as mussels are the most common source of the glucosamine used in supplements.
- **Chondroitin** helps the joint retain water and elasticity and inhibit the enzymes that break down cartilage. Chondroitin is a component of cartilage that's manufactured by the body, but chondroitin supplements are usually obtained from cow cartilage.
- **MSM** is an organic source of sulfur. The body uses it to form connective tissue.

Studies in humans have shown that glucosamine and chondroitin are effective in relieving arthritis pain and stiffness, and these findings can also be applied to dogs.

Other nutraceuticals that may help reduce joint pain include vitamins C and E and the herb yucca. Nutraceuticals can be effective for mild cases of joint pain, but it may take a couple of months before you see any improvement. If you don't see any change after a couple of months of giving nutraceuticals, your dog's pain and stiffness may require a more powerful painkiller.

Nutraceuticals for Itchy Skin

Allergic skin diseases are common in dogs, and their itching can be painful to watch. They occur when offending antigens—pollen, mold, certain foods, fleas, chemicals, or other irritants—cause the skin's defensive mast cells to release inflammatory agents. Studies have shown that supplementation with omega-3 fatty acids (found in oils from cold-water fish) can help reduce this inflammatory response. You may see results as early as two weeks after starting supplementation, but more often it takes six to eight weeks for the effect to kick in.

Holistic Medicine

You may hear some veterinarians distinguish themselves as providing holistic treatment. Holistic medicine is not necessarily synonymous with alternative/complementary medicine. What it means is that the veterinarian is open to using alternative as well as conventional treatments. A holistic veterinarian doesn't look only at your dog's symptoms but asks about diet, the home environment, behavior, and anything else that might be affecting the dog's health. Looking at the big picture helps the holistic veterinarian arrive at a correct diagnosis and provide your dog with the most effective treatment, whether that is pharmaceuticals, surgery, an alternative/complementary treatment, or a combination of these.

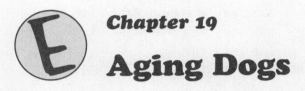

Chapter 19

Aging Dogs

The single drawback to loving a dog is his short life span. Depending on breed, diet, and overall health, the average dog lives to be about twelve years old. Giant breeds tend to have shorter life spans of eight to ten years, and toy breeds sometimes live into their late teens. Dogs in general are living longer, thanks to advances in nutrition and veterinary care. Some ways you can help ensure your dog a happy, healthy old age are to provide appropriate exercise, adjust his diet as needed, and take him for regular veterinary exams.

Signs of Old Age

We've probably all heard that seven years is the age that marks the beginning of the senior years for dogs. In reality, dogs are individuals and age at different rates, just like people. Lots of dogs are still going strong and looking young at age seven and beyond, while others do indeed live up to this stereotype. Signs that your dog may be getting old include the following:

- Graying of the muzzle and eyebrows
- A thinning coat
- A drop in energy level
- Weight gain or weight loss
- More frequent urination

Older dogs also tend to move more slowly because of stiff or painful joints. The lens of the eye becomes hazy, which is a normal part of aging, or is sometimes clouded with cataracts. Teeth become looser and more tartar-encrusted if good dental hygiene isn't practiced. You may notice that your older dog is less able to tolerate extremely hot or cold weather.

Preparing for the Senior Years

Regardless of whether your dog shows any signs of aging, it's a good idea to schedule a geriatric screening exam on that seventh birthday. The health values established at this exam—weight, dental health, blood chemistry, and so on—help you and your veterinarian establish a baseline for comparison as your dog ages. By screening for age-related health problems at this early stage, you're more likely to uncover health issues while they can still be dealt with easily.

The Geriatric Exam

Besides checking your dog for obvious physical signs of aging such as stiffness, heart murmurs, bad breath, and skin lesions, a complete geriatric exam includes blood work or other diagnostic tests. Blood work and a urinalysis are important to assess liver and kidney function, check for anemia or hidden infections, and otherwise assess body chemistry. If your young-at-heart dog suddenly starts acting old, it's definitely time to schedule a check-up. He may have a health problem that needs to be dealt with—fast!

FACT

Dogs age at a more rapid pace than humans. For every chronological year that passes, a dog ages the equivalent of five to seven years. This means that changes can occur more rapidly than you might realize.

As your dog starts showing his age, consider scheduling a veterinary exam every six months instead of once a year. He doesn't need a full work-up, but a physical exam and your veterinarian's trained and objective eye can catch things that you might otherwise not notice.

Good parasite control is also a must. The blood and nutrient loss caused by parasite infestation is more detrimental to an older dog's health than it might be to a dog in his prime. Keep your dog on an effective preventive for flea, tick, and intestinal parasites throughout his life.

Personality Changes

Besides physical changes, your dog may also exhibit various changes in the way he behaves. You may notice that he sleeps more and is less attentive to what's going on around him. His sense of smell may become less acute, leading to a reduced appetite. As he ages, it's more important than ever to provide your dog with a stable routine. This helps reduce stress, which is tougher on old dogs than young ones.

Nutrition

Just as puppies and canine athletes have special nutritional needs, so do older dogs. Because they're less active, they don't need as many calories to maintain a healthy weight. They do, however, need a high-quality protein food to make up for the digestive system's decreased ability to efficiently metabolize protein.

If your dog is doing well on his regular food, but you want to feed him less because he's gaining weight, add plain canned pumpkin (not the sweetened kind used in pies) to make up the difference. It's low in calories but high in fiber, so he'll feel full, and dogs like the taste.

The best food for an older dog contains about 25 percent protein and has a lower concentration of fat and calories than a regular dog food. Some diets formulated for older dogs—or for dogs that need to lose weight—are high in fiber, which helps reduce caloric density. A dog eating this type of diet will feel full, even though he's not getting as many calories.

Special-Needs Diets

Many health problems can be managed with the aid of a special diet. These include diabetes, epilepsy, inflammatory bowel disease and other digestive disorders, kidney disease, urinary tract problems, and some types of cancer. Some special diets contain ingredients that are believed to promote joint health, which can be beneficial for older dogs. At least one food marketed for older dogs contains antioxidants and other nutrients that may help fight the signs of brain aging or age-related behavioral changes. These types of foods are available only by prescription from your veterinarian. If your older dog has a health problem, it can't hurt to ask if a change in diet will help.

Supplements

Most veterinary nutritionists agree that a dog fed a complete and balanced diet doesn't need additional supplements. That's true in most cases, but when it comes to the aging dog, some supplements can be beneficial for certain conditions. For instance, dogs with reduced kidney function might need a B vitamin. The B vitamins are water soluble, meaning they aren't stored in the body. What isn't used is lost in the urine every day, so a dog that's urinating a lot because of kidney disease will need higher amounts of the B vitamins to replace what flows out with the urine. Another common problem of old age in dogs is dry, itchy skin. Adding vitamin E, zinc, or essential fatty acids to the diet may help. Ask your veterinarian if this type of supplementation could be helpful for your older dog.

Appetite Loss

Older dogs often begin to eat less. Their teeth might hurt or their sense of smell—which is linked to the ability to taste—might be reduced. Tartar buildup on teeth can cause pain, so consider taking your dog in for a veterinary cleaning if you notice lots of brown buildup on his teeth. You may be amazed when he starts acting like a puppy again because he's feeling so much better. If tartar buildup isn't the problem, try warming his food in the microwave before serving it. The heat increases the scent, making it easier for him to realize that there's a yummy meal sitting in front of him. (This works for dry food as well as canned.) Don't forget to test the food for hot spots with your finger before serving.

A study conducted over fourteen years concluded that dogs that ate a calorie-restricted diet lived a median 1.8 years longer than the average dog and were slower to develop chronic diseases such as osteoarthritis.

Be concerned if you try these tricks and your dog still doesn't have much of an appetite. He may have a hidden health problem, especially if he's rapidly losing weight. Take him to the veterinarian for a checkup.

Weight Gain or Loss

It's important to pay attention any time your dog suddenly starts gaining or losing weight. These can both be signs of an underlying health problem. Don't forget that what seems like a minor weight loss to you—say, a pound or two—is pretty significant for a small breed. That could be as much as 10 percent of his body weight.

If your dog is gaining weight, look at the amount of food you're giving him as well as the amount of exercise he gets. It's all too easy to slack off on walking or playing with an older dog, especially if he doesn't seem interested himself. If you're still feeding him the same amount he was getting when he was younger and more active, well, it's no wonder he's putting on weight. Unexplained weight gain can also be related to certain health conditions, such as hypothyroidism.

Unexplained or rapid weight loss can also signal health problems. For instance, if your dog eats ravenously but still loses weight, he may have diabetes. Picking up food and then dropping it can mean that your dog's teeth hurt. Weight loss can also be an early, subtle sign of cancer. Whether your dog is gaining or losing weight, take him to the veterinarian to rule out any health problems.

Age-Related Health Problems

There's no getting around it. No matter how well you take care of him, your dog will at some point begin to suffer the aches and pains and disorders of old age. In dogs, these can include arthritis, cancer, cognitive dysfunction syndrome (senility), congestive heart failure, dental disease, diabetes, hearing loss, hypothyroidism, kidney disease, and vision loss. While this litany of potential problems may sound depressing, the good news is that veterinarians now have more and better ways of treating them, especially when they're caught early. There's no reason why your dog can't have a long and comfortable old age.

Arthritis

At last count, more than 8 million dogs in the United States had been diagnosed with this painful degenerative joint disease, and more than 80 percent of them were seven years or older. Dogs with arthritis usually show the following signs:

- Stiffness when getting up or lying down
- Lowered activity level
- Reluctance to walk very far or to climb stairs
- Flinching or snapping when touched
- Swollen joints that seem hot or painful

Arthritis doesn't have a cure, but a number of medications are available to relieve the pain of those achy-breaky joints.

Medications for Arthritis

Your veterinarian can prescribe a nonsteroidal anti-inflammatory drug (NSAID) to relieve pain and inflammation. These drugs are similar to the ibuprofen or acetaminophen you might take for yourself, but they're formulated specifically for dogs. In fact, your ibuprofen or other NSAID can be toxic to your dog, so never give him anything like that without your veterinarian's okay. Canine NSAIDs are generally safe, but they can have side effects—vomiting, diarrhea, and liver or kidney damage—and some dogs (Labs in particular) are highly sensitive to them. Your veterinarian may need to adjust the dose or try a different drug if your dog develops these problems, and she will probably require periodic blood work to check liver and kidney values before renewing a prescription. Nutraceuticals (discussed in Chapter 18) can also help.

Other Ways to Relieve Arthritis Pain

If you have a small dog, lift him on and off furniture throughout his life, but especially as he gets older. This helps prevent cumulative damage to the joint. Keep your dog's weight at a healthy level to reduce stress on the joints. And consider providing your dog with a heated bed. Warmth is one of the best ways to relieve joint pain.

Cancer

Cancer is the word used to describe any malignant tumor. Malignant means that the tumor is capable of spreading and invading other tissues. Cancer occurs when cells grow uncontrollably on or inside the body. The risk of cancer increases with age, and common cancers seen in dogs include mammary (breast) tumors, skin tumors, testicular tumors (in unneutered males), mouth cancer, and lymphoma. Be concerned about cancer if your dog shows any of the following signs:

- Lumps that don't go away or that grow larger
- Sores that don't heal
- Unusual or excessive weight loss
- Lack of appetite for more than a day or two
- Bleeding or discharge from any body opening
- Difficulty eating or swallowing
- Unexplained lack of energy

Cancer is generally diagnosed with a biopsy, the removal and study of a section of tissue. Other diagnostic techniques your veterinarian may use are blood work and X rays.

Breast Cancer

Mammary tumors are the most common type of cancer in female dogs and are most often seen in older unspayed females. The tumors can be removed surgically, and your dog may also benefit from chemotherapy afterward. The best way to prevent or greatly reduce the risk of mammary cancer is to spay a female before her first heat cycle.

Skin Cancer

It's not unusual for older dogs to develop lumps and bumps on or beneath their skin. Generally these growths are harmless, but it's a good idea to have your veterinarian take a look at them to be sure. Always take your dog in for a checkup if a growth becomes larger or changes color.

Harmless but unsightly growths such as cysts, papillomas (warts), adenomas, and lipomas can be removed surgically. You might also want to do this if a growth is impeding your dog's movement.

Mast cell tumors are a common type of malignant skin cancer. They can develop anywhere on or in the body and resemble raised, nodular masses.

Mast cell tumors may feel solid or soft when touched. Most commonly, they develop in dogs that are eight to ten years old, although they can occur at any age. The best treatment is surgical removal, sometimes followed by radiation therapy to kill any remaining tumor cells. In advanced stages of the disease, chemotherapy may be helpful.

Testicular Cancer

Testicular tumors usually develop in male dogs that are at least ten years old, but they have occurred in dogs as young as three. Dogs with retained testicles (which remain up inside the body) are most likely to develop testicular cancer. Testicular cancer is treated surgically, followed by chemotherapy or radiation if the tumor has spread. Neutered dogs do not get testicular cancer.

Mouth Cancer

The most common mouth (oral) cancer in dogs is malignant melanoma. One out of every twenty canine cancer diagnoses is for this disease. Malignant melanoma is highly aggressive, so catching it early is important. That's just one of the many good reasons for brushing your dog's teeth on a regular basis—you're more likely to spot the signs of this disease, which include a mass on the gums, bleeding gums, bad breath, or difficulty eating.

QUESTION?

Will my dog lose his hair and become nauseous if he has chemotherapy?
Luckily for dogs, they don't suffer the same side effects from chemotherapy that people do. You may notice, however, that he's tired for a few days after each treatment.

Oral cancers are diagnosed using biopsies and X rays. They're treated surgically and may require a follow-up treatment of radiation therapy. A potential new approach to treating malignant melanoma is a DNA-based vaccine that's being studied at New York City's Animal Medical Center.

Lymphoma

If your dog has an unusual swelling or enlargement in the lower neck area, he may have lymphoma, a tumor of the blood-forming system. An examination by your veterinarian may show that all the body's lymph nodes are enlarged. Blood work, a biopsy, and chest and abdominal X rays may all be necessary to confirm the diagnosis and determine where the tumor is located and how large it is. Lymphoma usually responds well to chemotherapy.

Canine Senility

More formally known as cognitive dysfunction syndrome (CDS), senility can be described as an age-related mental decline that's not caused by hearing or vision loss, organ failure, or cancer. Dogs that are senile generally show it by wandering aimlessly, acting confused or disoriented, staring into space, changing their activity or sleep habits, or withdrawing from family members. Dogs can show signs of CDS as early as eight years of age.

Like any medication, the drug that helps with senility can have side effects. These include vomiting, diarrhea, hyperactivity, or restlessness. If you note these problems, tell your veterinarian so he can adjust the dose or recommend other changes that may help.

If you think your dog has CDS, don't assume nothing can be done. Take him to the veterinarian for a definitive diagnosis, first, to rule out health problems that can mimic CDS. These include kidney, thyroid, or adrenal gland disease. Then ask your veterinarian about medication that can help. You may also want to give your dog choline supplements, which are believed to help increase mental alertness. You can find choline supplements for dogs at holistic veterinary clinics, pet supply stores, online pet supply stores, and health food stores.

Congestive Heart Failure

When the heart is too weak to adequately pump blood, fluid accumulates in the lungs, causing a condition known as congestive heart failure (CHF). Your dog may have CHF if he coughs frequently, has trouble breathing, seems restless at night, or tires easily after mild exercise. It's most common in old, overweight dogs. There's no cure for CHF, but it can be managed for a time with diet, medication, and rest. Weight loss helps, too.

Dental Disease

Most older dogs develop some level of dental disease, especially if they are toy breeds with a mouth full of crowded teeth. It is, however, one of the easiest problems of old age to prevent—simply by brushing your dog's teeth daily. If you need more of an incentive, good dental health is related to overall health. When dental disease goes untreated, the mouth becomes a breeding ground for bacteria, which then enter the bloodstream and go throughout the body.

That said, some dogs just plain have bad teeth and will develop plaque and tartar no matter how much you brush. Take them in for veterinary cleanings annually to keep their mouth in good shape.

Diabetes

Diabetes is a common problem in older dogs, especially if they're overweight or have a genetic predisposition to the disease, as some breeds do. It's a disorder of the pancreas gland and develops when the pancreas doesn't produce enough insulin—the substance the body uses to drive glucose, or blood sugar, into the cells—or stops producing insulin altogether. When this happens, glucose levels build up in the blood stream instead of being used for energy. The term diabetes mellitus comes from the Greek and means "sugar sickness."

Diagnosing Diabetes

Your dog may have diabetes if he suddenly seems thirsty all the time and starts needing to urinate much more often as a consequence of drinking so much water. He may even have accidents in the house. Dogs with diabetes often have a ravenous appetite, but they lose weight despite eating everything they can find. If the disease goes long enough without a diagnosis, they may even go blind. If your dog shows any of these signs, take him in for blood work and a urinalysis. Among the breeds that have a tendency for diabetes are golden and Labrador retrievers, German shepherd dogs, keeshonds, poodles, and pugs.

Managing Diabetes

There's no cure for diabetes, but it can be managed with daily insulin injections and diet. Establishing the amount of insulin your dog needs daily will require some trial and error. Some dogs can get by with one insulin shot daily, while others need two. Your veterinarian can show you how to give the injection, and with a little practice it's quite easy—even if you don't like needles. Most dogs don't seem to mind the injection, especially if you give them a treat or a meal immediately afterward. The best diet for dogs with diabetes contains good quality protein and some extra fiber to stabilize blood sugar levels. Such diets can be prepared at home, but your veterinarian may prefer to prescribe a commercial diabetes diet for your dog. Home cooking is not always consistent and can make it more difficult to regulate your dog's insulin needs. Weight loss through exercise and diet is also important in managing the disease. Your dog will need periodic blood work to assess how well the disease is being managed.

Hearing Loss

Don't assume that your old dog is ignoring you when you call him to come and he doesn't respond. He may not be able to hear you. As dogs age, they experience degenerative changes in the inner ear and a stiffening of the eardrum. As a result, their hearing becomes less acute.

Diagnosing Deafness

If you suspect that your dog isn't hearing so well anymore, try this test. Walk up behind him and make a noise by clapping your hands or dropping your keys. If he doesn't jump up and whirl around in response, he may well have suffered partial or total hearing loss. Your veterinarian can confirm the diagnosis of deafness and make sure that it's not caused by a treatable condition such as an ear infection or neurologic disease.

Living with a Deaf Dog

Some simple adjustments can help you communicate just fine with your deaf dog. To let him know you're behind him, stomp your foot. He'll feel the vibrations and know where you are.

Make use of the hand signals you learned in obedience class. Many dogs respond better to hand signals than to verbal commands anyway. As for a dog that is partially or totally deaf, he'll simply make more use of his senses of sight and smell.

Finally, you may want to consider acquiring a canine hearing aid for your dog. Yes, they're available. If you have pet health insurance, check to see if your plan covers hearing aids, which cost about $400. Keep in mind, however, that dog hearing aids can fall out easily, so they may become lost.

If your dog is still a puppy as you're reading this, start teaching him hand signals now. They'll come in handy, so to speak, throughout his life. Two basic hand signals are a rising hand for sit and a raised hand, palm out, for wait or stay.

Hypothyroidism

The prefix hypo means less, so hypothyroidism is a decrease in thyroid function. It's the most common hormonal disorder seen in dogs and usually develops in dogs that are middle-aged or older. If your dog's level of thyroid hormones falls below normal, you'll see such signs as rough, scaly skin or skin infections; hair loss on both sides of the body or the rear end; and weight gain for no apparent reason. To diagnose hypothyroidism, your veterinarian will run blood work to check the levels of circulating thyroid hormones (T3 and T4).

Hypothyroidism is managed with a daily dose of synthetic thyroid hormone, which is available in the form of a chewable tablet. The amount your dog needs depends on how much he weighs. Your veterinarian will recommend blood work every six months to make sure the dose doesn't need to be adjusted.

Kidney Disease

Kidney disease is one of the most common problems in old dogs, second only to cancer. As the kidneys age, they become less efficient at removing waste products from the body, causing waste to build up instead of being eliminated with urine. Clearly, it's not good to have toxins remaining in the body, but until recently it wasn't possible to identify the problem until 75 percent of the kidney's function was destroyed. Today, however, a new screening test allows veterinarians to identify kidney disease in the early stages, when it's still possible to manage it with a special low-protein diet that won't overwork the kidneys. Your dog can live significantly longer if kidney disease is caught and managed early—another good reason for regular screening exams.

Although a low-protein diet is appropriate for dogs with kidney disease, it's not necessary to restrict protein for all older dogs. Your healthy older dog needs high-quality protein to stay in good condition.

Vision Loss

Common vision problems in aging dogs are nuclear sclerosis and cataracts. If the center of your dog's eye lens appears hazy or gray, he has nuclear sclerosis—a normal part of the eye's aging process. Nuclear sclerosis is caused by the formation of new fibers at the edge of the lens. These fibers push inward toward the center. Nuclear sclerosis isn't painful and it won't greatly affect your dog's vision, although he may have a little trouble focusing on objects close-up.

FACT

Cataracts can sometimes be removed surgically, but if that's not possible, you can help your dog navigate his surroundings by scenting furniture and other objects at his nose level. Be sure to test an inconspicuous area first to make sure that the perfume or other scent you use doesn't harm the finish.

Acquired cataracts—as opposed to juvenile cataracts, which are congenital or hereditary—are generally a consequence of aging or a side effect of diabetes. Cataracts cause the lens to become opaque, starting at the center of the lens and spreading outward, gradually decreasing the vision. Fortunately, dogs that are blind or have limited vision can get around quite well using their senses of smell and hearing. You can also learn to communicate with them using a whistle. Consult a trainer for advice on how to do this.

Keeping Your Old Dog Comfortable

When you notice that your older dog is becoming a little stiff and creaky—or even before he reaches that stage—take steps to help him stay comfortable. Here are some ways to do that:

- Put soft bedding in his favorite places so he always has a comfy place to rest.
- Get him a heated bed; the warmth will soothe old bones and painful joints.
- Lift him on and off furniture to protect his joints.
- Provide a ramp up to the bed, sofa, or car so he doesn't have to jump up.
- Install a dog door so he can go potty outside as often as necessary, or take him out more often.

- Keep a thin-coated dog warm during winter with a sweater, as old dogs are more sensitive to temperature extremes.
- Take him on short, easy walks every day to keep his blood flowing and his joints moving.
- Brush his teeth and schedule regular veterinary cleanings.
- Check him for lumps, bumps, or sores as you groom him.

All of these efforts will help ensure that your dog's golden years are happy and comfortable. Your dog will love you even more for it.

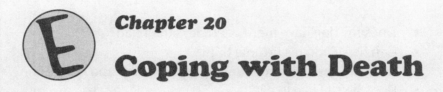

Chapter 20

Coping with Death

Choosing to euthanize an old or sick dog is the most difficult decision you will ever make as a dog owner. It's also the most loving. When your dog is no longer able to enjoy life, you can give him a peaceful release from pain. Because you know your dog best, this is a decision only you can make, but consulting your veterinarian and other family members will help. In this chapter, you'll find advice on how to know when the time is right as well as information on the euthanasia procedure, what to do with your dog's body, and how to cope during the grieving process.

Deciding on Euthanasia

It's never easy to know when the time is right to let your dog go. It can help to look at his overall quality of life. This means honestly evaluating his appetite, attitude, activity level, comfort, elimination habits, and interaction with people, especially family members. Ask yourself the following questions:

- Does my dog have more good days than bad?
- Can he still do his favorite things?
- Is he still capable of controlling his urination and defecation?
- Does he still like to eat?
- Does he act as if he's in pain more often than not?
- Does he still enjoy being petted and talked to?

If you answer no to the majority of these questions, it's time to talk to your veterinarian about euthanasia. Although it's difficult to face, sometimes a dog is so sick or old or severely injured that he will never recover normal health. When this is the case, the kindest thing you can do is to give him a quiet, humane death.

Talking to Family Members

Your spouse is probably aware of the same things you are regarding your dog's condition, but if he or she is especially close to the dog, it's easy to overlook or ignore the painful truth. Gently bring up the subject and discuss the questions above. If your spouse loves the dog, he or she won't want him to suffer.

Sometimes finances are a concern. Life-saving treatments or long-term medical care can be an economic burden. You need to discuss honestly and openly whether your budget can bear the strain. You may be able to meet the cost by making certain sacrifices, such as giving up meals out or cutting back in other ways, but that's not always possible.

If you have children, it's important to involve them in the decision. Even if they aren't old enough to fully understand all the implications, you can still explain to them that your dog is very sick and the veterinarian can't make him better this time. It helps to let them talk it out. Give honest, simple answers to their questions. Avoid using the phrase "putting the dog to sleep." This can frighten young children and make them afraid to go to bed at night.

Talking to Your Veterinarian

Your veterinarian loves animals. That's why she's in this field, after all. There's no one better to understand what you're feeling and the difficulty of the decision you're facing. It's hard for a veterinarian to euthanize a favorite patient, so don't worry that you're wasting her time with your questions and concerns. Although she can't make the decision for you, your veterinarian can help guide you by fully explaining your dog's condition, his chances for recovery, and his long-term prognosis. Armed with this information, you can make the decision that's right for you and your dog.

The Euthanasia Procedure

If you decide that euthanasia must be your next step, it will help to understand what's going to happen. The word euthanasia means "easy death." It's accomplished by injecting your dog with a drug, usually an overdose of barbiturates, that brings a quick and painless death by causing the heart to stop.

Take Time for Farewells

Sometimes you will have a day or two between the time you decide to euthanize your dog and the actual procedure. Whether he's at home or hospitalized, take this opportunity to spend some special time with your dog, gently petting him and telling him how special he is to you. If he's at home, make sure he's extra comfortable until you can get him to the veterinarian. Let him have a favorite food, such as ice cream or steak. Suggest that your children draw a picture of him as a way of remembering him after he's gone.

This is also a time to decide how you want to dispose of your dog's body. Your veterinarian can tell you what options are available through her office. Burial and cremation are just two of the possibilities you may consider.

At the Veterinarian's Office

Your veterinarian may suggest that you bring your dog in early or late in the day so you don't have to face a lot of other people. Whatever time works best for you will be fine, though. The staff will have you bring your dog into an exam room, or they may have a special room set aside for this purpose. If you have a large dog, don't hesitate to ask for help bringing him in.

Be aware that death sometimes causes the limbs to move or the dog to urinate. This doesn't mean that your dog is in pain or is still alive. It's simply a reflex action, but it can be disturbing for some people.

Your veterinarian will give you time to say your final farewells. Take as much time as you need. Although you'll probably cry, try not to scare your dog. He'll sense your distress, and you want this to be a peaceful time for him. Your veterinarian may also give him a tranquilizer to help him relax. When you're ready, the veterinarian or a technician will shave your dog's leg and insert an intravenous catheter. Then she'll inject the drug, and death will come very quickly. You may want to avoid looking at your dog's eyes as the drug is injected. It's very sad to see the light of life disappear from them. For many people though, there is a brief instant of profound peace before that light disappears which helps as reassurance that you have made the right decision.

What to Do with the Body

For thousands of years, people have accorded dogs the same rites of death they had for themselves. Dogs have been found in graves buried with people, and the Egyptians mummified dogs so they would be with them in the afterlife. Your dog can be cremated or buried in a pet cemetery or, sometimes, on your own property. There are other alternatives as well, including having your dog's ashes transformed into a diamond.

Burial

Evidence of ritualized burial dates to the Paleolithic period, the earliest stage of human development. Dog remains have been found at human burial sites, sometimes in the same grave. One burial site found in northern Israel dating to 12,000 years ago featured an elderly man cradling a dog in his left arm. Such burials may have been performed to ensure that the person had a guardian or companion in the afterlife or simply as a reflection of a special bond between the two.

FACT

The dog-headed god Anubis ruled over the Egyptian afterlife. Anubis was black and had prick ears and a long, pointed muzzle. The Egyptian city of Hardai, called the City of Dogs—Cynopolis by the Greeks—was the center of Anubis worship.

Egypt, of course, is probably best known for its ritualized burial practices. Although cats are most commonly associated with the Egyptians, they prized dogs as well. Pet burial sites for dogs and cats dating back 3,000 years were located along the Nile. Pets were also interred in the tombs of their owners and were just as elaborately mummified as the humans with whom they were buried. One pharaoh ordered that fine cloth, incense, and scented oil be used in the mummification of his favorite guard dog.

Pet burial lost favor over the centuries and wasn't resurrected, so to speak, until the time of Queen Victoria, who was a great animal lover. The grounds of Windsor Castle served as a cemetery for any number of her favorite animals, including many dogs, which were immortalized with life-size bronze statues. Of course, not everyone had an estate on which they could bury their dogs, and there were rules against burying pets in human cemeteries, so this led to animals being tossed out with the trash or thrown into the nearest river. This was unacceptable to the animal-loving Victorians and became the impetus for the establishment of the first public pet cemeteries.

Pet Cemeteries

Among the first pet cemeteries of the modern era were Asnieres, near Paris, and Hartsdale Canine Cemetery, in New York, founded in 1896, the oldest pet cemetery in the United States. Today, there are more than 600 pet cemeteries in the United States. The largest U.S. pet cemetery is Bide-a-Wee Home Association, located in New York.

FACT

Los Angeles National Cemetery, operated by the Veterans Administration, has two dogs interred on its grounds, a practice that's now prohibited. One is Old Bonus, adopted by residents of the soldiers' home, and the other is Blackout, a war dog wounded in the Pacific during World War II.

You can find a pet cemetery in your area by contacting the International Association of Pet Cemeteries (see Appendix A). Choose a cemetery that's located on land owned by the proprietors or the cemetery corporation. Check to see that the cemetery is deeded to prevent future land development or other non-cemetery use of the property. The cemetery should also maintain a care fund to ensure that funds will be available for maintenance of the grounds.

Most pet cemeteries have a transport service and will pick up your dog's body from your home or from your veterinarian's office. They offer cremation or burial and can work with you to choose an urn, headstone, and burial site. The costs for cemetery burial vary. You can choose communal burial, communal cremation, or individual burial or cremation. Communal cremation is the least expensive option, and your dog will be cremated at the same time as other animals. Communal burial is less expensive than individual burial, and your dog will share a grave with other animals. This is a common choice, according to the IAPC. Individual cremation allows you to have his ashes buried, stored at the cemetery in what's called a columbarium, scattered in a favorite spot, or kept at home in an urn. With individual burial you can visit your dog's grave whenever you like, but it's the most expensive option, especially in areas where land is scarce. If for some reason you aren't able to bury or cremate your dog in any of these ways, you can still purchase a memorial plaque at the cemetery, have a flowering tree planted, or place memorial statuary or a bench at the cemetery to provide a place where you and your family can visit and remember your special dog.

Home Burial

You may prefer to bury your dog at home. Certainly that's less expensive than commercial burial or cremation, and it allows you to visit your dog's resting place at any time, but it does have some drawbacks. Unless you plan to be in the same home for the rest of your life, you'll have to leave your dog's body behind when you move. And the people who buy your home might not appreciate having him there. You must also consider local or county ordinances or state laws that regulate pet burial. Health hazards are associated with burying pets in a yard, primarily the concern that other animals may try to dig them up. Your veterinarian or the local pet cemetery may be able to advise you on the legalities, or you can check with your municipal government. Home burial is most commonly permitted in rural and some suburban areas.

The loss of a pet often brings feelings of guilt and depression. If you find yourself crying frequently, feel as if there are knots in your stomach or a constant lump in your throat, and have no energy for day-to-day tasks, you may want to seek counseling for your depression.

If you bury your dog at home, place him in a nonbiodegradable container. You can purchase a wooden casket from a pet cemetery or use some other wood or metal container. Before you put the body in the casket, place it in a heavy-duty plastic bag. Bury the receptacle at least three feet deep. This helps prevent other animals from being attracted by the scent and digging up the grave. You can plant a tree, some perennial flowers (which bloom year after year), or another favorite plant at the site, or you can mark it with a plaque or headstone.

Cremation

Like burial, cremation—the burning of a dead body—is a death rite that has a long history. The practice of cremation dates to the Bronze Age, some 5,000 years ago. Fire was seen as a purifying agent, or perhaps as a way to light the path of the deceased to the afterlife. More practically, it prevented bodies from being scavenged by animals and didn't require the use of land that could be put to more productive use.

The Cremation Process

Cremation no longer involves actual flames. The body is exposed to intense heat, which reduces it to ashes. Pet cemeteries often maintain their own crematoriums. You can choose individual or communal cremation. Most pet cemeteries can also arrange for you to view the cremation. This helps bring about closure and assures you that you are indeed receiving the ashes of your own dog.

Ashes to Ashes

The remains—referred to as cremains—can be returned to you as early as the same day, sometimes accompanied by a certificate of cremation. You can store the ashes in an urn and have them placed in a columbarium at the cemetery, keep them at home in a pretty urn or box, or scatter them at your dog's favorite place. When your dog is cremated with other animals (communal cremation), his ashes are usually scattered in the cemetery's memorial garden.

Other Options

Although not common, the alternatives to burial or cremation include taxidermy, mummification, and diamond creation. Taxidermy and freeze-drying preserve a dog's lifelike appearance. They can be expensive, however, and some taxidermists do not work on dogs or other pets. You must also remember that taxidermy and freeze-drying preserve your dog as she was at death—not in her peak condition. A Utah-based company called Summum offers mummification for pets (and people), wrapping them in fine linens bathed with fragrant herbs, oils, and resins. The process takes two to four months, and the animal is returned encased in a bronze mummiform. The cost is high, ranging from $6,000 to more than $100,000, depending on the animal's size and the amount of custom work done for the bronze statuary. The newest alternative is having your dog's cremains turned into a diamond. A company called LifeGem extracts the carbon from cremains and heats it to extremely high temperatures under special conditions. The process converts the carbon to graphite, which is then placed in a diamond press where it's subjected to extreme heat and pressure, forming a rough diamond crystal. It's then faceted by diamond cutters to your specifications and certified for authenticity. The entire process takes about four and a half months. You can have the resulting gem set in a ring, necklace, or other piece of jewelry. The price depends on the carat size you choose and ranges from $2,500 to $14,000.

Dealing with Grief

Grief and sorrow are normal feelings after the loss of a dog. People often feel embarrassed about grieving for a dog, but the loss of any special relationship is devastating, especially if it's one that has lasted many years. Never be ashamed of crying or otherwise expressing sorrow over your loss. Your dog was your friend, and your feelings are natural and healthy.

Stages of Grief

Everyone experiences and expresses grief differently. You may cry, feel depressed, blame yourself because you couldn't do more or didn't recognize a problem soon enough, or even become angry. These are all normal reactions.

Don't be surprised if you find yourself bursting into tears for days or even weeks after your dog's death. It's not something you can control—unless you just want to walk around with a big lump in your throat all the time. Let yourself cry. It's part of the healing process. Your true friends and anyone who loves animals will understand. Unfortunately, not everyone does understand the hurt that comes from the loss of a beloved dog. They may not recognize the intensity of your feelings or the depth of your loss. If you're faced with someone who's unsupportive, don't waste your energy arguing with them or trying to justify your feelings. Just think to yourself how sad it is that they've never experienced such a special relationship.

There's no normal amount of time for grieving. Some people grieve for months, while others recover fairly quickly. Experiencing grief is a normal, natural response to any death. Never denigrate anyone else's response to a pet's death.

Sometimes anger is a part of the grieving process. You may feel angry at yourself, your family, your veterinarian, or even your dog for leaving you. While it's not wrong to feel angry, it is important to realize that you may say things in the heat of the moment that you'll regret later. Bite your tongue, count to ten, or write it down and then burn it instead. All of these tactics can help you refrain from saying something hurtful that you don't really mean.

A Child's Grief

Young children up to the age of five tend to have what is called magical thinking. They're still not quite clear on the differences between reality and make-believe. Give them concrete explanations about your dog's death, such as "Casey is dead. That means he's not barking, he's not playing, he's not wagging his tail. Now that he's dead, he can't ever come back to see us, but we can always remember him."

Children are more open about expressing their feelings than adults, and this can be helpful when it comes to dealing with grief. Assure your child that your dog died without pain and now doesn't hurt anymore. Encourage her to write a story about the dog or draw a picture of him. Writing and art are good therapy!

Rituals are important to older children. Let them help pick out where to bury your dog or choose a photo to have framed. They might also want to lead the family on a walk to all of your dog's old favorite places.

Grief Counseling

It can help to talk through your feelings about your dog's death. Dog-loving friends will understand, but if you have deep feelings of grief you may find it useful to speak to someone who's trained to understand the grief process. This can be a grief counselor, clergyman, social worker, or psychologist. Many communities have pet loss support groups or hotlines (see Appendix A). Sharing your feelings with other people who understand what you're going through is often the best way to let go of the sadness while still remembering all the special things about your dog. While you will always miss him, the grieving process helps you come to terms with your dog's death and accept that he's gone. It's painful to go through, but eventually you will be able to think about the good times with a smile.

Memorializing Your Dog

Doing something good for other dogs, or establishing a ritual to remember your dog may help to ease your grief. These can include making a donation in your dog's name to a shelter or to support veterinary research into canine health problems; lighting a candle; planting a tree or flowers in your garden; or making a scrapbook or photo album. Making a donation is a concrete way of ensuring that your dog's life stands for something. Lighting a candle on the anniversary of his birth or death, or choosing a specific day (such as November 1, which is celebrated as All Saints Day or Day of the Dead in some cultures) to remember all past pets helps focus your attention on memories of your dog. A plant or a photo album provides a visual reminder of the good times. And when you are ready, you'll get another dog. He'll never replace your previous dog, but your heart and mind are big enough for an infinite number of special dogs.

Appendix A
Resources and Web Sites

Health-Related Organizations

American Animal Hospital Association
12575 W. Bayaud Ave.
Lakewood, CO 80228
303-986-2800
✍www.aahanet.org

**American Kennel Club Canine Health
Foundation**
251 W. Garfield Rd., Ste. 160
Aurora, OH 44202-8856
888-682-9696
✍www.akcchf.org

ASPCA Animal Poison Control Center
1717 S. Philo, Ste. 36
Urbana, IL 61802
888-426-4435
✍www.napcc.aspca.org

American Veterinary Chiropractic Association
P.O. Box 249
Port Byron, IL 61275
309-523-3995

American Veterinary Medical Foundation
1931 N. Meacham Road, Suite 100
Schaumburg, IL 60173
800-248-2862, ext. 6689
✍www.avmf.org

Canine Eye Registry Foundation
Purdue University—CERF/Lynn Hall
625 Harrison St.
West Lafayette, IN 47907-2026
765-494-8179
✍www.vmdb.org

Morris Animal Foundation
45 Inverness Dr. E.
Englewood, CO 80112-5480
800-243-2345
✍www.morrisanimalfoundation.org

Orthopedic Foundation for Animals
2300 E. Nifong Blvd.
Columbia, MO 65201
573-442-0418
✍www.offa.org

PetCare Insurance
3315 E. Algonquin Rd., Ste. 450
Rolling Meadows, IL 60008
866-275-7387
✍*www.petcareinsurance.com*

Tellington Touch (TTouch)
✍*http://tteam-ttouch.com*

Veterinary Botanical Medicine Association
✍*www.vbma.org*

Veterinary Pet Insurance
P.O. Box 2344
Brea, CA 92822-2344
800-872-7387
✍*www.petinsurance.com*

Pet Loss and Bereavement

International Association of Pet Cemeteries
P.O. Box 163, 5055 Route 11
Ellenburg Depot, NY 12935
518-594-3000
✍*www.iaopc.com*

Pet Loss Support Page
✍*www.pet-loss.net*

Appendix B
Frequently Asked Questions and Vet Answers

Q. Will spaying or neutering change my dog?

A. Yes, but mostly for the better! Dogs that are spayed or neutered won't contribute to the pet overpopulation problem. The risks of mammary cancer are greatly reduced, and your dog will be free from uterine or testicular cancers. Dogs that are spayed or neutered are more likely to be happy staying at home, less likely to fight, and less likely to mark with their urine.

Q. Why is preventive care stressed?

A. Preventive care is important for many reasons. Your dog will be healthier if you prevent problems such as parasites and infectious diseases. Your checkbook will be healthier as some problems will be totally prevented and any others will be caught early on when treatments tend to be more successful and less expensive.

Q. What concerns should I have before breeding my female dog?

A. Only dogs that are top notch, healthy, good examples of their breed should be bred. Your dog should have passed all health screenings for her breed, have been evaluated by knowledgeable judges or breeders, and have a sound temperament. Be prepared to spend a great deal of time and money producing a litter, and realize your dog will be at risk for surgery (C-section) or even death. Have good homes screened and ready ahead of time and be prepared to take any puppies back—even ten years from now!

Q. How often will my dog come into heat?

A. There is a wide range of normal heat cycles in dogs. Some breeds only cycle once yearly, while others cycle every four months. Check with your breeder for the cycle history of your dog's dam. Many dogs follow their mother's schedule.

Q. I want the biggest, rowdiest puppy. Why is that not a good idea?

A. While the biggest puppy may grow up just fine, often the big puppies are at higher risk for orthopedic problems. The rowdiest puppy may end up being more dog temperament-wise than the average family wants to deal with. Look for the middle-of-the-road pup as a good family pet.

Q. What should I feed my puppy and how much?

A. Initially, your puppy should get whatever food the breeder was using. You may want to change over to a different food that you and your veterinarian feel would also be appropriate, but do so gradually. The amounts listed on dog food packaging are just guidelines—you need to adjust the amount to your specific pup and her lifestyle and activity level.

Q. Our family has health insurance. Why can't I get health insurance for my puppy?

A. Actually, health insurance *is* available for pets. As with your own insurance, you need to look carefully at the different companies and decide what plan makes sense for you. Some plans cover routine care as well as emergencies, while others are just for serious emergencies and medical illnesses. See Appendix A for resources.

Q. How often do I need to bathe my dog?

A. The number of baths your dog needs varies greatly with his coat type and length and his favorite activities. Shorthaired dogs may need baths to wash off mud and dirt. Longhaired dogs may need baths to help remove dirt and clean the hair. If your dog is groomed on a regular basis, he will need fewer baths. Some dogs with skin problems need frequent baths to keep their skin healthy. Check with your breeder, veterinarian, and groomer about suitable shampoos for your dog.

Q. Why does my dog need to go to the veterinarian every year even if she doesn't need any vaccines?

A. Just like us, it is important for your dog to have an annual physical (more often for older dogs or dogs with chronic health problems.) At this exam, your veterinarian will check for parasites, discuss your dog's diet and weight with you, and look for any early signs of health problems. Catching problems early means faster and often less expensive treatment.

Q. Which bones in my dog's leg are the same as my wrist? And my ankle?

A. Your dog's front legs are just like our arms. Our forearm comes down from the elbow and the next "bendable" area is the carpus, or wrist. Your dog's hind leg is similar to our legs. His hock, or tarsus (the joint that projects backward above the foot), is the same as your ankle.

Q. What is the difference between a tendon and a ligament?

A. Ligaments hold bones to bones, while tendons attach muscles to bones. Both are tough, fibrous connective tissues.

Q. Why does my dog cough if she has a heart problem, not a lung problem?

A. The heart and lungs work very closely together. If your dog has a heart problem that allows fluid to back up in the lungs, she will cough. That cough will not respond to cough medicines but is controlled by diuretics and heart medications.

Q. My dog's urine looks red in the snow. Should I be concerned?

A. Yes! Normal urine should show up yellow on snow. Red urine is a sign of blood or other pigmented substances like myoglobin (a muscle pigment). Neither of these is normal in urine.

Q. I have a busy work schedule, so I just leave a big bowl of food down all the time for my dog. Is that okay?

A. Leaving a bowl of food down all the time is not the best way to feed your dog. Food can spoil. Also, your dog may overeat, and you won't be able to tell how much he does eat every day. You could miss signs of illness such as a decreased appetite. It is more difficult to housebreak a puppy when fed like this as well.

Q. My dog loves to beg snacks from me. Can she have extra treats?

A. Many of our snacks are not the healthiest of foods. Giving your dog salty, fatty, or very sugary treats is not in her best interests. It would be better to keep a small bowl of her treats or food available to give her snacks if you want.

Q. Even though my dog has a strong immune system, my veterinarian says my dog has an immune problem. Why is this?

A. Unfortunately sometimes the immune system gets overstimulated or focused on the wrong tissues—the normal ones instead of outside invaders. When this happens, your dog shows signs of illness from the immune system attacking her own cells.

Q. I thought my dog just had a fatty tumor, but my new veterinarian says it is cancer!

A. Tumor simply means swelling—it could be a cancer, an abscess, or another kind of swollen tissue. A fatty tumor is a cancer, but luckily, a benign one!

Q. What is a core vaccine and why does my dog need any?

A. Core vaccines are vaccines that every dog should have. They cover the diseases that are very serious (even life threatening) and that most dogs will get exposed to. These include rabies, distemper, and parvo.

Q. My dog is drinking a lot of water. Is he diabetic?

A. Certainly diabetes is one disease your veterinarian will test for. Liver and kidney diseases may also make your dog drink more, as well as uterine infections, certain medications, and some endocrine problems.

Q. My dog has a squinted eye. Do I need to worry?

A. Eye problems can go from minor to serious very quickly. If you can't go to the veterinarian right away, at least flush his eye with some artificial tears.

Q. My dog has a genetic problem that is recessive. Would she pass it on to her puppies?

A. If your dog has a recessive problem, she must have two copies of the defective gene. This means she will pass a defective gene on to all of her pups. Depending on the genetic makeup of her mate, all her pups could show the defect. Or they might appear normal, but all of them will at least carry the defect.

Q. We found fleas on our dog. If we get rid of the dog, will the fleas all leave too?

A. Getting rid of your dog would be a drastic solution, and it doesn't work. There are flea eggs and larvae in your house now. Unless you treat the environment, soon *you* will have flea bites, too. Why not just treat your dog and your house and then start on one of the excellent new flea preventives?

Q. My dog just had abdominal surgery. Can I give her an aspirin for pain?

A. You need to discuss this with your veterinarian. While aspirin can be excellent for pain, it might increase your dog's chances of oozing around her incision. Your veterinarian can prescribe the safest and most effective pain medications.

Q. My veterinarian has suggested acupuncture for my dog's pain. Don't those needles hurt?

A. While some dogs do flinch at first from the acupuncture needles, the needles are very small and sharp. Most dogs quickly learn that they feel better from their acupuncture treatments and ignore the needle pricks.

Q. My dog just got hit by a car! What do I do?

A. First, stay calm. Call your veterinarian's office and tell them you will be on your way. Check quickly for any broken bones that need to be stabilized, any bleeding areas where pressure needs to be applied, and that your dog is breathing. Feel for a pulse or heartbeat, and do CPR if needed. Transport your dog carefully and safely, using a muzzle if needed.

Q. My dog obviously just loves chocolate as she always begs for some of mine. Why shouldn't she have any?

A. Chocolate can be toxic to dogs—especially dark chocolate and unsweetened baking chocolate. Carob is a safe alternative she can enjoy.

Q. My dog is very old and seems to be in pain. What do I do now?

A. This is a good time to talk to your veterinarian about hospice care and eventually euthanasia. Discuss ways to make your dog as comfortable as possible, giving him good quality of life for the time he has left.

Q. My dog hates getting her daily medications. Help!

A. Check with your veterinarian to see if her pills can be hidden in treats. Then give one or two normal treats, the doctored treat and another normal one. If that doesn't work, look into getting her long-term medications compounded. There are companies that make medications into treats or even gel to put in her ear.

Q. My male dog is aggressive with other dogs. Would breeding him help?

A. Absolutely not! Your male dog may become more aggressive after being used for breeding, and no matter what, you don't want to pass that aggressive temperament on.

Q. I work eight hours a day plus have commuting time. Can my four-month-old puppy be left that long?

A. No, most pups that age can only hold their urine for about four or five hours. Also, that is a long time for a baby to be left with no company. Arrange for a friend, neighbor, or pet sitter to let him out about noon.

Q. My dog has really bad breath. Can I use my mouthwash for her?

A. Human mouthwash is not good for dogs. They tend to swallow, not gargle, swish, or spit. You need to do some detective work to find out why your dog has bad breath and treat the cause. He may need a dental cleaning or could have a health problem.

Q. My dog sheds all year round. I thought dogs only shed in the spring and fall.

A. It is true that on a natural schedule, dogs would shed primarily in the spring and fall. But companion dogs live inside and don't get all the natural stimulus for shedding, as they are in a controlled climate. So many of them will shed some hair all year round, with slightly bigger shedding amounts with seasonal light changes.

Q. My dog has been diagnosed with hypothyroidism. How serious is this?

A. Hypothyroidism means not enough thyroid hormone is being produced. If this condition was left untreated, it could cause problems for your dog. Luckily, most dogs respond very well to inexpensive thyroid replacement medications.

Q. My dog picks berries off our bushes. Is this okay?

A. Many dogs seem to love strawberries, blueberries, and raspberries. As long as your dog isn't picking any toxic berries, this is fine. And how clever she is to pick her own!

Q. My dog has bluish purple areas on the pink skin of her belly. Should I worry?

A. Yes! These areas could easily be hemorrhages under the skin. You should head right to your veterinarian to have her checked for autoimmune problems or bleeding disorders.

Q. My dog has cancer. Can she be treated?

A. Treatment will depend on the exact type of cancer, but most dogs can handle cancer therapy quite well. Chemotherapy, radiation, and surgery are the most common treatments, alone or in combination.

Q. My puppy just vomited up a long white worm. Do I panic now?

A. Panic is never a good solution. Save the worm (carefully in a plastic Baggie) and take it with a recent stool sample and your pup to the veterinarian. He probably has roundworms and will need a dewormer.

Q. My dog is holding his one ear tipped over. It seems sore, too.

A. There is a good chance your dog has a hematoma—a blood-filled swelling of his ear. This happens when dogs scratch or shake their ears and break blood vessels. Your dog will need surgery to drain the blood and keep his ear in a normal shape. Your veterinarian will also look for the underlying cause of the shaking or scratching.

Q. A neighborhood dog may have bred my bitch, in addition to the purebred stud I paid for. How do we tell if the pups are purebred?

A. You can do a DNA profile of the possible sires, dam, and puppy. Comparing profiles will show which puppies had which sire.

Q. My dog got a bee sting and her muzzle is swollen!

A. First, make sure your dog is breathing normally. Breathing may be a little faster than normal due to excitement, but normal otherwise. If she is breathing faster, apply a cold compress to her sore muzzle. You may also want to contact your veterinarian about an antihistamine or steroid to reduce the inflammation. If her breathing is labored, hustle to your veterinarian, as she may be having a reaction.

Q. My dog is stiff in the morning. Is this just old age?

A. Certainly stiffness when getting up can be a symptom of aging. You should have your dog checked for arthritis and look into medications to make him more comfortable.

Q. Why is hydrotherapy good for dogs recovering from lameness?

A. Hydrotherapy (using a pool or pond) helps keep your dog's muscles fit while keeping weight off the joints.

The EVERYTHING® SERIES!

BUSINESS & PERSONAL FINANCE

Everything® Budgeting Book
Everything® Business Planning Book
Everything® Coaching and Mentoring Book
Everything® Fundraising Book
Everything® Get Out of Debt Book
Everything® Grant Writing Book
Everything® Homebuying Book, 2nd Ed.
Everything® Homeselling Book
Everything® Home-Based Business Book
Everything® Investing Book
Everything® Landlording Book
Everything® Leadership Book
Everything® Managing People Book
Everything® Negotiating Book
Everything® Online Business Book
Everything® Personal Finance Book
Everything® Personal Finance in Your 20s
    and 30s Book
Everything® Project Management Book
Everything® Real Estate Investing Book
Everything® Robert's Rules Book, $7.95
Everything® Selling Book
Everything® Start Your Own Business Book
Everything® Wills & Estate Planning Book

COOKING

Everything® Barbecue Cookbook
Everything® Bartender's Book, $9.95
Everything® Chinese Cookbook
Everything® College Cookbook
Everything® Cookbook
Everything® Diabetes Cookbook
Everything® Easy Gourmet Cookbook
Everything® Fondue Cookbook
Everything® Grilling Cookbook
Everything® Healthy Meals in Minutes
    Cookbook
Everything® Holiday Cookbook

Everything® Indian Cookbook
Everything® Low-Carb Cookbook
Everything® Low-Fat High-Flavor Cookbook
Everything® Low-Salt Cookbook
Everything® Meals for a Month Cookbook
Everything® Mediterranean Cookbook
Everything® Mexican Cookbook
Everything® One-Pot Cookbook
Everything® Pasta Cookbook
Everything® Quick Meals Cookbook
Everything® Slow Cooker Cookbook
Everything® Soup Cookbook
Everything® Thai Cookbook
Everything® Vegetarian Cookbook
Everything® Wine Book

HEALTH

Everything® Alzheimer's Book
Everything® Diabetes Book
Everything® Hypnosis Book
Everything® Low Cholesterol Book
Everything® Massage Book
Everything® Menopause Book
Everything® Nutrition Book
Everything® Reflexology Book
Everything® Stress Management Book

HISTORY

Everything® American Government Book
Everything® American History Book
Everything® Civil War Book
Everything® Irish History & Heritage Book
Everything® Middle East Book

HOBBIES & GAMES

Everything® Blackjack Strategy Book
Everything® Brain Strain Book, $9.95
Everything® Bridge Book
Everything® Candlemaking Book

Everything® Card Games Book
Everything® Cartooning Book
Everything® Casino Gambling Book, 2nd Ed.
Everything® Chess Basics Book
Everything® Crossword and Puzzle Book
Everything® Crossword Challenge Book
Everything® Cryptograms Book, $9.95
Everything® Digital Photography Book
Everything® Drawing Book
Everything® Easy Crosswords Book
Everything® Family Tree Book
Everything® Games Book, 2nd Ed.
Everything® Knitting Book
Everything® Knots Book
Everything® Motorcycle Book
Everything® Online Genealogy Book
Everything® Photography Book
Everything® Poker Strategy Book
Everything® Pool & Billiards Book
Everything® Quilting Book
Everything® Scrapbooking Book
Everything® Sewing Book
Everything® Woodworking Book
Everything® Word Games Challenge Book

HOME IMPROVEMENT

Everything® Feng Shui Book
Everything® Feng Shui Decluttering Book,
    $9.95
Everything® Fix-It Book
Everything® Homebuilding Book
Everything® Lawn Care Book
Everything® Organize Your Home Book

EVERYTHING® KIDS' BOOKS

All titles are $6.95
Everything® Kids' Animal Puzzle & Activity
    Book
Everything® Kids' Baseball Book, 3rd Ed.

All Everything® books are priced at $12.95 or $14.95, unless otherwise stated. Prices subject to change without notice.

Everything® Kids' Bible Trivia Book
Everything® Kids' Bugs Book
Everything® Kids' Christmas Puzzle
  & Activity Book
Everything® Kids' Cookbook
Everything® Kids' Halloween Puzzle
  & Activity Book
Everything® Kids' Hidden Pictures Book
Everything® Kids' Joke Book
Everything® Kids' Knock Knock Book
Everything® Kids' Math Puzzles Book
Everything® Kids' Mazes Book
Everything® Kids' Money Book
Everything® Kids' Monsters Book
Everything® Kids' Nature Book
Everything® Kids' Puzzle Book
Everything® Kids' Riddles & Brain Teasers Book
Everything® Kids' Science Experiments Book
Everything® Kids' Sharks Book
Everything® Kids' Soccer Book
Everything® Kids' Travel Activity Book

KIDS' STORY BOOKS

Everything® Bedtime Story Book
Everything® Fairy Tales Book

LANGUAGE

Everything® Conversational Japanese Book
  (with CD), $19.95
Everything® French Phrase Book, $9.95
Everything® French Verb Book, $9.95
Everything® Inglés Book
Everything® Learning French Book
Everything® Learning German Book
Everything® Learning Italian Book
Everything® Learning Latin Book
Everything® Learning Spanish Book
Everything® Sign Language Book
Everything® Spanish Grammar Book
Everything® Spanish Phrase Book, $9.95
Everything® Spanish Verb Book, $9.95

MUSIC

Everything® Drums Book (with CD), $19.95
Everything® Guitar Book
Everything® Home Recording Book
Everything® Playing Piano and Keyboards
  Book

Everything® Reading Music Book (with CD),
  $19.95
Everything® Rock & Blues Guitar Book
  (with CD), $19.95
Everything® Songwriting Book

NEW AGE

Everything® Astrology Book
Everything® Dreams Book, 2nd Ed.
Everything® Ghost Book
Everything® Love Signs Book, $9.95
Everything® Numerology Book
Everything® Paganism Book
Everything® Palmistry Book
Everything® Psychic Book
Everything® Reiki Book
Everything® Spells & Charms Book
Everything® Tarot Book
Everything® Wicca and Witchcraft Book

PARENTING

Everything® Baby Names Book
Everything® Baby Shower Book
Everything® Baby's First Food Book
Everything® Baby's First Year Book
Everything® Birthing Book
Everything® Breastfeeding Book
Everything® Father-to-Be Book
Everything® Father's First Year Book
Everything® Get Ready for Baby Book
Everything® Getting Pregnant Book
Everything® Homeschooling Book
Everything® Parent's Guide to Children
  with ADD/ADHD
Everything® Parent's Guide to Children
  with Asperger's Syndrome
Everything® Parent's Guide to Children
  with Autism
Everything® Parent's Guide to Children
  with Dyslexia
Everything® Parent's Guide to Positive
  Discipline
Everything® Parent's Guide to Raising a
  Successful Child
Everything® Parent's Guide to Tantrums
Everything® Parent's Guide to the Overweight
  Child
Everything® Parenting a Teenager Book
Everything® Potty Training Book, $9.95

Everything® Pregnancy Book, 2nd Ed.
Everything® Pregnancy Fitness Book
Everything® Pregnancy Nutrition Book
Everything® Pregnancy Organizer, $15.00
Everything® Toddler Book
Everything® Tween Book
Everything® Twins, Triplets, and More Book

PETS

Everything® Cat Book
Everything® Dachshund Book, $12.95
Everything® Dog Book
Everything® Dog Health Book
Everything® Dog Training and Tricks Book
Everything® Golden Retriever Book, $12.95
Everything® Horse Book
Everything® Labrador Retriever Book, $12.95
Everything® Poodle Book, $12.95
Everything® Pug Book, $12.95
Everything® Puppy Book
Everything® Rottweiler Book, $12.95
Everything® Tropical Fish Book

REFERENCE

Everything® Car Care Book
Everything® Classical Mythology Book
Everything® Computer Book
Everything® Divorce Book
Everything® Einstein Book
Everything® Etiquette Book
Everything® Mafia Book
Everything® Philosophy Book
Everything® Psychology Book
Everything® Shakespeare Book

RELIGION

Everything® Angels Book
Everything® Bible Book
Everything® Buddhism Book
Everything® Catholicism Book
Everything® Christianity Book
Everything® Jewish History & Heritage Book
Everything® Judaism Book
Everything® Koran Book
Everything® Prayer Book
Everything® Saints Book
Everything® Torah Book
Everything® Understanding Islam Book

All Everything® books are priced at $12.95 or $14.95, unless otherwise stated. Prices subject to change without notice.

Everything® World's Religions Book
Everything® Zen Book

SCHOOL & CAREERS

Everything® Alternative Careers Book
Everything® College Survival Book, 2nd Ed.
Everything® Cover Letter Book, 2nd Ed.
Everything® Get-a-Job Book
Everything® Job Interview Book
Everything® New Teacher Book
Everything® Online Job Search Book
Everything® Paying for College Book
Everything® Practice Interview Book
Everything® Resume Book, 2nd Ed.
Everything® Study Book

SELF-HELP

Everything® Great Sex Book
Everything® Kama Sutra Book
Everything® Self-Esteem Book

SPORTS & FITNESS

Everything® Fishing Book
Everything® Fly-Fishing Book
Everything® Golf Instruction Book

Everything® Pilates Book
Everything® Running Book
Everything® Total Fitness Book
Everything® Weight Training Book
Everything® Yoga Book

TRAVEL

Everything® Family Guide to Hawaii
Everything® Family Guide to New York City, 2nd Ed.
Everything® Family Guide to RV Travel & Campgrounds
Everything® Family Guide to the Walt Disney World Resort®, Universal Studios®, and Greater Orlando, 4th Ed.
Everything® Family Guide to Washington D.C., 2nd Ed.
Everything® Guide to Las Vegas
Everything® Guide to New England
Everything® Travel Guide to the Disneyland Resort®, California Adventure®, Universal Studios®, and the Anaheim Area

WEDDINGS

Everything® Bachelorette Party Book, $9.95
Everything® Bridesmaid Book, $9.95

Everything® Elopement Book, $9.95
Everything® Father of the Bride Book, $9.95
Everything® Groom Book, $9.95
Everything® Mother of the Bride Book, $9.95
Everything® Wedding Book, 3rd Ed.
Everything® Wedding Checklist, $9.95
Everything® Wedding Etiquette Book, $7.95
Everything® Wedding Organizer, $15.00
Everything® Wedding Shower Book, $7.95
Everything® Wedding Vows Book, $7.95
Everything® Weddings on a Budget Book, $9.95

WRITING

Everything® Creative Writing Book
Everything® Get Published Book
Everything® Grammar and Style Book
Everything® Guide to Writing a Book Proposal
Everything® Guide to Writing a Novel
Everything® Guide to Writing Children's Books
Everything® Screenwriting Book
Everything® Writing Poetry Book
Everything® Writing Well Book